SCHUMACHER

SCHUMACHER

THE LIFE OF THE NEW FORMULA 1 CHAMPION

TIMOTHY COLLINGS

BLOOMSBURY

First published in Great Britain 1994

This paperback edition published 1996

Copyright © by Timothy Collings 1995

Bloomsbury Publishing Plc, 2 Soho Square, London W1V 6HB

A CIP catalogue record for this book is
available from the British Library

ISBN 0 7475 2242 1

10 9 8 7 6 5 4 3 2 1

Typeset by Hewer Text Composition Services, Edinburgh
Printed in Britain by Cox & Wyman Ltd, Reading, Berkshire

CONTENTS

Acknowledgements   vii

1   Spa-Francorchamps
     A Dramatic Entrance   1

2   Kerpen-Mannheim
     Growing up and Karting   18

3   Macau and Fuji
     Flings of Eastern Promise   42

4   Stuttgart
     On the Road with Mercedes-Benz   54

5   Silverstone
     Welcome to Eddie's Green and Pleasant Land   76

6   Monza
     An Overnight Move to the Family   91

7   Witney
     Learning from Martin, Fighting with Ayrton   111

8   Enstone
     A Technical Year with Riccardo   131

9   Monte Carlo
     A New Life, a New Challenge   147

10   Imola
     Death, Disaster and Leadership   157

11   Hockenheim
     A Sad and Controversial Summer   167

12   Adelaide
     The End of the Road   178

13   1995   189

Michael Schumacher Fact File   221
Index   229

ACKNOWLEDGEMENTS AND THANKS

This book would not have been possible without the generous help and co-operation of many people, particularly those who gave up precious time to recount the part they played in the Michael Schumacher story. Above all, however, I am indebted to Michael himself for making full use of his extraordinary natural talent by winning the Formula One World Drivers' Championship. He also, wherever possible, helped in ensuring the details of his early life in particular were recorded accurately. All of the following, in no particular order, contributed to the research and writing of the book: Flavio Briatore, Eddie Jordan, Ian Phillips, Trevor Foster, Andrea de Cesaris, Jochen Neerpasch, Willi Weber, Martin Brundle, Heinz-Harald Frentzen, Peter Sauber, Gustav Buesing, Christophe Schulte, Karin Sturm (and her paperback book *Michael Schumacher Superstar*), Michael Schmidt, Derek Warwick, *Autosport* magazine, *Motoring News*, *Motor Sport*, Riccardo Patrese, Richard Grundy, Steven Tee, Tom Wilkinshaw, Jurgen Dilk, Udo Irnich, Mathias Brunner, Guido Dilk, Mark Skewis, Tony Jardine, Jochen Mass, Bruce Jones, Max Welti, Roberto Moreno, Mika Hakkinen, Eddie Irvine, Corinna Betsch, Leo Reiss, Ross Braun, Harry Hawelka, Tim Wright, Fred Rodgers, Pat Symonds, Max Fluckiger, J.J. Lehto, Joe Verstappen, Joan Villadelprat, Frank Dernie, Stuart and Diana Spires, Patrizia Spinelli, Maria Bellanca, Rae Turkington, Jessica Salisbury, Damon Hill, Rod Vickery, Steve Madincea, Dick Scammell, Duncan Lee, Victoria Flack, Stan Piecha of the *Sun*, Maurice Hamilton of the *Observer*, Derick Allsop of the *Independent* (and his book *Designs on Victory*), Oliver Holt of *The Times*, Bob Constanduros, Alan Henry, Nigel Roebuck, David Tremayne, Fred Petersens, Heinz Prueller, Helmut Zwickl, Gerald Donaldson, Achim Slang, Wolfgang Neumayer, Malte Jurgens, Tony Dodgins, Mike Doodson, David Smith, Joe Saward, especially Jonathan Noble and Kate Bouverie for patience and editing skills, Kathy Rooney, for faith in the idea, and Ruth Collings, for making it happen on time. Special thanks must also go to every member of the Mild Seven Benetton Ford Team for generously allowing access to their factory, offices, motor home and garage throughout the year and for putting up with so many odd questions at often inconvenient times. Finally, I acknowledge and thank Steven Tee of LAT and Ulrich Sonntag of *Autobild* for contributing the vast majority of the photographs used in the book and apologize to anyone whose help has been overlooked.

Timothy Collings
November 1994

1 SPA-FRANCORCHAMPS

A DRAMATIC ENTRANCE

I remember the start of 1991 being fantastic. Mercedes actually came to me to ask if I would drive for them. It was like Christmas and my birthday all rolled into one. All the journalists said to me 'you must surely drive in another series, in F3000,' but for me that wasn't so. Formula 3000 is so hard. It's crazy. If I'd had the money and made tests with a couple of English or French teams, then maybe. In the end, I thought the best chance for me to get to Formula One, and it proved right, was through Group C. If you have success in any international arena, then there must be a possibility of getting to Formula One. If I hadn't been successful, I could have done Formula 3000 in 1992, when I would have been only 23. The advantage I had then was that time was on my side.

Michael Schumacher assessing his career prospects in late 1992.

A MIST STILL HUNG IN THE TREES and the overnight dew had barely cleared. Campers were awake and moving around amongst the trees which surrounded their tents and covered the slopes of the valley. The smells of dawn wafted through the Belgian Ardennes: coffee, pastries, cheese, the first *frites* of the day and the pure pine-needle natural whiff of the local Francorchamps air. Some of the roads which form part of the Spa-Francorchamps circuit remained open to public traffic, some were damp under heavy cloud cover and others were dry. It suggested the typical wet-dry changing conditions of 'Spa', a circuit loved by those who went there on a regular basis and especially those who remembered the old daunting road track. To most Formula One drivers, Spa has long been regarded as one of the most challenging race circuits in the world as well as the longest in the Grand Prix calendar. It combines raw high speed with fast corners, slow corners, straights and swooping dips, rises and falls, changes of camber and surface, in a way which makes it unique and dangerous. The Eau Rouge, loved and feared, is often claimed to be the most fearsome corner of any circuit in the world. On 23 August 1991, this 6.940 kms (4.312 miles) track was as daunting as ever and was expected to be a particularly severe initiation to the highest echelon of motor racing for Michael Schumacher.

At only 22 years, seven months and 20 days, he was in line for his Formula One debut with the 7-Up Jordan team in opening qualifying. He had been drafted in as a late replacement for Bertrand Gachot, who was facing a jail sentence in England after being convicted for assaulting a London taxi driver. Gachot, the son of a Brussels Eurocrat, claimed his actions were in self-defence, but he lost his case. The action had been a controversial one in Europe and Gachot's English girlfriend Kate Palmer had raised protests in Belgium, where the Gachot family lived, in Luxembourg and in France. As a result, the Formula One paddock, sprawled across the tarmac within the confines of the triangle inside La Source hairpin, was alive with intrigue and rumour. Slogans had been painted onto the track near the famous Eau Rouge corner and leaflets were handed out to spectators, drivers and team officials.

Until this day, Gachot had been a much better-known racing driver than his replacement, Schumacher, who was a relative unknown building a reputation in the World Sportscar Championship with Mercedes after establishing his credentials in karting, Formula Konig, Formula Ford 1600 and the German Formula Three championship. Gachot had been with the new Jordan team from the start of the year, had shared in their first points-scoring success at Montreal and had, as someone who grew up in Belgium, looked forward to this weekend as a very special occasion. Instead, he was in a Brixton jail cell, awaiting transfer to the Ford open prison, and his car, number 32, was occupied by a young German debutant for whom Spa-Francorchamps, this weekend, was to become the springboard to greatness.

No one knew what to expect from this boy, and those who had an inkling of his talent and potential were keeping their counsel to themselves. After all, Schumacher had never gone round the Spa-Francorchamps circuit before, let alone raced on it. More to the point, he had never raced a Formula One car before and had only briefly tested for Jordan, at Silverstone just a few days earlier. Yet this young man, not much more than a boy, slim and wiry, fresh-faced and fit as a flea, had only a cursory advance look at the fast and vast circuit on a bicycle. For him, it was enough.

Peter Sauber, the man whose Group C Mercedes team had guided Schumacher for the previous two years, knew what to expect. Of course. He had seen it all before and it did not matter if Schumacher was about to drive a single-seater Formula Three, Formula 3000, Group C car or a Formula One car. It was always the same. 'As soon as he got into the car, he was fast,' recalled Sauber of Schumacher's first run with him in Group C. 'He did not need a long adjustment period. He produced great times from the start. Over time, the others often gained on him. At the end, their differences were often minimal, but Michael always produced a fast early lap. At least once. That raised him above the rest.'

This explosive early speed was to be Schumacher's hallmark. He stunned spectators and competitors with his sudden fast times, at the start of a practice or qualifying session, early in a race or a test session, gaining both a technical and a psychological advantage. It had always been the same, from karting to Group C. A raw speed, a braveness and a confidence which set him apart. It was the only way he knew how to approach the hobby which, almost by surprise, had become his job. And in addition to the speed, Schumacher had also an immense well of determination and a single-minded focus on his own ambitions. And at only 22 years old he brought these qualities with him to Spa-Francorchamps to amaze Eddie Jordan and his team and to stun everyone else.

Despite lacking an intimate knowledge of the circuit, he was able to clock a time early in the first session which made him fourth fastest at that time before he slipped down to 11th as other drivers made the most of their soft rubber. He made an immediate impact and whenever he steered his car out on to the track, there was an air of anticipation. 'The relationship between me and the team is quite fantastic,' he said, in the English he had acquired through working for Mercedes and in the manner he had acquired through media relations practice with the German factory team. 'They accepted me and that's quite important for me. And working together is nice. There's not so many political things in the team, because it is a really small team. There are a lot of good people there.'

It was the confidence with which he performed as much as what he did which impressed. Immediately, he was described as arrogant, Teutonic, super-confident or cool. It was hard for his contemporaries and critics to accept what he did. His teammate Andrea de Cesaris was pushed beyond his own normal limits. For everyone, it was hard to believe that this boyish-looking slim-as-a-wisp driver could achieve such times in such a confident fashion. His aloofness, his remoteness, his self-centred confidence made it worse and virtually every reporter in the paddock who came into contact with him was to be intrigued. This German boy, who came from sportscars, was blasting a hole through the Formula One establishment, handling himself with ease in and out of the car and oozing confidence. What made it even more difficult to accept was the simple fact that it was all natural. Yes, he really was that good.

'On Friday, I never tried Eau Rouge flat. I nearly braked and at first I took it in fifth gear and then in sixth. That was a problem, to get used to a part of the circuit like this where you can do it flat, but without experience so you do it slowly, step by step,' Schumacher recalled later. 'With my first set of qualifiers, I was just on my lap when Eric van de Poele went off and practice was stopped. The second time I tried with the same set of tyres and Prost blocked my lap. He was starting his quick lap. I braked at the limit for me, but he braked a bit too early for me and there were only two possibilities. Crash into him or use the escape road . . . I thought it was better to use it.'

And on the second set of tyres? 'The time was not at the limit. Not 100 per cent. But maybe 98 per cent, really good. But I liked to take it easy, because I wanted to qualify the car, and not more. I didn't want to take any risks.' Schumacher's fast initial qualifying time was set on his 22nd lap of Spa-Francorchamps, including pit-stopping laps. It placed him eighth on the overnight grid. This meant he was five places ahead of his teammate Andrea de Cesaris, who was qualifying for his 160th Grand Prix. The effect was to make his driving the talking point for everyone that evening, throughout the coniferous valleys. And on Saturday morning, he delivered more of the same. Eau Rouge was taken flat in sixth. He topped the times for much of the morning session on race tyres and then, using qualifying tyres, improved on his grid time by two seconds to finish up fifth in the session. Few at Jordan, let alone in the rest of the paddock, could believe their eyes, the late Ayrton Senna included. Unfortunately, for Schumacher, he did not quite match his best time again in the afternoon when it mattered. 'The first run was clear, but there were some points where it was not really at the limit. It was okay, but it was also a lap which I wanted to take easy to have a time and then with the other one you can take a little bit more risk. On the second one, I did this section better, but at the chicane I had to overtake and lost maybe one second. I think I maybe could do a time in the middle 50s,' he concluded.

Schumacher's explosive start that weekend was not, as we know, quite as unrehearsed as it seemed. This racing driver had been addicted to speed with a pedal kart since the age of four, later crashing a kart – motorised by his father with an old motor cycle engine – by going too fast and hitting a lamp-post. There had always been hints of an embryonic champion, another Senna, a man obsessed by a single goal. From then on, like Senna, Schumacher had support: financial, emotional and technical, to ensure his precocious talent would not be wasted. His father, a bricklayer, helped him with his early karting career and, when he could no longer afford the repair bills and the new engines and parts, Michael was lucky to receive support from a friend of his father, Gerd Noack, who sponsored him, and later from Jurgen Dilk, whose backing helped carry him from karts to Formula Three and the management of Willi Weber. From there, he moved into the hands of Mercedes, the International Management Group (IMG) and Jochen Neerpasch, nominally Mercedes Sporting Director, but a man of far-reaching influence in German and European motor racing. So, with this management behind him already, it is fair to say that Schumacher arrived at Spa-Francorchamps as well-prepared for such a debut as anyone could have been.

Formula One was as ready for Schumacher as he was for the move to the top. So too was Germany. Indeed, Germany was almost desperate for the arrival of its wunderkind after so many barren years with so little Grand Prix racing success. For a country which manufactured such revered cars as those built by Porsche, Mercedes, BMW, Audi and Volkswagen, it was a mystery that no German had ever won the Formula One Drivers' World Championship. There was a hunger, a deep-felt need for a German racing star and Schumacher, from an ordinary background in the north, was in a position to satisfy a national urge.

Before Spa, he had been contacted by Jordan and invited to England for a test at Silverstone. It was the Jordan team's first season and had been successful but incident-filled. The 191, powered by a Ford-Cosworth V8, was a competitive package, well-designed and engineered by Gary Anderson and, in the hands of Gachot and the Italian Andrea de Cesaris, had proved to be capable of claiming quick times and points. It was fast enough and reliable enough and Eddie Jordan believed Schumacher was the boy around whom he could consolidate and build for the future. What Eddie and his team did not expect was the sheer speed of Schumacher and the events which arrived in its wake. At his first Formula One test, he was called in and told to slow down. Not once, not twice, but three times . . .

'I remember those first laps at Silverstone,' said Schumacher. 'I was in the car and I was thinking "This is crazy – here I am in an F1 car and I am only 22 years old." Everything had happened so quickly and I was really, really nervous. I thought that it was going to be really hard to get used to this thing. The first three laps were incredible. But after that it started to be okay. Sure, it was special, but at the same time it was extra-special. The step was not so great because the power and the speed in sportscar racing helped to prepare me for this.

'But at Spa, I had no experience of the circuit and there are places such as Eau Rouge which you have to take flat if you are going to be quick. At first, I nearly braked. Then I took it up in fifth gear. Then sixth. My feeling was to do it slowly, step by step. Then I was taking it flat and it was no problem. After that, to qualify seventh was like a dream. All I had really thought about was getting into the race and then finishing. Nothing more.' Schumacher qualified seventh, but he retired from the race at the first corner, La Source.

Such bare statistics explain the stunning quality of his qualifying and why, within days, he was to be the subject of an unprecedented tug-o-war between two teams as, in a remarkable move, Camel Benetton Ford, swooped like a bird of prey to steal off with the new star. Throughout the whole weekend of that first Belgian Grand Prix, Schumacher shone like a rough diamond. A year later, on the same circuit, he won his first Grand Prix, proving how accomplished one man could become in 12 months of Formula One motor racing.

'The first time I remember seeing him was at the Silverstone south circuit on the Tuesday before the Belgian Grand Prix – in the test,' recalled Jordan's Commercial Manager Ian Phillips. 'He was mind-blowing. I'd done a lot of testing at the south circuit, particularly when I was with March. We were the team that probably used it the most. There is what I consider to be an incredibly dangerous left-hand kink where you stand to do the signalling and, from there, you can judge whether someone is doing a good job by how early they brake for that kink. Schumacher went through it flat on his fourth lap and it was the most terrifying thing that you've ever seen in your life. I said to Trevor [Foster]: "Call him in, slow him down." He said: "You tell him, you tell him, this man's something special." I did exactly that. Twice more during the test Trevor had to call him in to slow him down. The Sunday prior to that when Eddie phoned me and said "I've done a deal with Michael Schumacher," I, along with

99 per cent of the motor racing world, didn't really know who he was. I'd heard the name. I knew he had won Macau and he was a bit special in a sportscar, but it wasn't the name that immediately sprung to mind in the situation we were in then.

'But Eddie's great strength is pulling these people out of nowhere. To this day, I believe there is not another Grand Prix team which would have given him that chance. He was negotiating with Neerpasch and I was talking to Keke Rosberg, Derek Warwick and Stefan Johannson. The old favourites, if you like. I'd been left to deal with them while Eddie talked to this unknown Schumacher kid. Suddenly, he said "I've done a deal and he'll be there tomorrow . . . Get him in the car, give him a contract and run him on Tuesday."

'He came on Monday afternoon. I'd met his manager Willi Weber before because he was touting him around. I think he was in Brazil. That was when the name was first mentioned. I didn't know. I had no idea what to expect. He was very young to look at. He was 22, I suppose, which until we signed Rubens (Barrichello) a couple of years later, was the youngest thing that there was in Formula One then.'

Like everyone at Spa-Francorchamps that weekend, Phillips was as struck by Schumacher's self-control, his coolness under pressure and his self-awareness as by his speed. In and out of the cockpit, he was a measured, confident and remarkable young man. 'The thing that was immediately apparent was how in control of the situation and himself he was,' Phillips remarked. 'Spa was like a home race for him, so there was a lot of pressure. But he handled it all.' Mercedes paid for Schumacher's initial drive with Jordan, at an agreed rate of £150,000 per race for Spa and the rest of the season. 'Mercedes were paying and they had some space on the car,' said Phillips. 'The money was paid and a man turned up on their behalf at Spa saying "I've got stickers to put on", and that was it really. Eddie agreed the money and that was the deal for the rest of the year. No problem. I'd anticipated people crawling all over him, but it was an absolute doddle. He handled everything. He closed the shutters on the garage. He was able to conduct himself very well. It just wasn't a problem. He was a very young man, but very obviously in control of everything he wanted to do, both inside and outside of the car.'

This assurance was such that Michael, on his debut weekend, felt confident enough in his first session not only to tangle with Prost, then at the peak of his career with Ferrari and a contender for the world championship, but also to claim that the Frenchman was effectively blocking him when he was later called to explain himself before the Stewards. 'Michael was called in and asked what he thought he was doing,' recalled Phillips. 'And he replied that he was too slow and "he was in my way". He was in control, he knew just what he was doing. Alain Prost, in the Ferrari and contesting the world championship, was in this 22-year-old new boy's way! He had only ridden a two wheel bicycle around Spa the previous day and here we were after the first session. Everybody had seen, without doubt, that this guy was good. Most people had never heard of him, let alone could spell his name and here he was . . . It was a good car, very easy to drive. At the time, we had never qualified well and we asked questions and we have done ever since really about our ability to qualify, because it has taken us the best part of three years to better that performance.'

There were signs too of Schumacher's breezy outlook on life outside racing as Phillips learned. 'The Paddock Club at Spa is situated up at the hairpin. I had to take him there to do a speech for the 7-Up guests and I thought "Oh, my God, he ain't gonna like this." To get there, you had to walk through public areas and God knows what. "No problem," he said. There were 400 people there having lunch and Michael Schumacher arrived. But he was great. No problem at all.'

It was a measure of the stunning effect of Schumacher's qualifying performance at Spa (seventh on the grid for his first race on arguably the world's most daunting Grand Prix circuit) that many people refused to believe or accept it. One was Schumacher's veteran Italian teammate Andrea de Cesaris. 'Andrea was distraught at the end of that qualifying,' said Phillips. 'He was just shocked. "I know I didn't drive well, but one and a half seconds!" he said. "It is not possible. Not possible." And then Andrea proceeded to have what was perhaps the finest race of his career. He started 14th and to be honest would have won it. Michael would have won it if he had not burnt his clutch out at the first corner, but Andrea got to the point of disputing the lead with Senna from 14th place and Andrea is a very proud man. He was so devastated after qualifying that he drove the race of his life.'

Trevor Foster, later to join Lotus, was at that time the team manager at Jordan. He remembered how struck he was by Schumacher both at the Silverstone test and at Spa and his effect on de Cesaris. 'We felt that the Jordan tradition was to go for the young unknown driver so Gary (Anderson) and myself voted to go for Michael, and Eddie went along with it too. When he came over, he was very self-assured. No problems with anything on the car. We told him it was the race car and also that engines were not aplenty at that time because, obviously, we were working to a pretty tight budget. The idea for the test was to do a half-day at Silverstone south circuit, on the Tuesday, I think, and then we were going to Spa.

'So we went over there and off he went, almost literally. After about six or seven laps, he was flicking the car through a chicane and I had Weber with me and I said "This is his race car and it must be ready tonight at four o'clock and we've got to reach the start so we have really got to calm him down a bit." So, we brought him in, sat him down and said "Look, you've got to support me on this. There is plenty of time. You are only 22 years old. You've got a long way to go." And he said "I do not understand what the problem is. I am in control." I mean, he never looked out of control. But he looked, for a young guy, with only six laps behind him in an FI car for the first time, he looked, well, I mean . . . we were flabbergasted really. And he did the same thing again in another ten laps or whatever it was. It was just a natural speed that he had all the time. We ended up doing 20 or 25 laps and it was so natural to him. We called him in three times!

'But there was another thing we were concerned about, which was the over-running the engine on the down-change because that was the engine which was scheduled to do the two days of qualifying and had he overrun that engine there, even by mistake, which even the best drivers are capable of doing, then that would have been it. We would have lost another engine and the team could not afford that sort of thing. So, we stopped after those early laps and it was incredible because he had been so quick, as quick as we had ever been around there.'

Foster was just as amazed as everyone else the following weekend. 'We went to Spa and I said "Have you ever driven round this?" and he said "No." I said "Well, we had better wait for Andrea and I will get him to go round with you in a road car and show you round the track. I got some notes out from the year before, from the F3000 race, and we worked out the gears we were going to go for and, for some reason, Andrea was late. I think he was talking to Eddie about negotiating his contract and he got into a sort of wrangle and in the end Michael said "Don't worry, at six o'clock I'll get my bike out and I will go round on my bike." So, off he went. Afterwards, I told him to wait and that when Andrea and Eddie were finished, I will make sure they give you a run round later. Anyway, it got later and later and later and it just never happened and he said "Don't worry, before it gets dark, I will go round again on my bike" and he did. Then he came back and said "Don't worry. I'll see you tomorrow."

'He turned up in the morning and he was immediately on the pace. I cannot remember exactly, but he was so self-assured and so fast. One of the things which impressed me was his control. Normally, when you get a young guy like this, one of the difficulties is to restrain them. They get super carried away with it all, you know, and Spa, which has one or two very dangerous spots, left us quite worried. About him. And I said to him, about half-way through the first session "Michael, are you sure you are not driving over the edge?" And I always remember him saying to me "No, I'm not over the edge. I am on the limit, but I am not over the limit." That was it. And what happened was that Andrea was not happy with his car, so he jumped into the spare and part-way through the session, we developed a water leak on the water pump, which meant the engine had to be changed. I said to Gary "Can we use Andrea's car to get the laps up?" and he said "Yeah, no problem – Andrea thinks the spare car is better anyway." So we put him in Andrea's car and he immediately passed Andrea. He ran that car until the end of the session and then we changed the engine and he went out in qualifying and at the end of it, he had obviously done a really good job and we were all very impressed.

'There were some very interesting points, again, which struck me. One was that on a particular part of the circuit, Andrea was in a quandary. If he kept it in fifth gear all the way through the section, the car got very high on revs and very nervous. And he said "If I try it in sixth gear then, likewise, the car bogs down." He was talking about the bit where the track comes down from the top of the circuit, where you come into the first one in fifth and then take the second part of it in sixth and, obviously, to change gear in the middle of it was difficult . . . I said to Michael, in the debrief: "Do you have the same problem?" He said, "Well, I did for three laps and then I realised that what I do is go into it in sixth gear and I just left-foot brake and it just steadies the car in the middle and then I just take both corners in sixth." And he had not even mentioned it. He had just worked it out all for himself. For him, it was perfectly natural. He was simply driving the car.

'There was no issue. He had not come in and said "Look, I've found this a problem or that. And there was no mention of anything at all. As far as he was concerned, it was the fastest way to get the car round those two corners. He had worked out all the other options and none of them were ideal. But this was the best compromise. There was also another bit, coming back to the "Bus Stop" chicane, the two very quick left-handers, which was interesting. If you looked at the section times, he was very quick there. Although he was in the top seven or eight all the time, he was always about second or third quickest. Andrea was unhappy with that section in his car. He said that "As you lift, just as you turn in, it gets a bit unsettled on the bumps", and I remember I talked to Michael about it. "Yeah," he said. "But it is okay if you just drive it flat. The lift actually destabilizes the car and if you keep it flat it's okay." Sure enough, it was.'

De Cesaris found it difficult to cope with all these unexpected lessons in technique from the novice, but the experience – as Nelson Piquet, Martin Brundle, Riccardo Patrese and J.J. Lehto were to find – did push him to improve his own performance. His race that Sunday was his finest in Formula One, but, back at the factory the following week he was still filled with concern and agitation. 'We had lost Michael to Benetton by then, I think, and Andrea knew we were obviously going to put another driver in the car, so he wanted Michael's car,' Foster recalled. 'Immediately we asked him why? It always causes so many problems, so much greed, these things. One lot of mechanics had built that car and these things end up causing a lot of ill feeling. Andrea said he wanted to change because there must be something better about the other monocoque, because there was no way Schumacher could be that quick. "He cannot be that much faster than I am," he said.

'We had several, very heated meetings about swapping the monocoque over. First Eddie said "No" and then he tried Gary and he went on and on. It drove us mad for about two weeks. I still think it took Andrea a long time to concede that Michael *was* that good.'

As ever, Schumacher had performed all his racing duties without raising more than a glow on his cheeks at Spa-Francorchamps. This was to prove as typical of Schumacher as the speed with which he made all his subsequent moves, including the rapid switch from Jordan to Benetton that followed. He and his advisers knew that there was a world of difference between Jordan and Benetton. It was like moving from a happy shared apartment, among students and friends, to a fine country house, as Phillips recognized. 'We were staying in a holiday camp place,' said Phillips. 'It cost us five pounds a night and it was just outside Spa, the town. A holiday camp. But it was more like a prison camp. It was positively the most awful hotel you could stay in. But it was five pounds a night and as far as Jordan were concerned this was the business. Ironically, two weeks later, the night we realised we had lost him, and the next time we saw him was in the Villa d'Este by Lake Como where he was staying at Benetton's expense. He wasn't paying his own expenses this time. And there could never have been a greater contrast.'

Michael's race at Spa ended early. As early as possible. A burned-out clutch saw him rolling to a halt just after Eau Rouge. And that it was a clutch should be remembered. Afterwards, having overcome his disappointment, he and his manager Willi Weber, who had remained with his protégé since his first German Formula Three season, came back to speak to the team, said goodbye and left the circuit early. The Jordan team were so excited by Andrea de Cesaris' stirring drive-of-his-life that they broke off only briefly to bid adieu. Schumacher and Weber left them behind, left the five pounds a night holiday camp hotel and the jolly bright, clean and green machine, and headed home, thinking ahead, planning the next step in what was clearly to be a spectacular career. On the surface they were pleased. But Weber had learned that Jordan were interested in forming a partnership with Yamaha for 1992 and Benetton, like everyone, had shown delight in Michael's debut. Many business cards had been exchanged and men like Weber, Neerpasch and Flavio Briatore (of Benetton) are not in Formula One for fun. It is the most serious business in international sport and Benetton, the Ford factory-supported team, were not at all happy at seeing the young upstarts at Jordan, a new team in their first Formula One season, performing so well.

For Eddie Jordan himself, 1991 was an amazing year. A year of thrills and education. But, even three years on, he found the pain of the Schumacher affair still stabbed from time to time. 'I think I first saw Michael in a car in 1989,' he remembered. 'I just liked the way he moved around the paddock. He had that strange appearance, but at the same time an arrogant or confident walk. He walks in a definite way. He's a lovely boy. I still think that, despite our problems, which have been a considerable upset to the team. My first contact with him came in Formula Three where he won the championship. At that stage, he was part of a sportscar programme with Mercedes . . . I remember it well.'

So he should. Jordan not only recognized Schumacher's talent for Formula One before anyone else, he had also seen the value of the Mercedes-trained trio and had hired Heinz-Harald Frentzen, Schumacher's contemporary and rival, for his Formula 3000 team. 'I had an idea of what was going on,' said Jordan. 'Dave Price and I always chatted about drivers because I liked to be kept in touch on that side. It was basically seen that Frentzen appeared to be the quickest, Wendlinger could do the same time as

Schumacher, but with more mileage, and that you could see these kids were getting a very good grounding and were very good. But no one had ever taken anyone from sportscars to Formula One before . . . but, I'd been watching and whilst I would have formed my own opinions anyway, I met Willi Weber and Gerd Kramer from Mercedes who said to me 'Listen, please do keep an eye on Schumacher for the future – he could be a good one.' And he was right.

'He was in a line of two or three guys who I really felt had enormous potential, but not just because of Formula Three. It was based on that and sportscars, how he applied himself, his mannerisms. All this type of thing. It was cumulative. I put it all together. I watched him as the season went on and then the opportunity arose because of the problems with Gachot. We felt he was going to get out on appeal, but I couldn't take the risk, so I spoke to Schumacher, through Jochen Neerpasch, at the race in Hockenheim on the qualifying Saturday. I asked them about a release and they were very excited. They said Mercedes would pay a certain sum of money per race through Sauber. It was agreed that if the opportunity arose, I would use him. I discussed it with my people here and while some of them thought I'd gone off my head, I had some support. I usually make a choice and when I make a bad choice, I say I've made a bad choice. But, to be fair to this team, we always like to give younger guys a chance.

'We had to give him a test and we did it here on the south circuit on the Tuesday and immediately he was very quick. Then, in the afternoon we heard about Gachot and we had a letter of support from the Irish Prime Minister. We have had them too from Nelson Mandela and from Ayrton Senna as well, just before he died. There is a lot of goodwill towards this team . . .'

Proud, sensitive, enthusiastic to a fault, Eddie Jordan made a bold, brilliant decision to sign Schumacher and in his boldness and brilliance overlooked the dangers of rivals moving in to poach his signing as he and the team revelled in their unexpected good fortune in the build-up to Spa-Francorchamps. 'Gachot didn't get out of jail,' said Jordan. 'I thought he would. So we had to rush to get a letter of agreement to Schumacher. We'd supplied him with a contract in English, but he wanted it translated into

German. He'd signed it and a letter came through from Sauber to agree to how much they would pay and we went ahead. We told our sponsors and everyone and to be fair a lot of people were amazed. They didn't know him. They had not heard of him and they could not spell his name.'

What followed was a brilliant first outing by Schumacher and a long wrangle over contracts, involving lawyers, other drivers and other teams. But in Belgium, the first and most noticeable event was Schumacher's driving in the Jordan. 'It was a wonderful, wonderful performance,' recalled Jordan, his eyes misting with emotion. 'Seventh on the grid and I don't think there had ever been a debut on a circuit you've never ever seen before, as good as that, in a car that was quite good, but not from a top four team. To qualify seventh was an outstanding performance.'

There were back-slaps all around. No-one's confidence had been misplaced. Weber was satisfied. Kramer was satisfied too. Raising the money in the middle of the year to satisfy Jordan's demand for £150,000 was not as easy as it had seemed. Weber knew it had to be done and Kramer encouraged him. 'If necessary do it with a bank guarantee. Or credit. But somehow you have to do this.' Kramer recalled that Weber was prepared to raise the money himself for Schumacher's debut and on the weekend before Spa-Francorchamps, the phone lines between the Nurburgring, where Schumacher was racing with Mercedes, and the Jordan base at Silverstone were humming with activity. The Nurburgring race was bruising and memorable for Schumacher – he even became entangled in a temperamental confrontation with Derek Warwick – but all is forgotten by Sunday night, when, after an early retirement, he is informed of his chance to race for Jordan at Spa.

A few weeks earlier, there had been talk of Schumacher joining Footwork, but it had not happened. This time, when the talking started, followed by the denials, it did. 'We just knew there was a chance to do it,' Schumacher told Adam Cooper, in an interview for *Autosport* in late August 1991. 'They didn't involve me really in what was going on, because they wanted me to have a clear head in the Nurburgring race. But after the race, I heard that I had to go to England. I was to go anyway as I had a meeting with

Jackie Oliver. We talked together – we were in contact before – and after that meeting I went to Eddie and heard that I could do the race.'

The race itself was so brief, it merits no description other than that of Schumacher's car rolling to a halt, the clutch gone after he had burned his way up to sixth from the grid. For a moment, it seemed the man who had brought the Midas touch with him from Kerpen to Spa may have lost his way. Even he agreed, such good luck as his could only go on for so long. It could not last forever, particularly after such a wonderful 1991 to that point. 'It will happen,' he admitted. 'Every time you have a high point, you can come down to a low point. But you have to handle the situation and come back up to the same point or maybe a higher one.

'Maybe I won't qualify the car or something like this. That would be a situation where I think it would be really good from the press for them not to push me too hard, do not push me to a level I have not reached yet. If there comes a time when it is not so good, don't make it too hard for me. In Germany, the press is like this. They push so hard and if you lose then you fall down so quick and so deep . . . But, for me, the future is to do Formula One. Nothing more. I cannot do Sportscars and Formula One next year, so I hope I can concentrate only on Formula One. If I can do Formula One, I will. If I cannot, then I will continue in Sportscars. Let us wait and see.'

2 KERPEN-MANNHEIM

GROWING UP AND KARTING

My helmet carries the German national colours of black, red and yellow, with some blue. I wanted the national colours, but arranged in my design, and that is how it has turned out. I had a friend in Germany who painted cars and I said that I wanted a design. I just told him to do something, I had no ideas. He brought me the helmet with the blue and the stars on it and that was the starting point. There was something on the side that I didn't like so we took that off and did something else. That was in 1986 and it's been like that ever since. I didn't really have that much input into it.

Michael Schumacher talking about his helmet design in 1993.

THEY CALL THE AREA WEST OF COLOGNE, off the motorway towards Aachen and Liege, the flatlands. It is an unkind description, full of innuendo. Certainly, the landscapes around Kerpen are not those of Switzerland, but neither are they as dull and dreary as some detractors would have you believe. This area is industrial and agricultural. It is productive, filled with hard-working people, fields of cereal crops and sugar beet, sprinkled with small factories and broken up by a network of small roads linking the many villages. This is rural, provincial Germany. This is the ordinary heartland of the north and the place where Michael Schumacher grew up, discovered his love of karting and motor racing and learned his way in the world.

Michael was born in Hurth-Hermuhlheim on 3 January 1969,

his father Rolf, a bricklayer, and his mother Elisabeth, adding another racing-mad son to their family in younger brother Ralf, some years later. For the Schumachers, life was simple and modest and Michael's upbringing was filled with the traditions and habits of any typically suburban German family. He loved his mother's apple-strudel, chocolates (later to become the forbidden luxury of the Formula One motor homes), visits to the local Italian cafés and bars, sessions at the local kart track and straightforward pop music. This is not a land of introspection or pomp, but a land of ordinary people, community values and simple pleasures in which obedience, respect and discipline are valued.

The Schumachers like it that way. Father Rolf has always resisted temptations to take a share of the limelight offered by his son's celebrity status. Mother Elisabeth prefers to remain at their modest family home in Kerpen-Mannheim, close to the local kart track where Michael learned his way, where she has a fast-food stall and where Rolf is much involved, helping with the organization, the repairs and the maintenance, making sure young kart enthusiasts, as Michael was, have a reliable machine to hire and in which to practise as they start their careers. They are a well-known and a well-liked family. At the local fire station, any request for directions towards the family home, or to the Europa Moto Drom, the track where the Schumacher kart club settled after being ousted by noisy protesters from its original site, is met with a polite smile, plenty of arm-waving directions and a proudly-presented souvenir brochure of Michael's achievements. If you are lost in the district, the assistance is likely to extend beyond directions to a personal direction service, a proud local leading the way. Kerpen, it is clear, has taken much pride in the achievements of its local hero.

At the Europa Moto Drom kart track, even on a quiet Monday, there is much activity and interest. There are two circuits, both laid on ground salvaged from a sand and gravel pit surrounded by newly-planted coniferous trees. It is a hot, dry place in summer, filled with the smell of asphalt and old rubber tyres, alive with wasps and ambitious teenagers in overalls and helmets trying to learn to do it the Schumacher way. From the roadside, this place looks unattractive and tough. There are caravans and dogs. But down the hill, near the small circuit, near to the snack bar run by Elisabeth Schumacher who dispenses sausages and French fries to hungry drivers, fans and curious visitors, there is a different atmosphere. It is the corporate touch of Ford and Dekra, left behind by promotional days in support of Michael Schumacher, the Formula One driver. It is clear that Michael's success has caught on and caught the imagination, but with typical modesty he maintains a level-headed association with his old friends, his old club, his old kart track. And no-one in Kerpen has ever had a bad word to say about him.

This kart track remains an important part of Schumacher's life and he returns there to visit, purely for fun, as often as he can. Regrettably, for him, it is not often enough. But he still feels it is the place where he can rediscover himself most easily when the pressures and worries of Formula One threaten to overwhelm him. It was here, after all, that he first took on the world – in the form of the richer boys with better karts – and won, in his own machine constructed from other boys' rejected parts. 'My karts were not so much made from second or third-hand parts, but from 10th or 12th-hand parts,' he joked. 'But I was so enthusiastic about karting, I would be there all the time. I would spend hours there practising, and if I had taken the chance I could have gone professional. I never really thought of anything else.'

Michael's first introduction to speed had come with a pedal-kart which was later improved with the addition of a small engine. When he was only four, he crashed for the first time – into a lamppost – and in the process instigated his father's decision that his son, clearly at home and happy on motorized projectiles, should be introduced to a proper way of doing things at the local kart track. Michael recalls it well. 'My father took away my nice "kick" go-kart, I remember,' he said. 'He had an old motorcycle engine and put it in the "kick" go-kart. That's the way it started. First we went to the green and then on the pavement until – and you know this story – I had a meeting with a lamppost. Then we changed to a race circuit, the first proper one was quite close to home – 10 or 15 kms away at Kerpen-Horrem. When I joined the club and became a member there, I was the youngest driver and I came straightaway into the newspaper. From there, everything started. I was four at this time and when I was five I got what I think was the cheapest go-kart ever built.'

This kart, built by his father, was created from second-hand pieces of equipment thrown away by other people. 'But it did run,' stressed Schumacher, 'and we even won races with it. That was the most important thing. It had a 100cc engine. My father actually had to cut a piece out of the middle of the chassis and glue it back together again because I was too short to reach the pedals. It did work in the end.'

And so the Schumacher career began at the old Graf Berghe von Trips go-kart circuit in Kerpen-Horrem. 'The club is at Kerpen-Mannheim now,' said Schumacher. 'It is the same club, but we had to move because the people living near to the old circuit started to get angry . . . My father used to work at the first circuit. He started to work on go-karts, renting them at first. He built up rental karts there. Suddenly, he was offered this work, which he could do alongside his job. At that time, I was probably seven, so I had probably been a member of the club for two or three years.'

Rolf took more than a passing interest in the karting and by combining his work and a part-time job at the circuit, repairing and maintaining the karts, he could help Michael. With Elisabeth also working there, Rolf knew that at least the family could keep a safe eye on their oldest son.

Predictably enough, Michael took to karts like a natural. He loved it and he practised all the hours he could. By the age of six, he was club champion for the first time and displaying a rare ability. His machines were never of the quality of those of boys from wealthier families and most of his rivals were older than him. Yet, whatever the opposition, he won, and his success soon brought with it a new set of problems for his father as Michael's demands for better karts grew with increasing intensity. Tyres, for example, were a source of perceived performance enhancement for the young competitors and many went to buy new ones imported from Italy, throwing their old and out-of-fashion tyres onto the rubbish heap. Michael would go to the rubbish heap and salvage the best of those he found, discarded by his rivals, and still beat them on the track.

As time passed, it became increasingly apparent to Rolf Schumacher that his son's hobby was going to cost him rather more than he could afford if he was to support him as he wished. Not only tyres, but also engines had to be purchased and the karts themselves had to be overhauled, maintained and kept in the best possible condition. The breaking point arrived when Michael wanted a new engine which cost 800 Deutschmarks. His father informed his son that he could not afford to buy it for him and, for a moment, Michael faced the end of his career as a wunderkind in karting in northern Germany. The moment did not last long, however, as the Schumacher family soon found a new way of funding their son's extraordinary talent by gaining sponsorship from friends and local businessmen.

One of the first offers of financial assistance came from Gerd Noack, a friend of Rolf Schumacher who had made money in the carpet business. His support was invaluable in the early days, but it was the more significant longer-term sponsorship from Jurgen Dilk, a man who had succeeded in the slot-machine scene, and from Willy Bergmeister, in whose garage Michael worked after school and who also gave him the benefit of his own racing experience, which enabled Michael to enjoy not only a long and successful karting career, but a secure path towards single-seater racing and beyond. For the young Schumacher, it was an ideal platform as he never had to borrow money to gain a chance to race. This form of funding, used by Niki Lauda, for example, at the start of his career, would have been abhorrent to the family. 'I was raised never to spend more money than I had,' Michael often remarked later, when referring to his childhood. He would also add, with just as much frequency, that he felt an obligation to his sponsors. 'If they have helped me, then the least I can do to repay them is to always try my best to succeed. I cannot slacken off and relax, can I?'

Karting dominated the formative years of Michael Schumacher, though he did go to school, the Otto-Hahn Realschule, where he showed promise in many academic subjects including English and mathematics and demonstrated plentiful talent in several sports, particularly judo. When the time came for him to leave, not having shown any inclination or desire to go to university or any other form of higher education, he chose to take up an opportunity to become an apprentice mechanic at a local Volkswagen and BMW garage. 'In car racing, that can only be an advantage for a driver,' recalled Schumacher later. 'If you have a good knowledge of technology, you can describe what a car does much more easily. You may also have ideas about what can be changed or improved. But it was something I did not particularly enjoy. Quite a lot of the work can be really boring.

'I think I was about 17 and a half when I left school. I had nothing planned. I was not top-class at anything, because the only thing I really concentrated on was go-karting. I loved it. I became good at it because I did it constantly and I had the talent for it. I just did not have the same talent for judo or football, which I also did. Well, not as much talent as you need to become as good as I had to for Formula One. That is how I left school. I went to the garage and I did my normal exams in the garage, it lasted two and a half years. At the same time, I was following a course which suggested I might become a professional go-kart driver or something like that. I was so keen. I was also asked to test a Formula Ford 1600 car, but I went on and passed my exams. I thought it was necessary to have some qualifications. If nothing happened, I knew I would need something, so I was planning and preparing for that.

'I did not really enjoy working with the cars very much. Just changing oil filters and so on, washing cars, it was not that interesting. Around that time, after I left school, I also had one year away in Darmstadt where I spent nearly half the time in the wash garage, cleaning cars. Then I stood up once and said 'Hey, guys, I'm not here to learn to wash cars. I'm here to learn to repair cars and they said okay and I started to repair cars.'

In typical Schumacher fashion, even the task of a two-and-a-half year apprenticeship in a garage had to be cut down to size and dealt with quickly. The garage he worked in was connected with a dealer who had supported his kart career, but Michael was not content with this and after one year he returned home to Kerpen where he became involved with Willy Bergmeister, who ran in the European Saloon Car championship. Bergmeister gave him a perfect opportunity to learn his trade well as a mechanic in his garage and, as a result, he was able to finish his course and pass his exams in only 18 months instead of the prescribed 30 months. 'He was incredibly helpful to me,' said Michael, for whom Darmstadt had been a valuable growing-up experience away from home, although it was the place where he also, as he admitted, nearly lost his fluent grasp of English. 'I forgot a lot in 1986,' he said. 'I wasn't travelling and I wasn't in school any more.

'I really didn't have any English needs, I didn't have to speak it at all. For one year, I did not speak in English really and when I came back to do some more karting events and then the Formula Ford, in Europe, I built up my English again, but it was difficult. Darmstadt was an important time for me. I was away from home and I had to handle my own life. I had been around with girls and that stuff and I had £200 a week to live on and I went home at weekends, to work with my father and to earn some more money. It was my time really, quite interesting for me and it was very useful to get a different life. It was quite a good growing-up time for me.'

Asked if he had ever made any mistakes, or let the handbrake slip on his phenomenal self-control, he replied adamantly: 'No, I never did. I never spent any money which I didn't have and I never did things which took me out [of myself]. I have seen other people and that is why probably I have never done it myself. There is nothing interesting about this time in that way.'

Michael's teenage years were nothing unusual, except for his obsession with speed and karting. 'That's how he always was,' said his close friend Udo Irnich, who recalled meeting the 'baby' world champion when he was still a frail child at the kart track. 'He was so small then, just a little boy – he weighed less than 50 kilos – but he drove the karts so fast,' he said. 'He was interested only in them. He would go to school, he had some friends, some girlfriends too, and he would go to the cinema, or play football, or sometimes go to a party, but most of his time he was at the kart track or training. That was his life. You have to remember, he entered the German, the European and the world kart championships, so he was away all weekends and when he was not away, he was training and getting ready, preparing himself and his kart for the next race. He liked cycling too, but he was very professional about everything he did, even as a little child. All the way, he has been the same.'

Jurgen Dilk was the most important figure in the life of the young Michael Schumacher, according to the journalist Christoph Schulte. 'He was like a second father for Michael,' he said. 'He looked after him from when he was a schoolboy and always supported him in his racing. He really loves Michael. He helped him so much. When the family did not have enough money to go on with the karting, when Michael was I think about ten, his father told him he could not pay for everything anymore. Mr Dilk had two sons and one of them was a go-kart driver, but he did not work too well. Mr Dilk said "Well, I will do something" and he bought a new kart for Michael. He bought it and then at about the same time, he realized that Michael was a true hot-shot, so he decided to give him all the equipment he needed. I think he was also the person who did the most for Michael to get into Formula Ford and into Formula Konig as well.

'Willi Weber did not become involved until Formula Three. That is where he came in. Willi was a Formula Three driver himself, before. Then he built up his own team, the WTS team: Weber, Trella and Stuttgart. And it was a good racing team. Trella was very good on racing set-ups with Michael, but that came later of course.'

Michael also recalled how close he was to Mr Dilk and his two boys. 'By 1983, when I was 14, we knew each other quite well and we had become friends and I was helping his sons and he saw the problems that I had. I just could not continue, if I did not have a sponsor. At that time, he was in a good business and he said "Okay, I'll do it, and the only thing I want to have is your trophies." So I said "That's fine for me – I can drive and you get the trophies."

'And we became closer, as friends, and it was just a very good time altogether and all this happened really from 1983 to 1986, when I went to Darmstadt. When I lived there, the relationship went off a bit because it was not necessary any more for him to pay me. I did not get paid, but I was driving in a kart for nothing for the dealer in the European championship. Then, I went to Formula Ford 1600 and Mr Dilk and I were together again, because again I needed a sponsor, and he agreed to do it. He just signed the contract for me, which was for very little money. It was £10,000 for ten races, not much, but I could not have signed it because I did not have £10,000. I did not even have £100 – so he signed for me and everyone knows the rest of my career from there. He was very important for me and he is still very important to me and still comes and joins me at the races sometimes. In 1993, he came to three or four races and he came to two more in the first part of 1994.'

Mr Dilk's influence was to remain significant. As a genuine fan and supporter of Michael's unique talent, he launched the official Michael Schumacher Fan Club and became its first president. In that capacity, he was at the 1994 Belgian Grand Prix at Spa-Francorchamps with more than 100 members, camping beneath the trees in heavy rain, hoping for an outstanding win from his young hero. Schumacher delivered, of course, but his car was later to be declared illegal, much to the disappointment of the man whose support had carried him through his karting years.

Bearded, open-faced, bespectacled, Mr Dilk oozed respect for Michael's achievements as he talked in the Fan Club's official campsite. Flanked by his son Guido, at 27, two years older than Michael, Mr Dilk talked with warmth of his memories. So, too, did Guido, who as a boy of 14 had been, in motor racing parlance, blown away by the rising star. 'We saw him every day at the kart track,' recalled Guido. 'We used to race and play together and it became a friendship. My father saw he (Michael) was a very good driver and so he invited him to go with us and we went racing in all of Germany together. We went to every kart race we could at that time, always together, and we slept in the van. It was good. We had some very good times.

'At 13, or maybe 14, he was a very, very good driver. By that time, after a couple of years of this, I had started my job in a coal mine and I stopped racing. Michael carried on, of course, and my father carried on taking him to the races. But not me. My family was able to help him. My father was in a business with the machines in amusement arcades – juke boxes, flippers and so on –

and so he could help him. But he did not only do that, he also went out and found sponsors for Michael too.'

These early sponsors ranged from Mercedes dealer Bodden Gerd, to any local butcher, baker or candlestick-maker with the funds to help their local boy. 'Michael was always a popular guy, very nice and easy to get on with,' said Guido. 'He taught me about karting later and he started to train hard too. He took himself seriously and when we went away, or he was away with my father, he would always go to bed at 10 o'clock. He had no time to play around then. Not with us or with the girls. Racing was his life. It was all his life.'

Mr Dilk and Michael shared many adventures with trips across Europe for karting events from Brands Hatch in England to circuits in Italy, Spain, France and Belgium. All the time, Michael gained experience, mechanical sympathy and racecraft. It all came in useful. 'One day, in the German championship for juniors, Michael was leading, when, on the second lap, he knew he had a problem,' recalled Mr Dilk. 'He put his hand back onto the engine, where he felt he had a carburettor problem. He left his hand there for 18 laps, driving with one hand on the wheel, and he won the race. Afterwards, he told me what was wrong. Apparently there were two small screws loose on the fixing of the carburettor. That victory helped him win the German championship, when he was about 15 or 16, I think. It showed too what a great feeling he had for engines.'

Mr Dilk, together with his wife and Michael travelled to among other places, Le Mans in France, a trip which typified their weekends across Europe. They learnt all about one another. Michael was like one of the family. Indeed, as Mr Dilk said later, Michael would refer to him when asked as being like 'my father, teacher and my pastor rolled into one.' Mr Dilk was so close to the Schumacher family that they agreed he could, on Michael's behalf, be responsible for making protests and dealing with them at races as Michael was under age. When Michael later embarked on his single-seater career, he again needed Mr Dilk's reassurance.

'It was when Stefan Bellof was killed,' said Guido. 'After that my father said I cannot go with him in Formula One because of my fears from this accident. But Michael called him back himself and he said "Please come with me, I want you to be with me in Formula Konig", for the trials at Hockenheim. He went to meet him there, but he was one hour too late and Michael was very down, very disappointed. He thought my father was not coming, but he did.' Mr Dilk remained a loyal Michael Schumacher supporter and did all he could. 'It was not my money which I gave him,' he said. 'It was my time and my heart. I did what I could and I helped him to find sponsors.' Emotive words, but true, from Mr Dilk who continues to wear around his neck a chain from which hangs a small kart, a momento of those days they spent together. 'There was only one other made – and that one is Michael's,' said Guido. 'For me it was always so nice to work with Michael,' said Mr Dilk. 'He had an open mind. He listened to all that was said. There was always a good feeling in working together on anything because he is a wonderful person. Everything I have given him through those years, from my heart, he has given me back.' To this day, Michael makes sure that Mr Dilk is never required to pay whenever he travels to watch Michael racing in a Formula One Grand Prix.

Michael's karting days gave him the insight and the feel he needed to develop into the great racing driver he became when he was older. But they were never able to give him total satisfaction and he found, particularly on the European circuit, that it was difficult to compete well against rivals who were far better financed. In this period, he undoubtedly realized that he needed his sponsors and their patronage just as much as they needed him. He also learned that success came through hard work, something bred in him through his family. At this time he collected a series of karting titles. He was German Junior Champion in 1984, at the age of 15, repeating the feat the following year when he was also runner-up in the world championship. In 1986, aged 17, he was third in the German senior karting series and third, also, in the European series. In 1987, at 18, he was German and European champion. It was obvious he was something special.

'I was only young,' he remembered. 'It was the end of the year. I was staying with a family and this young guy who lived there took me to a disco. We had a lot of fun! Of course we had a lot of contact with girls. I was on my own at the time. I didn't have a girlfriend of my own so I was free to do what I wanted. But I did not go with any of those girls, even if they were attractive and fun. I was – and still am – very well aware of the dangers of going with just anyone. Things like AIDS and so on are a real threat to us all and I did not want to take those sort of risks. So, we all had a good time dancing and talking – and that was it. I know everyone thinks all drivers are like playboys, but that is not the way it is or was for me. I am not the sort of guy who is interested in one night stands at all. I like to have fun, yes, but just fun. There is nothing to be proved in going with a girl for one night. I have seen it and I know it is not for me.'

By 1988, when he was 19, he was looking further afield and considering a switch from karts to car racing. Once again, he needed help – financial help – and again it arrived thanks to the support of Jurgen Dilk who, together with a Lamborghini dealer named Hoecker, smoothed Schumacher's path into the German Formula Konig championship and the German and European Formula Ford 1600 series. Typically, he learned fast, showed an uncanny natural ability to drive fast immediately, exploded onto the track and made the transition with ease. Within almost no time at all, he was a proven winner in all classes. He was runner-up in the European Formula Ford 1600 series behind Mika Salo and sixth in the German series. His talent became the talk of the junior formulae; spies watched him racing and, before long, began talking of the next logical step as being an early move to Formula Three, a critical and often difficult move for any driver.

Luckily, for Schumacher, he was spotted early and given his chance by Willi Weber without having to find the 650,000 Deutschmarks usually required in sponsorship to reach the first rung of the ladder to Formula One. Weber had heard of him and his speed and Schumacher had won the Formula Konig title and impressed in Formula Ford. Weber knew, as he searched for a replacement for Joachim Winkelhock, who had just won the German Formula Three title with his team, that Schumacher might be the boy. Having asked around, and after talking to, among other people, Domingos Piedade, the Portuguese AMG Mercedes chief – a man with a long involvement with Formula

One having worked with Michele Alboreto and Ayrton Senna in the past – Weber settled on Schumacher. Piedade, who had two sons racing in German karting, knew what he was talking about and told Weber: 'There is one driver who is in a class of his own – Michael Schumacher. He is the one you want.' Gerd Kramer seconded this view and pushed Weber towards the boy from Kerpen.

So, Weber took a look and was impressed. The impression was made at the Salzburgring, at a Formula Konig race, in 1988, in heavy pouring rain. Conditions were diabolical, Michael was seventh on the grid, but he was confident, his driving assured and clean, and after the first lap he was in the lead. He drove beautifully. 'The precision with which he drove impressed me,' said Weber. 'He had a clean line and he kept it, absolutely and identically, in every lap. He had a complete mastery of his car and the conditions.'

Weber had seen Schumacher racing in Formula Ford, but he was not bewitched until he saw him that day at the Salzburgring. 'The way he drove impressed me completely,' he recalled. 'It wasn't only that he was quick. It was the way he handled the car on the limit. He just pulled away as if nobody else was behind him. He was driving his own race. He impressed me so much. So, I sent somebody to his team. He came to see me face to face, then we spoke and I asked him to race Formula Three. He said "Yes," but said he wanted to know why I chose him. He was completely out of control – he was too happy. We made a date for him to test the car and make a seat. Then we met at the Nurburgring. The way he handled the car was absolutely unbelievable. Then we called him in and made some changes. After only an hour on the track, he was already 1.5 seconds quicker than my driver. Afterwards, I asked him if he wanted to race for two years in Formula Three, but he said he couldn't because he had no money. So I said "Don't worry about that. You just drive the car." Under these conditions, we drew up a contract and I said to him "Help me to get my money back" and six years on we are still together.'

Weber had watched the young Schumacher, in Formula Ford, in both Mainz-Finthen and in Hockenheim before he was totally convinced. 'I recognized that he was something special, so good he deserved a very special chance. Everything he did on the track was superior, playful and easy for him. I had to offer him that chance.' On the same night that they agreed on racing in Formula Three, Weber offered to take care of Schumacher's career and they agreed a 10-year management contract.

Aware of Schumacher's background, Weber decided to do all he could to help him develop his talent and potential inside and outside the car, encouraging him to grow in self-esteem and confidence. He barely needed to make the effort; Schumacher was such a natural, in all respects, that he made no enemies, could charm anyone and could, at the same time, drive a car to distraction. After three races of his first season in Formula Three, he led the championship, having scored three thirds and having established himself as a strong newcomer to the series. At Hockenheim, he also killed off all suggestions that he might be a softie when he resisted a challenge from Michael Bartels, who collided with him. 'Bartels drove into me,' said Schumacher. 'I was angry and it was unacceptable.' It was a signal of things to come and many other drivers were to learn that Schumacher would not be intimidated.

It also proved that Schumacher had overcome his own self-doubts, according to Christophe Schulte. 'Early on, he was worried,' said Schulte. 'It was one of the few times, or periods, when I have seen him worried. He came to me once and he just did not seem normal. He did not have the wide grin he usually has. He said he felt he may have to go back to go-karts. He said "I am not sure I am able to do this." He had lost his confidence. He had lost his way, briefly. But he soon found his determination again. That is how he is. He listens, he learns, he is confident and he is determined.'

By the time of the fifth round of his first season in Formula Three, Schumacher had made a name for himself. Fast enough to have outstripped his WTS teammate Frank Schmickler, he was established as a championship contender as the teams headed towards Zeltweg, the fast Austrian circuit, for a race in the pouring rain and an exciting duel with another fast-rising young German driver, Heinz-Harald Frentzen. Born two years earlier in Monchengladbach, Frentzen had maturity and experience on his side. He had raced against Schumacher before too, in karts, and had won. But on that day, it was to be the 20-year-old from Kerpen who triumphed in the wet. 'He was so young and he still had so much to learn that I worried that he might allow his success to go to his head,' said Weber. 'But it never did and it never has.'

As that summer went by, Schumacher's form ebbed and flowed and Frentzen and another future Formula One star and friend, Karl Wendlinger, took control of the championship. They were, together with Schumacher, a formidable group and one recognized by many in Germany as a trio for the future. But few expected they would be taken together to form the Mercedes junior team as was to happen the following year. For each it was a surprise, but for Schumacher, who had little interest in the history of motor racing or the wider aspects of the sport, it was like a great adventure. In the summer of 1989, for example, he watched his first Formula One race, the Monaco Grand Prix, and was bored rigid. Such was his feeling for the so-called top formula of racing. 'I did not race there, but my teammate did,' he remembered. 'So I went there because I knew I would race there the year after. I just went to see what it was like and we were camping there. I went with the camping van and I was there with my girlfriend and with some other friends.

'I closed my ears because it was so noisy and I can remember I watched a quarter of the race and then I left because it was just . . . well, it is always interesting to drive, but to just stay in one position and just watch it, to see just one car passing like that is nothing. I did not get any satisfaction at all. I went home and I watched it on television. I knew who was first, but I didn't know who was second so I just watched it on television. My father never took me racing. I always enjoy taking part, but I prefer watching go-kart races to Formula One. I stood at the Casino, to watch in Monaco. I was interested in Joachim Winkelhock.'

Schumacher's own racing in that first year of Formula Three was consistently close and exciting. It seemed the championship would be decided between Wendlinger and Frentzen, with Schumacher chasing, as they went to the Nurburgring for the penultimate round. There, however, Bartels became involved again, colliding with Frentzen in a move which took him off the circuit, damaged Wendlinger's hopes and, in the process, opened the way for Schumacher to claim his second victory. It also set up a thrilling and controversial final race at Hockenheim where Bartels claimed victory and Wendlinger the title. Schumacher finished third, ending the championship with 163 points, equal with Frentzen, but one less than Wendlinger.

'I was not too unhappy at the outcome because it meant Michael could race for me for another year,' said Weber. 'We had a new goal. If he had won that title in his first season, it would not have accomplished much really and I would not have known what to do next. The way it was, it allowed us to stay together for another go at the title.' And they did. But little did they know that it was to be a year in which Michael's talents were to be recruited by Mercedes as well and from then on he was to be described no more as just the boy from Kerpen, but as 'the Mercedes youngster'.

It was a description he could not ignore. Despite a poor start to the season in 1990, at both Zolder and Hockenheim, and then a fifth place after much commotion at the Nurburgring, Schumacher recovered his poise and form and the results flowed. He won five of the next six races. It was much as before, a mixture of extraordinary speed with occasional errors, but too many spellbinding moments for anyone to ignore the arrival of a natural star. At Zolder, for example, Schumacher dominated qualifying in his Reynard-VW 903, clocking his fastest time in only a handful of laps before sitting back to watch from the pits. Peter Zakowski finished second fastest alongside him, but was left almost for dead at the start as Schumacher led away and into the first corner, building up a six second lead in the opening seven laps. He looked unbeatable, but then 'unexpectedly understeered into the tyres' at Turn Two, according to a report in *Autosport*. On the way back to the pits, he hid his disappointment as he bumped into Jochen Maas, by then one of his sportscar teammates at Mercedes. The conversation was not recorded. A few days later at Hockenheim, it was much the same story. Schumacher took pole, but spun off during a chaotic first lap on a wet track and ended up 19th, following repairs. The

Nurburgring was the scene, however, of a memorable drive by Schumacher's standards. His car had been adjudged underweight by 1.8 kgs by the scrutineers and he had started from the back of the grid, but he produced a storming performance which was to typify many similarly spirited outings in difficult circumstances later in his career.

After three races, he was 42 points behind the championship leader Wolfgang Kaufmann, but he kept his nerve to come through and win so strongly. 'The most important thing then was to stay in control, not to lose my nerve, not to try to use any force after a bad start, but to work calmly and consistently and keep working at it,' said Schumacher. He did and it worked. His good run began at Avus, in Berlin, where in a slip-streaming battle with Otto Rensing and seven other drivers, he came through to resist a last-gasp attack from Ellen Lohr, almost forcing her into the rails on the run towards the chicane, to win. It lifted him to fourth place in the championship with 26 points to Kaufmann's 50. The chase was on. Schumacher had recovered from his early-season problems.

'There was something important in this season,' said Schulte. 'The way he recovered. There was something in him which reminds me now, looking back, of Martin Brundle. He just would not be put off. He had to make up for the disappointing start to the season and to make the most of it. And you could see him doing it, in his face and his actions. At the start of the season, everyone had told him that he was the new champion. He had the best car, the best engine. This was the Michael of 1990, a good young driver with a Reynard with a Speiss VW engine, not an Opel. It was something well done by Willi Weber. He got Michael the best car and the best engine. He had good connections and he did a good job for Michael.'

For Schumacher, however, this was no normal year. In addition to the work required for success with Weber in Formula Three, he had to handle the pressures of coping with his Mercedes opportunity too, and all that it brought with it. 'There was a lot of pressure on Michael then with this package,' said Schulte. 'He had to win in Formula Three and on the other hand, he had to try and cope with Group C too. And there he had some problems as well. He just wasn't able to do all he wanted. For example, he was disqualified in some races, and in Monaco he was not allowed to take part in the Formula Three race, which he had wanted to do, because he had a Group C licence.'

Not that Michael allowed it to bother him. Concentration, on a single goal, on a single lap, on a start, on achieving a prescribed level of fitness, had always been one of his strengths. Thus he was able, on 3 June 1990, at Wunstorf, to score the second successive victory of his Formula Three season, with a lights-to-flag performance from pole position, only a fortnight after being excluded from the Empire Trophy Sportscar meeting at Silverstone, where he had been driving with Jochen Mass for the Sauber-Mercedes team. The disappointment of Silverstone was a blow, but one from which Schumacher recovered with rapid aplomb after being adjudged, individually, to have not worn his seatbelts on his return lap, after stopping on the circuit during an untimed Saturday morning practice session when the gearshift on his car broke.

Schumacher was in the C11 at the time, attempting to change to fifth on the pit straight. He could do nothing and the car coasted to Copse in neutral before he steered into the infield by the pit exit road to be greeted by a group of running team members and mechanics, led by team manager Max Welti. Schumacher climbed out, but resumed after jamming the gearbox into third and then drove back round the circuit to the pits without a gear lever assembly. The faulty part was carried back to the pits by his crewmen, no-one realizing what was to follow before final qualifying began.

After a studious read through the rule book, the FISA Stewards at the meeting had found Article 13, paragraph (c), of the World Sports Prototype Championship regulations. This said that 'any repairs outside the pits must be carried out by the driver alone using any tools or parts carried in his car . . .' And in paragraph (f), it added that 'with the exception of the driver, . . . no-one is authorized to touch a car which has stopped outside the pits.'

Schumacher himself, according to an official who alleged he was not wearing seatbelts, had infringed another part of Article 13 and had to be excluded. Both Welti and Jochen Neerpasch, the

Mercedes motorsport director who had brought Schumacher into the new 'junior' team, argued against the decisions and said it was not clear where the pit-lane stopped. 'The marshals pushed Michael's car into what we thought was still the pit-lane zone,' said Welti. 'But the stewards decided that this was no longer the pit-lane zone. It was certainly not defined in the rules. We didn't work on the car at all. We just opened the door and had a look at what was broken and we told Michael to try to put it into a gear and in the end, he was successful. I touched the car myself, but I did not work on it.'

As to the seatbelts, Schumacher complained in the strongest possible terms that he had, in fact, done them up and that the officials were mistaken. But it was all to no avail. 'They said that I didn't have my belts done up,' he said. 'But I got into the car, started it, closed the door and then did the seatbelts. Then I came round to the pits and before I stopped the car I undid my seatbelts and opened the door – only then the guy could see that my seatbelt was undone, of course. They just did not believe me . . .

'The problem, I think, is that we were in England. It was not a major mistake for me and I have no bad feeling with the mechanics. We are all people, we all make mistakes. If I had gone to the mechanics and said they were stupid, then what? We all thought the car was in the pit-lane. It was 150 metres from the track. There was no regulation to say where the beginning and the end of the pit-lane was until this problem. It's crazy. I think England was the problem.'

Given the trouble that Schumacher was to experience at the same English circuit in the summer of 1994, he might have selected Silverstone as the source of his misery, not England. 'They disqualified me because I wasn't wearing a harness,' he went on. 'But I was. When I started the car, I only had the belts around me, as I said, but when I closed the door I clicked them shut. When I stop it is my routine. You open the belts, then the door. But forget it. That's why I think the problem was only because we were in England.'

In common with many other occasions in his career, when he was to brush with controversy, Schumacher held an immoveable belief in his own position. To those who admired him, it was clearly a strength. To those who saw him race, it was clearly an asset, as he was able to shrug aside all outside influences as soon as he sat in a car. But some saw it as arrogance. It happened in Formula Three, it happened in sportscar racing, it happened on the weekend of his Formula One debut with Jordan and again at Benetton and it happened again and again after that. So, to those who knew what had happened to him at Silverstone, but who understood the character of this extraordinary young racing driver from Kerpen, there was nothing very exceptional in seeing him so dominant at Wunstorf, where his masterful 20-lap win moved him into the forefront of the Formula Three title race 14 days later.

He followed that with a good second place, in his WTS Reynard, behind Otto Rensing's VW Motorsport Ralt-VW, in Norisring's 44-lap race, on 30 June, before taking the championship lead outright on 15 July at Zeltweg in his West-liveried car. Schumacher had taken pole again at the Osterreichring and had the race virtually won in five laps thanks to another flying start. Marco Werner came home second and Rensing was sixth, allowing Schumacher to top the points table with 83 to Rensing's 78 with three races remaining. A week later however, Schumacher had other business: back on the Sportscar racing scene with Mercedes at Dijon.

This time, it all went right for Schumacher. No alarms, no breakages, no disqualifications. Sauber-Mercedes were happy too, delivering a crushing one-two in searing heat which proved that fitness was as much a necessity as durability and skill in their battle with the Silk Cut Jaguar XJR11's. *Autosport*'s report by Adam Cooper said that Schumacher had enjoyed the honour of leading the race for three laps and that he had 'done an excellent job in the second Merc, running quickly and bringing back fuel.' It also pointed out that this contribution by Schumacher had ensured Mass had sufficient fuel to run with extra turbo boost for the final session of the race. It ended with Jean-Louis Schlesser winning in the leading Mercedes by just 3.8 seconds from Mass, after a race of 127 laps lasting more than two and a half hours. In Schumacher's curriculum vitae, it meant he had learned his first big lesson in sportscar racing and was maturing rapidly. Yes, bad news for those rivals awaiting his return to Formula Three two weeks later at Diepholz.

By any measure, it was a startling performance and a fine victory at Diepholz. Seventh on the grid, three rows behind Jorg Muller who had claimed his first pole position in his Reynard-VW, Schumacher made a flying start and was up to second by the end of the first lap. He set his sights on Muller and outbraked him to take the lead on the fifth lap, never to be threatened, winning by four seconds. It was a demonstration of determination and strength of mind. His lead in the championship was stretched to 13 points over Rensing and then increased to 18 points at the Nurburgring with his fifth victory in round nine, having claimed his fifth pole of the year for the race. Nothing, it seemed at the time, could go wrong for Schumacher. The man of the 'Silver Arrows' was enjoying a golden touch and it shone brightly that Sunday, on 19 August 1990, when he won the Formula Three race in the morning and then proceeded to demonstrate the full range of his talents in the Mercedes team in the afternoon.

On the same circuit, but in his other guise, he continued to prove his credentials among the men as he and Jochen Mass, in their C11, finished second again behind the victorious Sauber Mercedes of Schlesser and Mauro Baldi. This time, Michael proved himself by qualifying and racing supremely well. Described by his critics as an 'L-team' junior, Schumacher was given his opportunity when Mass was struck by electrical problems at the start of the first session. As the team worked feverishly to find the cause, Schumacher climbed into the T-car for his first run on soft tyres with boost – an experience, *Autosport* reported, he had never had in testing. The usual reliable Schumacher response was supplied: two very fast consecutive laps which had tongues wagging. The best was 1:21.013 which, to the delight of the team, was good enough for pole at that time. When Schlesser, his nose perhaps disjointed, tried again he cut three-tenths off that time, leaving Michael with a challenge he could not meet on his second run. 'I had never really used qualifying tyres before and I did not know how to get the best out of them,' he admitted, satisfied, naturally, that his time was better than the restored Mass could manage.

The race was equally interesting. Schlesser started from pole and had little trouble in pulling clear of the troubled Mass who fell into a scrap with Martin Brundle, in his XJR11, for second place. Mass had opted for a soft compound front right tyre and it was not working. Indeed, it was a decision he lived to regret as he struggled with the Mercedes T-car, Schlesser out in front pulling into a 20 second lead by the end of lap 15. Brundle was only three seconds behind Mass and threatening the C11 when Mass decided to end his own agony and make an early pit stop after 26 laps. Enter Schumacher.

After a rapid pit-stop during which the car took only 67 litres of fuel on board, Schumacher rejoined the fray in 15th place, a lap down on Schlesser – who had lapped everyone bar the top six – but just behind the Jaguars on the road. In confident mood, after his Formula Three success that morning, he soon latched onto Jan Lammers and made the most of the improved handling of his C11, now fitted with medium tyres all round. On lap 31, he unlapped himself from Lammers. On lap 32, he unlapped himself from Brundle. There was no doubt Schumacher was doing a good job and as the places ahead of him began to change through pit-stops, he took advantage, reeling in his rivals with a clinical efficiency which belied his years.

Mauro Baldi, Schlesser's team-mate, was hamstrung by poor tyres and was soon devoured by Schumacher who led from lap 52 until he pitted on lap 67. He closed the gap again on the two Jaguars, lapping Andy Wallace on lap 56 and Alain Ferte on lap 58. Gradually, he built up a clear lead on Baldi of nearly 15 seconds before coming in, with two litres of fuel left showing on the computer after his fast and economical run. Mass resumed, just in front of Baldi on the road, but almost a lap down. Were they impressed? They were. The race continued with Mass unable to win, with Schlesser victorious; but the real star was the new boy, the óne with 'L' plates who had contributed so much in car number two.

He may have benefited from a weight advantage after his entry into the race, as with only 67 litres he was running a lighter load than that of Baldi, who took on 86 litres of fuel when he stopped, but he certainly made the most of it. He always did. When he travelled to Le Mans for the FIA European Formula Three race, he also pulled off a victory over a small field which revealed more of his considerable range of qualities. Unfortunately, the result did not stand in the record books as RC Racing protested at Schumacher's decision to swap to his spare car with a different engine type when the race was red-flagged and victory was handed to one of his future Formula One rivals Alessandro Zanardi.

The penultimate race of the German Formula Three season took place at the Nurburgring where Schumacher was declared the provisional champion, having finished fifth, revised to fourth, following an often acrimonious duel with Otto Rensing, who was disqualified for passing under a yellow flag. It was a mighty race on yet another soaking wet day, so many of which have produced the finest drives of Schumacher's career. Schumacher led from the start, chased by Rensing, and the two title contenders made contact at the first corner. Schumacher spun, losing ten places, while Rensing stayed on the road only to spin a few corners later and drop back to 21st.

The championship celebrations had to be put on ice, however, until VW's protests for Rensing were rejected and Schumacher had the pleasure of racing in the final round at Hockenheim as champion. A final victory did not come, unfortunately, as Mika Hakkinen, making a guest appearance with the West Surrey Racing team, won pole and the race to issue a warning of what to expect at the Formula Three classic race in Macau a few weeks later. The title chase ended with Schumacher on 148 points, Rensing on 117.

Another disqualification was to work in Schumacher's and Mass's favour a few weeks later when they were handed victory at the Hermanos Rodriguez circuit in Mexico City in the final round of the fuel-formula sportscar championship of that year. Again, it followed a heavy rainstorm and a race on a near-flooded track. This time, refuelling irregularities were the culprit, Baldi and Schlesser being excluded after coming home ahead of Mass and Schumacher in their C11. It was a memorable race for all sorts of reasons, not least because Schumacher led from lap 47 to lap 79 and that he ended up as a winner. He also clocked the fastest lap of the race to justify his decision to be the only man running on pre-heated tyres.

As he had at the Nurburging, Schumacher excelled in the conditions in Mexico, pulling ten seconds clear of Schlesser, one of the men from whom he was learning his lessons, and showing adroit skill in all areas. This was best shown when on lap 66 Oscar Larrauri spun at full speed on the last turn in his Porsche and ended up facing the wrong way in the middle of the track. The first car upon the scene was Schumacher's and he successfully avoided the 962 to stay on the track and out in front, keeping his lead with impressive comfort until he came in on lap 79. Alas, it all seemed to no avail when heavy rain turned the race into a lottery, Baldi making an early pit-stop to steal the advantage which would have won the race had his car not been found guilty, by just 0.1 litres of fuel, of infringing the strict regulations. It was not the way Mass or Schumacher wanted to win the race, but it provided some justice as they had appeared to have been in such control before the rain intervened.

It was also a result which confirmed beyond all doubt that Schumacher was a rising star, not only of the German Formula Three series, but of international racing. He had proved himself among the grown-ups, in the heavy turbo-charged cars of Group C, and he had survived. Indeed, he had survived with ease and the only blot on his record in 1990, which irritated him and Willi Weber, was the way in which Hakkinen had come to the Hockenheimring and won in the final round of the Formula Three series: It was something the boy from Kerpen wanted to put right.

3 MACAU AND FUJI

FLINGS OF EASTERN PROMISE

I had a really good feeling for Macau. Normally, I think that maybe I have a chance to win, but that year [1990] I knew there was definitely a chance. After first practice, I was very surprised by Mika (Hakkinen) who was on pole. His time was crazy. I thought mine was fantastic, but his was unbelievable. . . . In the race, I never believed he would do that [attempt to pass]. If he stayed behind, he had the race won. He knows the mistake was from him. Not from me. Somebody said I went off the gas, but I never did. I just went to the right a little, but not so much. If he was in my position, he would have done the same. I didn't speak to him directly after the race. Emotions are running so high then. In the evening I apologized. But he said: 'No, no. It's okay. It wasn't your fault.' I had a good relationship with Mika before the race and I still have.

Michael Schumacher on his rivalry with Mika
Hakkinen, looking back in 1992.

O N THE OTHER SIDE OF THE WORLD from Michael Schumacher's home in Germany, a long way from the Eiscafé Giorgio in Bergheim, where he often stops for an ice-cream and a coffee, are two race circuits where Schumacher wrote his name into the record books and left no doubt about his status as Germany's most promising driver in decades: Macau and Fuji. Macau, a far-flung Portuguese protectorate amid the shanty towns and humidity of China, across the water from Hong Kong; a place where the food is cheap, gifts are even more modestly priced and the packed casinos and colourful bars and clubs exude an oriental atmosphere often enjoyed by many through a haze supplied by the imported *vinho verde*, was hosting in 1990 its annual Grand Prix on its own famous road circuit.

This was a race for Formula Three cars and, to those involved in the European series in Italy, France, Britain and Germany, it was regarded widely as the international showdown, more important than Monaco, more meaningful to the Formula One spies waiting to study the results and the performances. The outcome of this annual race, on the demanding track near the shanties, below the trees which hung close to the old fort, down by the harbour and up the hill, meant something special to Michael Schumacher too. If he won the 37th running of the Macau Grand Prix, and coupled his victory with another win at Fuji, on the beautiful circuit below the snow-peaked and even more beautiful Mount Fuji, so often lit by sunshine, he would not only leap towards stardom, but claim the prize money on offer of £20,000. For Michael, like the rest, it was a passport to Formula One.

Michael had been to Macau the previous year where, in a night-club known as the Starlight Disco, he had met two of his future colleagues at Camel Benetton Ford, Richard Grundy and Tony Jardine. Grundy, who was to take a leading role in Camel's marketing through Formula One, recalled the impression Schumacher had made on him in 1989. 'It was his first year in Formula Three,' he said. 'And he had not come from Formula Ford, but from Formula Konig, which was not quite as sophisticated. It was also his first year in Macau, but he did a really good job. He qualified well. I think he finished second in the first leg [He actually won it!] and was running a strong second in the second when he had a gearbox problem and stopped. It was a shame because he was up there with the best of them and he looked totally in control. Very smooth. Very clean. Not on the edge at all. Well away from the walls.

'I saw him after the race in a night-club, the Starlight Disco, and he was sitting at the bar, with his back to it, and I introduced myself. We chatted about Formula Three and what he was going to do the following year. We talked about various things. Then I asked him how old he was and I was astonished when he said he was 19, because he came across as such a mature young man. I thought he was about 24 or 25. The way he spoke, the clarity of his thoughts and his self-confidence. He knew exactly what he wanted.'

Mika Hakkinen, who had beaten Schumacher in Hockenheim, also badly wanted to win in Macau. He wanted to prove his superiority. He wanted to show he was the master, not Schumacher. And, of course, he wanted the money too. After taking the British Formula Three championship, he was full of confidence when he arrived. He had won 11 races in all and, by shining this time for West Surrey Racing, he wanted to make up for a disappointing showing at Macau the previous year, when he qualified only 15th out of 30 for Dragon Motorsport. Another victory over Schumacher, Hakkinen knew, would be the perfect result.

Otto Rensing, Schumacher's German Formula Three rival, had taken pole in 1989. There was much for both of the new young and successful drivers to fight for and Hakkinen, just like Schumacher, liked to set the pace. It was always going to be a classic confrontation and so it was.

On Thursday morning, Hakkinen set the pace in his Theodore Racing-entered Ralt-Mugen. He lapped the tight, twisting and undulating street circuit of 3.8 miles in two minutes and 23.5 seconds. It was 1.12 seconds slower than Rensing the previous year, but good enough to put him 1.26 seconds clear of Schumacher, in his WTS Racing Reynard-VW. Frentzen was third-fastest, in an Alan Docking Racing Ralt-Mugen. Rensing lost a wheel after crashing into a wall in his VW Motorsport Ralt-VW. Others tried to stay in touch. None could. This was the way it would be.

In official qualifying, the first time, Schumacher set the pace when the field was split. He clocked 2:22.0. 'I looked at my pit-board and couldn't believe the time,' he said. 'It didn't feel any quicker than the others at all. I didn't even get a tow.' Schumacher had been a heat winner at Macau the previous year but, like Hakkinen, he desperately wanted to improve on that and to win outright. That time put him 0.57 seconds in front of Eddie Irvine, driving for West Surrey Racing in a Ralt-Mugen, but left him concerned about Hakkinen, who ran in the second part of qualifying.

Irvine, later to become a Formula One rival for Schumacher, knew of the young German, but at this time had never spoken to him. 'He impressed me with the way he drove in qualifying; he was quick, but so were a lot of people in Formula Three,' he said. 'It does not always mean that much. Sometimes, people can be sensational in Formula Three in qualifying, but do nothing else. He was on the limit, but never hit anything. He was a bit different.'

Laurent Aiello, who had won the Monaco Formula Three race, lapped in 2:22.98 in his Racing for Europe Ralt-VW. It was fast enough for second-best only . . . Hakkinen, in his red-and-white Ralt, clocked a record-breaking 2:20.88. It was only a fraction slower than the outright record set by Formula Atlantic cars in the past. Schumacher knew now what to expect.

On Friday morning, he improved his Thursday best to 2:21.8, topping the times. Hakkinen, with one flying lap, was 0.04 seconds slower. It seemed impossible for Michael to outpace him. When Friday afternoon came, the groups were reversed and Hakkinen's group went first. Hakkinen was soon into the 1:21's or 2:21's again, but then Frentzen, Schumacher's old rival and a fellow-German, crashed. The track was only partially obstructed, at the Maternity bends, but it was enough to upset the young Finn. He managed only 2:20.89, slower by 0.01 seconds than his previous best, and had to sit and wait, muttering about oil, debris, poor tyres, lack of tow . . . Aiello improved to 2:21.81 to join him on the front row of the grid pending the outcome of the second group's qualifying efforts.

In the second session, Schumacher's chief rival was Irvine, who ended up fourth on the grid with a best lap of 2:21.86. His chief ambition was to improve and he did it. He clocked 2:21.59, knocking out Aiello from the front row, to claim his spot alongside Hakkinen for the first heat, which began in blazing sunshine as the lights flicked to green. On such a circuit as

Macau, they all knew that both grid positions and good starts were critical and Irvine had learned the lesson better than most. He was swiftly past Schumacher and up to second behind his Theodore Racing-entered team-mate immediately, leaving Schumacher trailing behind in fourth. It was exactly the start Michael did not want.

At the end of the first lap, Hakkinen was clear by 2.35 seconds with only 14 laps to go and Schumacher was third, fighting and gasping to stay in touch, as the cars streamed round the narrow steel-lined streets like a swarm of bees. By the end of the third, Hakkinen led by 5.49 seconds and Schumacher was diving past Irvine for second place and starting his chase. It was a soul-destroying task, but Michael kept at it, showing all his doggedness and on the way clocking a fastest lap of 2:21.19 (3.43 seconds quicker than the equivalent fastest lap in 1989) and cutting the Finn's lead to just 2.66 seconds at the finish.

Heat two approached like a thundercloud for Schumacher. He had to win. He had to succeed. There were problems on the grid for Frentzen with his starter-motor. Poor Frentzen. Always a problem or two. Then came the Chinese carnival. Dragons writhed and wriggled to a wild drum-beat, the drivers were introduced to the Governor of Macau, hundreds of firecrackers assaulted the ear-drums. It was hot, tense and loud. And then it was over and the race began. They were off and Schumacher made another poor start. This time, however, he did not allow it to matter. He recovered quickly, kept Hakkinen in his sights and chased him as if it was all his life was worth. And then, suddenly, like 'a slingshot' according to Bruce Jones in *Autosport*, he went past the Finn and into the lead on the run from R Bend to Reservoir. A lap later, he remained in front. Fighting for the honour, hardly believing he could hold on to such success. 'When he was able to stay with me, I knew he was going to win the race,' said Schumacher. 'I was quicker than Mika through the city, but he was quicker on the straights. I thought he was playing with me and he could have passed me when he wanted.'

By mid-distance, after seven of the 15 laps, Schumacher was still only half a second ahead and working every sinew. Both men were lapping faster than the pole time. Spectators were open-jawed. Schumacher, thanks to all that experience, all that natural talent, all those laps, hours, days and weeks of training and practice with Mercedes and Weber and the rest, was smooth, smooth everywhere, measuring each corner, kissing the barriers but never embracing them, while Hakkinen, with more power on the straight, was faster through the speed trap, down the straight and into Lisboa, the corner where he put most pressure on the heat leader.

To claim outright victory, Hakkinen had only to stay where he was. He could even have backed off a little and still been the overall winner. But such a calculated style of achieving success, driving like an old champion like Alain Prost, was not Hakkinen's style. He wanted to win the heat. He wanted to win both heats. He wanted to be a real hero . . . and he paid for it at the start of the last lap. By then, his superior straight-line speed had moved him closer still to Schumacher as they rounded the right-hand kink past the pits.

Then, Hakkinen pulled out to the right to jink past Schumacher. To lead. To win. To claim the glory. Schumacher saw him coming. He moved across to the right, just a fraction, to block him. Hakkinen clipped the back of the Reynard with his Ralt, a touch which sent Hakkinen spearing away to the barrier, spinning off across the track and into retirement. It was almost unbelievable. There was an air of shock at what had happened. Hakkinen had thrown it away. He jumped from his car, hurled his gloves to the ground in an act of spontaneous despair and faced the truth. Had he been patient, taken second place and overall victory, it would have been a success, even if he had not equalled Ayrton Senna's record of 13 wins in a season of Formula Three. Schumacher, with his rear wing destroyed, was then left to steer his car home eight seconds ahead of Aiello to join a joyful party with the WTS Racing crew. 'I think he was crazy,' he said with a broad grin. 'Nobody takes anybody on the last lap. Not without a fight. I spent the whole race thinking he would win, so I am even more delighted now.'

Hakkinen was not amused. Looking back four years later he kept a straight face. 'In the second heat Schumacher got past me and because of that I just decided to stay behind him. I felt I was quicker so I decided to just keep him under pressure and wait for a mistake. He certainly made one in the last part of the race. He gave me an opportunity to pass him quite early in a straight line. Maybe he was tired. I don't know. And we came to this high-speed corner in fifth gear and we are both doing 240–250 kph, until I am very close behind, planning to pass him on the inside when at the same time he moved. This incident was very clear. Just as I moved to pass him, he moved in front of me and caused a big accident. I crashed into him, lost the front end, hit the wall on the left-hand side, hit the wall on the right-hand side – and at a very high speed. It wasn't a very pleasant feeling. I lost everything.

'For that Macau, I always have sad feelings and good feelings. I was already the British F3 champion, I had been to Italy and Germany and won. I knew I had something big coming up and I felt quite good. I accepted it though. No bad feelings. I knew I had to, so I did. That's just racing.'

Later Schumacher summed up that Macau race and its importance with more objectivity. 'I had a really good feeling for Macau. Normally, I think maybe I have a chance to win, but this year I knew there really was a chance. But after first practice, I was very surprised by Mika. His time was crazy. I thought mine was fantastic, but his was unbelievable. In the race, I never believed he would do what he did. If he stayed behind, he had the race won. He knows the mistake was from him. Not me. Someone said I went off the gas, but I never did. I just went to the right a little, but not so much. If he was in my position, he would have done the same, there was no way to pass there. I knew I was out of the whole race, but I wanted to win that heat anyway. You never let somebody pass in that situation and I think he knew that.

'I didn't speak to him directly after the race. Emotions were running so high then. In the evening, I said "I'm sorry", but he said it was his fault and it was okay. We have always had a good relationship.'

Why did Hakkinen make that fatal attack? 'I was used to going to races to win,' he said. 'I was not used to the idea of backing off. I thought he was slower than me, maybe 10 kph slower and it would have been completely unnatural for me NOT to have overtaken him. So the reason I tried to pass him was simple. I am a racing driver and I wanted to win. For me, it was an easy opportunity to pass him. So why not do it?'

Mika also recalled how he had raced against Michael when they were both boys with karts, in 1983 and 1984. 'I remember those races,' said Hakkinen. 'The first was at his father's circuit at Kerpen. The idea was to hold a Junior World Championship race there at that time. It was unfortunate for us, the Finns. We had some problems with the entry. It was a silly mistake and it was a sad situation because there were about five Finnish drivers, who had come all the way from Finland to Germany to race that weekend. Very expensive. It was bad for everyone. But finally they told us we could race, but not for points in the drivers' championship, only for the teams' championship. I won all the heats in the team races and we won the European Championship in the teams' section. Then in 1984, I remember we raced again in a Junior World Championship race at Laval in France. I remember he [Schumacher] won the first day, and I won the second day, but then some Italian guy took me off at Number Four Corner. That was Laval.'

Just as delighted and thrilled on the other side of the world, at home in Germany, was Christoph Schulte, the motor racing reporter and friend of Schumacher's who had been following his career. 'That was the greatest race of them all for me,' he said. 'It was an extraordinary achievement. He was right on the limit. It was the last lap and it was a big effort from Mika to try and overtake Michael, because he wanted to do it. He needed to do it. Michael just couldn't do anything. Mika was going to be the winner and Michael just wanted to show him who was the boss. That is why Mika took the risk to overtake him then and there. Michael realized what was happening and he said that no-one would allow this to happen, so they tangled. It was just fantastic. I saw it and it was amazing. I am sure they will have such a big competition in their careers in Formula One. Since that day, I think Mika has been waiting for a chance to get his own back on Michael. Just one good chance.'

The Macau win was to have a remarkable effect. Michael was

already well-known in Germany. His stunning progress in Formula Three and his attachment to Mercedes had made sure of that. It had, among other things, been the reason Schulte was deployed by his magazine *Auto Bild* to report on the achievements of the youngster from Kerpen. 'Really, the big interest in Michael started when he first went to Group C, to the Mercedes junior team,' said Schulte. 'For me, it was a very interesting story and a double task. I had to follow him through his Formula Three season and also through Group C. It was a big story. There were these kids – and that is all they were – being called in to drive these big 800 horsepower Group C cars and with very little experience at all. It was an enormous step for them and for me it was absolutely fascinating to see how they would manage it and what Mercedes Benz would do . . . If you have seen pictures of Michael at that time, you will understand: he was just a little boy from the flatlands, from Kerpen. Just a boy. A boy from nowhere really as Kerpen is a very small place in between Aachen and Cologne . . . I don't mean this in any discrediting or disrespectful sort of way. They were just an ordinary family, from an ordinary place at a certain level and then, quite suddenly, he was a works driver for Mercedes Benz.'

So the boy from nowhere was arriving on the crest of a wave in Macau and now headed towards Fuji for the second leg of the Euro-Macau-Fuji Challenge, as it was billed. It was to be, as Bruce Jones reported in *Autosport*, 'without doubt, the best Formula Three race there's been for years . . . with slipstreaming, overtaking and heartbreak.' The pain was for Steve Robertson of England as he drove the race of his life, but missed out on a famous victory to Schumacher, on the circuit remembered so vividly for its rain during the final Grand Prix of 1976 when James Hunt won the Formula One World Drivers' Championship.

A typhoon, known as Typhoon Page, had hit the Philippines, 1,000 miles to the south and spread some of its weather effects to the north on the opening day of qualifying which was declared a complete washout. Schumacher, along with everyone else, was left to loiter around in frustration that Friday, but woke on Saturday morning to revel in the sight of Mount Fuji, snow-capped peak and all, bathed in sunshine. The weather was fabulous and the paddock was filled with anticipation as everyone prepared for action on the challenging track, with its long straights, fast bends, chicanes and hairpin.

The first session was untimed. Yoshimi Fujinaga was fastest, but 11 seconds distant from the dry circuit record. Rickard Rydell was top European, third-fastest. In all, not very meaningful. There was still far too much water from the storm on the track. But it dried out and when official practice began, it was Schumacher who set the pace. He clocked an early fast time of 1:31.806 in the WTS Racing Reynard and it looked good enough for pole until Formula 3000 exile Mauro Martini clocked 1:30.993 for the Ikegami team. For Schumacher it meant a place on the front row.

Heat one began in bright but cold conditions, thanks to a biting wind from the west. It lasted less than a lap as a collision on the grid resulted in the race being red-flagged. After the re-start, Schumacher was away first, created an early gap and then pulled clear for a comfortable victory. Heat two was also red-flagged on the opening lap and this time it was Robertson who was first to pull away in his Bowman Ralt-Speiss VW. Victor Rosso burst past in his Ralt-TOM'S Toyota, followed by Schumacher, and the race developed into a thriller with the lead changing hands frequently as it became a duel between Schumacher and Robertson by the end of lap six. The Englishman stayed in strong contention until his engine died and Schumacher was able to relax and coast to a famous victory. 'It was a very interesting battle with Steve,' he recalled. 'When he came back at me I thought "Aieee!" and I was lucky.'

This time the broad grin stayed stuck on the long face with the chin that was later to become famous. The Macau-Fuji double had been an unexpected triumph and it brought with it unexpected extra pressures and fresh offers. But Schumacher had signed already for Mercedes, was part of their long-term strategy and he knew where he was going next – another season of Group C racing. He explained why: 'I've learned a lot from driving for Mercedes. You get another driving style and you can use some of this in Formula Three. It helps a lot, especially for finding the feel of a car and for using the tyres in the best way.

But the biggest success for me was the braking technique. It has taught me to brake later and to keep the car on the limit.

'Driving the Mercedes now, I find the power normal. Sometimes, the team thinks I'm mad, because I come in and I say the engine isn't working properly, when it is really. The best time is when you can use big boost. It is so much fun . . . And driving with Jochen, Jean-Louis and Mauro has been fun too, because they are so funny. They have fun before and after the race all the time, but are serious in it. It is good, I think. I know the normal way to Formula One is through Formula Three and Formula 3000. But it is not so easy to get a good car and team in Formula 3000. I am not able to get it right for 1991, as my name is good in Germany, but nowhere else. Yes, after winning in Macau and Fuji, I will be better known internationally, but I've already signed to do a full year with Mercedes.

'My way is safer. It is normal that only the top two drivers in Formula 3000 get Formula One contracts, but I can win races for Mercedes, which is important, get paid and get given a car. Then, maybe, maybe, Mercedes will go into Formula One. Maybe after two years. And this will be just right for me . . .'

At the time, Michael also admitted that Weber and he had talked about a plan for him to do some Formula 3000 races with WTS, as preparation for the future. But, he stressed, it was Mercedes first for him at this time. 'Maybe in 1992, we will do a full programme in Formula 3000, but there is always the problem of finding money in Germany. Everyone there thinks only of *Tourenwagen*. The top Formula 3000 teams are from Britain, France and Italy, not Germany, so I have the problem of no team, no money and we have no race in Germany. It is like a circle, a bad circle.'

But Schumacher knew too how lucky he was. 'I cannot believe I am here now, in Japan, with next year all planned. It is amazing, as I was just an apprentice mechanic and started racing with no money. Nothing. First Jurgen Dilk helped me, like a second father, and then Willi. I have had so much luck.'

For Weber, the Macau-Fuji double was the first small dividend following his investment in Schumacher's future. He had seen the potential, backed it with his team, his time and his money and he was able to see the way ahead. 'I think that I have a good feel for people and especially for drivers,' he explained. 'I get enthusiastic about someone because of the way he handles a car. Someone who really wants to do it as a career cannot always put the blame on others when he fails, for example.

Weber had chosen Schumacher in 1988 and he had chosen wisely and well. His protégé was performing perfectly. They had enjoyed two years of progress and success, culminating in the memorable Macau-Fuji double. 'For me, they were his outstanding drives at that time,' said Weber. 'The two heats in Macau were very special. The track is so difficult there. It makes Monaco look like a highway and the way Michael won was just unbelievable. Then he did it again at Fuji. No-one could believe it. The organizers had said that if he won both races he could have £20,000. We did it, but the money was not there because they were so surprised that someone could do it. Nobody had ever done it before and it was not expected. After that, though, everyone started to speak about Michael Schumacher.'

4 STUTTGART

ON THE ROAD WITH MERCEDES-BENZ

Racing with Mercedes was an incredible experience. You were not only racing high-tech machinery as powerful as Formula One cars, but you also worked with very experienced team-mates. You worked together with them, not against them. Jochen Mass was particularly important at the beginning of my stint in sportscars. He did so much for all the juniors. He is not a man who holds back on some of the important things and he taught me a lot. That was not only on the driving side, but also with the press, the media, with my English, with everything.

Michael Schumacher on life with Mercedes, looking back in 1993.

DOWN THE AUTOBAHNS TO THE SOUTH, beyond Frankfurt and towards Munich, where it is hot in the summer and the sunlight sizzles, straddling the river Neckar, lies Stuttgart. It is one of the modern industrial cities of Germany, a place of manufacturing and progress, creativity and high standards. It is the home of the German car industry and the place where Mercedes-Benzs are produced, where they have always been produced and where the company was born. The city may still have trams, old quarters and charm, but it also has bustle and business and foresight, thinking for the future all the time, as Jochen Neerpasch did in 1988 when he formulated his scheme for a Mercedes Junior Team. The team was not announced until the following year, when Christoph Schulte set eyes on Schumacher for the first time.

'I first saw Michael there when they announced their plans. It was in Stuttgart. It was the announcement of the Junior Team,' said Schulte. 'I remember it well, but for the details, you need to ask Jochen Neerpasch. He was behind it all . . . Previously, he established a BMW Junior Team. It was a special team and it consisted of Marc Surer, Eddie Cheever and Joachim Winkelhok. It worked out well and they all got to Formula One. This success was the main idea behind his similar strategy with Mercedes. He wanted to create a platform just for the boys, the three new ones – Schumacher, Karl Wendlinger and Heinz-Harald Frentzen – to get more experience and interest in international motor sport. When Neerpasch left BMW, he had the same idea in his brain and so, when Mercedes decided to return to motor sport more seriously, he was ready.'

Neerpasch was more than ready. He was fully prepared. He had researched carefully, building up gradually for the time when everything was ripe, and Schumacher was part of these plans. 'I do not remember exactly what year it was, but the first time I saw Michael was in a Formula Three race . . . To get the drivers we wanted, we looked at Formula Three very carefully. In Formula Three, you tend to find drivers who have proved that they are talented and have the mind to be a professional driver. Happily, that year, there was a good championship in Germany and we looked at the first three drivers and one was Michael Schumacher.'

The year was 1989. It was not long after seeing Schumacher on the track that Neerpasch decided to meet him. Their first meeting was in a restaurant at a race meeting. 'There were lots of people around and he did not seem to be that much different to the other drivers, but he was very clear in his mind what he wanted. The idea of sportscars was something that he did not like. At that time, he was very close to Mr Weber and both came to the conclusion that it was not a good idea. I think at that time if they had the chance to go to Formula 3000 they would have taken it.

'But once they had started testing, they all changed their minds. They all realized – I mean all three of the young drivers – that it would be good for them. The engineers did a lot of mileage with the drivers, so in conjunction with them, you could say we kept it all in the family. It was a very technically oriented team and it was just like a family. They all found that, despite the heavy car, they could learn a lot about high-speed driving and the technical side of their jobs. After the testing programme, our strategy was to have them run in a race programme as well. That is how Michael did Formula Three at the same time as he did the sportscars. And Michael was the one who took up the challenge 100 per cent.'

Clues to the course Mercedes were planning to take appeared gradually in the run-in towards the announcement. In 1988, the Sauber-Mercedes Sportscar team appeared with sponsorship from AEG, the electrical manufacturing giant, and the car was blue with a new design. AEG were always closely related to Mercedes and it was immediately considered to be a signal that something was happening. It was. Behind the scenes, Neerpasch was planning ahead with Mercedes and the programme was for testing, testing and more testing with the boys. All in an unpressurized environment, with no media, but gradually to introduce the simulated pressures of top-level competition, demands from sponsors, partners, the written press, radio and television as time went by; in short, to prepare the boys for the highest levels of competition. The boys were to be given their own cars, crews, tyres, all they needed. It was a unique scheme and it was kept top-secret. 'I knew little bits of it, I heard things, but it was a struggle for me to get the story at all,' commented Schulte.

Eventually, the announcement came. Germany was stunned to learn that these three talented boys were to be thrown in together with factory driving jobs at Mercedes Benz. The three, including the boy from Kerpen, were nearly as surprised themselves. Summoned to Stuttgart, they were to be drawn into a new career programme which was to change their lives. When they were called in the first time, it was to fly in a private plane from Zurich to the Paul Ricard circuit at Le Castellet in the south of France, for what was effectively a private test session. The second was to Jerez, in southern Spain, for what was effectively an initiation test in February, 1990. With their own overalls, helmets and kit, they looked like young volunteers as they joined up with the élite corps from Mercedes for the flight south across Europe. 'Of course, there was a big competition between the three kids,' recalled Schulte. 'The first time we saw them together in the cars was at Jerez. They were very keen to be faster than each other. They wanted to impress. Heinz-Harald was the first, I think, and at once he was quick. Very quick. And with very low fuel consumption, which was so important in Group C then. Michael went to see him and to watch him and he said "He's so quick, very quick – and more than that he doesn't need any of the fuel. It is incredible." So he went to see Heinz-Harald and asked him how he did it, because he felt it was impossible. "I'm able to do such a time, but I am not able to do the time *and* to have such low fuel consumption," he told him. And they talked together, seriously, about driving and Heinz-Harald told him how to drive smoothly, to avoid heavy braking and ragged driving. How to let it go. And Michael told me he went back to his car and he thought about this and then he tried it. He thought this must be the way. And it worked for him immediately. He did it straight away.'

The first Jerez test took place in an environment constructed by Neerpasch. A race weekend environment, but without any real pressure. Even the media were requested not to write about it. Mercedes wanted total control of everything at that stage. But it was difficult for the German media. It was clear that not only was this a unique scheme, but also Mercedes were building up for something special. It turned out to be nothing less than what everyone expected – a planned return to Formula One after an absence of more than 35 years.

'I was there in February 1990 and I managed to get the story about the Mercedes-Benz development,' said Schulte. 'Peter Sauber – and this was an interesting thing – said he did not want to have the three kids. He said my job is to become world champion, not to be a teacher of these young drivers.' For Schulte, it was a good twist to a fascinating story. Here were three young drivers, considered to be the best in Germany of their age, being groomed for stardom by a Group C team owner who did not want them. Sauber, however, was in for a surprise, and after watching the boys he began to change his mind. He began to see their potential and it was a difficult feeling for him to understand and to express. 'He is normally a world champion in saying nothing at all,' said Schulte. 'But he came to see me – and up to then we had not had any real contact – and he said "Have you seen what they are doing?" He was astonished by their progress.'

Not only Sauber, but many others at Jerez for that first test found it scarcely credible that these three scrawny boys could climb into the high-powered turbo-charged sportscars and drive them with the skill and speed which they so clearly demonstrated. Sauber was struggling to understand how it could happen. 'It must be the Formula Three series which has prepared them,' Sauber told Schulte. 'Because there they have no power and you need to go smoothly. If not, you don't have the speed on the straight or the lap times.' It was the same for Group C, but it was not through their brief experience in German Formula Three that these boys, Schumacher included, had learned their speed. It was as a direct result of their raw talent and this, more than anything, brought great satisfaction, especially to Neerpasch.

'You could see the pleasure on his face,' recalled Schulte. 'It worked so well that first weekend in Jerez. Only one thing did not work out as planned. You know Jochen Neerpasch is very interested in modern art and he invited Frank Stella, who is a very good friend of his, to join him for dinner. He thought it would be a good idea to introduce the three kids too. He thought they might learn something. I was very interested too. I would have liked to have been invited, so I said to them the next morning – how was your dinner? They said it was very nice and I asked "Who was the guy on the table?" and they just did not have any idea who he was. And Stella was then very well-known in modern art! It was just like that.'

From that first test, the idea began to emerge in the media that Mercedes had created a special school which laid on lessons in speech, drama, media-relations, personal appearances and a whole range of off-track skills for these three boy-drivers, but none of this was true. Some attention was paid to the off-circuit needs, but the programme was based solidly round driving and learning how to improve in the cockpit when at the wheel of a high-powered sports racing car. For the boys, it meant testing, testing and more testing. Nothing formal was arranged for improving their English, teaching them one dish from another at dinners or how to address large groups of guests from important sponsors.

'I remember in 1990, there was an invitation from Ford and Michael was invited, together with some other young drivers, to a very good restaurant in Zolder, in Belgium, which was famous for its cuisine and for its wine-cellar,' Schulte recollected. 'It was a nine-course meal with a lot of different wines and I remember Michael saying to me "How does this work? Where does it begin?" There was so much cutlery on the table. So, I told him there was nothing to worry about – just eat from the outside to the inside . . . and then, at that time, I realized how little he knew.'

It was an incident typical of Michael's early life in which he showed as much willingness to learn and to work as to obey. He was also never too shy to ask about anything and never humbled. He was confident, inquisitive and ambitious, but always courteous. The smile, which has since graced the podiums of the world, was never far away. 'It was the most interesting thing about Michael,' said Schulte. 'The way he learned. He would realize straight away what something meant to him and then he would do it immediately. He would learn it so quickly. It always happened like that. In all my life, I have never seen a man who could learn things so quickly. I was so impressed I went away and had a discussion with one of my editors and I told him we had to do a big feature on him and on this aspect of him. Michael was not a person with much education, he had not travelled, he knew nothing – but he was prepared perfectly for racing. He took no interest in other things. He had no time. We went to Macau, for example, in 1989, and he was not interested in anything outside the car or off the track. He had no time at all. He knew the circuit, but nothing else.'

The Mercedes-Benz experience was a vital one for Michael, but it was one that few seasoned observers expected to succeed. 'Most people at that time said "No, no way" can this happen,' explained Gustav Buesing, one of the longest serving members of the

Mercedes Benz press and public relations team, who was involved in the development of the 'junior school' with Schumacher. 'But Jochen [Neerpasch] did it. He proved you could take these kids from Formula Three, only used to 170 horsepower and take them to Group C with 900 horsepower. Everyone said it was too much and there was no way anyone could do it, but Jochen's scheme with all the testing really worked. And they had a good tutor, of course, which was what they needed, in Jochen Mass. He knew the territory and he knew all about long distance races which were one of the biggest worries.'

Neerpasch, aware that sportscar racing was likely to move to a 3.5 litre formula, convinced everyone at Mercedes that his scheme was right and that the young drivers would be perfectly prepared for the new formula when the turbos were phased out. But it was important for everyone that Mass agreed to join the project, to help the boys, to race with them and to train them for what lay ahead. Mass, nearing the end of his career which included 105 Grands Prix, was fascinated by the idea and worked with enthusiasm. He was supported fully by Neerpasch who revelled in seeing the development of his protégés. 'It was a big advantage for them all to work with someone like Jochen Mass,' he said. 'To be in the same team and to learn the race strategy in the same car as Mass, gave them a lot. Michael was very constructive technically at this time. It was not long before he could explain the technical situation better than the other drivers could.'

Neerpasch's plan was to see two of the three graduate from his junior school all the way to the proposed Mercedes Formula One team. Unfortunately, Mercedes decided against running their own team in 1991 and this decision sparked the moves which ultimately saw Michael join the 7-Up Jordan team and, subsequently, Benetton. It was a rapid endorsement of the success of his preparation for the job by Mercedes from the start.

'I first remember Michael at Jerez, at the first "driving school" session, when those three guys came up with their Formula Three driver suits and then climbed into the sports cars,' recalled Buesing. 'It was fascinating to see, but they were so quick from the beginning. Jochen was so happy about this. He always felt it was his brainchild and they were good immediately. They also learned straight away how to save fuel and tyres. In fact, I think they did it better than some of the old guys and with better lap times too. They had to learn to run on a set of old tyres for a long time with good lap times. They did it well. Their driving style was so much more precise.

'It was marvellous to see. They had learned about smooth driving, I think, from Formula Three. How to go into corners smoothly. Both Michael and Heinz-Harald were quick immediately. They were there in new cars, on a new track and in new surroundings and after just two or three laps they were on the pace and quick. Karl took a little bit longer. Maybe five, six or seven laps, but then he got there. It was always like that with the three of them.

'Michael was the one who was always fastest. He was always in the car and then almost immediately quick. To someone like me, it was obvious he had a special talent. It was the same for all three of them, but with Michael there was something. It was so automatic. He learned so fast. He also, like the others, had to learn the way to be fast without burning up the fuel. Group C was a fuel formula and that was important then. And there were always big differences between the drivers, I can tell you. Sometimes there was a difference of up to ten per cent between them for the same lap time. I mean one driver would use ten per cent more fuel than another!

'Michael was so quick to learn and he did it well. When I look back now and I think of the race at Barcelona [the 1994 Spanish Grand Prix], where he drove most of the race in fifth gear, it was the style he used in sportscar racing. He took wide angles, tried not to lose any speed in the corners – by braking and accelerating – and drove in smoothly, helping the speed and braking just at the last moment. All that was learned from Group C and it was the only way he could do the whole track in the Benetton in fifth gear.'

To begin with, the 'drivers school' was run at tracks all over Europe. Michael was living in Kerpen and he travelled all over the continent, learning much about a variety of things, but chiefly the life of a driver. In the first winter, they all drove more than 5,000 kilometres in testing with the team, mostly at Mercedes' two favourite circuits at Le Castellet, between Marseille and Toulon in the south of France, and at Jerez. Hockenheim and the Nurburgring were both considered too cold for the task in winter.

Schumacher, like the other two drivers, threw himself into his work with a will. His whole life began to revolve around the Mercedes sessions, the outings to Willi Dungl's health and fitness clinic in Austria, where he learned about diet and athleticism, training and conditioning, how to eat and live in the right manner, and meetings with the staff for discussions on all aspects of the life of a top driver, including media and public relations. 'They had fitness sessions in the mountains with Dungl, running and cycling and skiing and that sort of thing, with the other drivers too, and they were all monitored. The whole lot went, including the touring car guys,' remembered Buesing. 'Of course there were a few escapades from time to time, but nothing serious.'

Searching for evidence of any wild behaviour off the track by Schumacher is a fruitless task. None of his friends, colleagues or rivals can recall him losing his famed self-control. He has often been described as having an old head on young shoulders and that was as apparent at Mercedes in the early days as with Benetton when he began to chase success. But, as with any healthy young man, there were a few moments of high jinks. One story, recalled by Frentzen, was about a fast drive from Dungl's to a local hospital or clinic, where the young drivers were to have a full physical check, including pulse rates. This particular drive took place during winter, when the roads were covered by much heavy snow, and Schumacher and Frentzen travelled together. Schumacher sat in the driver's seat. 'He drove very fast, on these snowy roads, with only the wheel-ruts to drive in. I was nervous, very nervous, because we were going so fast,' said Frentzen. 'I mean we were driving at very high speeds indeed and I felt quite frightened. We were going faster than I felt was safe. When we got to the clinic, we went in for our check-ups and we had our pulses tested. They took my pulse and it was 100 or 120 or something and they said "Hey, are you all right, and what have you been doing?" and I said I had been a little bit excited, but I would be better soon. I suggested they took Michael's pulse to see what I meant after the drive we had just had and when they took his pulse it was normal. I mean it was only 60 or 70 or something. It was just incredible.'

Buesing recalled another Schumacher 'fast' story. 'I remember one test at Le Castellet. Michael arrived late. He was really very much off the schedule and he did not have his car, his own road car, but had arrived by train. He was supposed to have driven down to the test in his road car from Mercedes. It was a 2.5 16V. A good car. So, he arrived without his car and we asked him: "What happened?" And he had to admit that he had just come down by train. "Has the car broken down?" we asked. "No" he said. Then, he had to admit he had been speeding on the motorway and the French police had caught him. They had told him to leave his car, to cool down and to travel by train to complete his journey. In fact, the police confiscated his car. This happened somewhere in France and he was left to do about 300 kms by train to come down to the testing session.

'At the testing, he had to report to Neerpasch. He was in charge. I remember, I was there when all of this happened. Jochen was a calm person. So he took Michael to one side and they went for a little walk and in the not-very-crowded paddock area at Le Castellet, between the trees, he explained that this was not the behaviour to be expected of a Mercedes factory driver. Not the behaviour he wanted at all. He said that if it is in the newspapers that you were doing 200 kph on a French motorway where the limit is 130 kph, it is not very good PR. He just said, don't do that. Michael is not a crazy guy, but then he was a young guy of just, maybe 21, and really, who would not have done the same thing? I think, overall, it was quite normal behaviour.'

Thankfully, yes, it was normal behaviour. Who could be so perfect as to always avoid temptation, particularly the temptation of driving your own company car, a Mercedes 190, towards its maximum on beautiful roads on a fast trip to the south of France? Buesing was right. And it proved that Schumacher was human, fallible and a regular guy. After all, he enjoyed his life, his friends, his fun. He took a few risks. The idea that he was some kind of ice-man, a Bjorn Bjorg of motor racing, was one he never enjoyed and it was not true. He was just an ordinary boy from Kerpen, given a nice car and a steady wage, who liked the life of good hotels, travel and racing that his job with Mercedes-Benz had given him.

While off the track, in testing, everything seemed to go smoothly for Neerpasch, it was not quite so good when the racing started. First of all, there were the problems of Heinz-Harald Frentzen, who was tempted by Camel sponsorship to try and include a Formula 3000 programme in his opening year with Mercedes; and then there were the difficulties with Schumacher being disqualified at Silverstone for not wearing seat belts. Both events figure prominently in Buesing's recollection, but less vividly than another famous Schumacher 'happening' a year later, in 1991, at the Nurburgring when he became involved in a disagreement with Derek Warwick, on the eve of his F1 debut.

'Derek was very, very upset,' said Buesing. 'Practice was finished, or nearly finished, and I think they went side by side and then, I think, they hit each other. Derek was so upset he jumped out of his car straight out of his pits and went after Michael who just walked from the garage to the transporter. Derek followed him, and so too did Jochen Mass, because he feared there would be some fist-fighting. Derek was so upset that he slammed the door behind him, so none of the gathering group of journalists could see anything. They closed the door and they had a big argument.

'Jochen [Mass], who was the only witness of all this, told me Michael was extremely cool in his reaction and that Derek was exploding with rage and that he lifted his arms. Michael just said "I don't see it like this. No, I don't agree" or something like that. All very cool. But what a situation! I think both were in the wrong because there was enough space on the track and there was no reason for the two cars to bump into each other at all. It was a typical motor racing incident.'

Others had different versions of the same story. According to Karin Sturm, a German motor sports reporter who has followed Schumacher's career closely, Michael wanted to do particularly well in this race on what was virtually his home track at that time. 'But things were not progressing well at all,' she said. 'Even during practice, Mercedes reported three engine problems and on

Friday, during that qualifying session, Schumacher, who was already irritated, had to face more problems. He felt Warwick had held him up on his previous fast lap and, in an act of retaliation, he made sure he "closed the door" on him himself when Warwick was on his fast lap. There was trouble!'

Warwick was psychologically battered anyway, following the death of his younger brother Paul four weeks earlier. He had been very close to Paul, supporting his career as much as he could before he was killed at Oulton Park in a Formula 3000 race. The Nurburgring meeting was Derek's first return to racing since then and, as he admitted, he was not in his best condition. After the incident in qualifying, he was furious. 'He drove into my car. That is not acceptable,' he roared. 'I did not deliberately slow him down. I don't do things like that. At the most, it was a misunderstanding. But what he did to me was intentional.' Later, Warwick admitted: 'I was very close to punching him. The only thing that stopped me and spared me a fine was that I suddenly saw a child before me. I looked at him – and I saw Paul. It stopped me in my tracks. But he was lucky that our team chief Tom Walkinshaw was not there at the time. There would have been a protest and more unpleasantness. Guaranteed.'

Mass, Michael's leader and the observer of all that happened, remembered it clearly too. 'Michael didn't say much. Warwick did most of the shouting and he yelled at the top of his voice in the transporter. I was just there listening to him and he was pretty calm. Michael would just say "No, you're wrong there" and Derek would be shouting again at the top of his voice. He went on and on. Then he said "sorry" and left. And after he left, I asked what it was and Michael said it was nothing. "I was on my line and if he is upset about it then that is his problem," said Michael. It was all a lot of nothing really.'

The following day, Schumahcher apologized. He was cautioned by the Federation Internationale du Sport Automobile (FISA) and Warwick admitted: 'I felt bad. I am not exactly proud that I reacted that way. But I was under a great deal of pressure at that time and there were so many emotions in me. It was difficult.' To cap an extraordinary weekend, charged with feelings, Warwick won the race after Schumacher had retired early with engine problems. In his cockpit, Warwick wept. 'I only thought of Paul. At the same time, it was such a wonderful victory. So terribly important for me.' The same evening, Schumacher learned he was to fly to England for talks with Eddie Jordan, the first move towards Formula One and the big time.

Buesing felt that initially the three boys were 'just wanting to enjoy it all. To play around. To do silly things. But when they were in the paddock, or near the Mercedes-Benz motor home, or near to Jochen Neerpasch or Peter Sauber, or those people, the father figures, then they behaved very good, just like they were sitting at school. But when no-one was looking, they messed around – like any young person of that age. They still had to learn a lot about behaviour in public and we helped them a bit, but not formally. There were no lessons, or seminars or meetings. But it was part of my job sometimes to practise a little bit with them. I used to follow them and listen when they were approached by journalists and I would just give them some tips. How to tell people what you want to say and not what they want to hear. Say you want to answer a question this way, not that way.

'Michael listened to this and he learned it well and quickly. Now he is one of the best with the media. He did not have a big group of hangers-on, which some people had. He was not that sort of guy. He did not change at Mercedes. He still has not really changed much in Formula One. He is the same. He has never shown signs of stress, never upset people. We sometimes find that difficult to accept, I know, but you have to remember he started racing at the age of four. I can well remember after a Nurburgring race once, I did an interview with him in the big Mercedes guest tent and there were about 1,200 people there, including a lot of people from the Mercedes board.

'I asked him about his fantastic race and how it was possible for such a young guy to be so mature and to be able to run such a faultless race. He was 21 or 22 then. He told me to "forget about it – I have been racing now already for 17 years . . ." And everybody laughed. But he meant it. And he was right. He had started racing from the age of four and he was used to the pressure and all the other things which revolve around the racing, even on a minor scale in kart racing. It was already his world. So, it was not such a big step mentally for him as anyone thought it was. He knew about drinking at night too, from his kart career. He had learned when he was very young that if you get drunk the night before, then the next day you will be in big trouble.

'I think he must have learned all this in his karting days because I never saw anything at all of this when he was at Mercedes-Benz. And you know, it is amazing too that I have never seen him lose his self-control or his composure at all. I have seen him really relaxed and I have seen him really happy and enjoying life with the race technicians and the staff, but without ever losing control.'

Both 1990 and 1991 were to be important and formative years for Schumacher as he made the transition from Kerpen's boy-hero into a young man with Stuttgart connections. He grew up on and off the track, learning to form stronger and more adult relationships both professionally and personally. Leo Reiss, for example, was the senior engineer involved with Schumacher during his sportscar career and well recalled seeing the boy develop into a man.

'I remember when I first saw him. We were together on a private plane. There was Schumacher, Frentzen and Wendlinger. It was a private charter from Zurich to Paul Ricard. They [the boys] didn't know where they were going or why, really. They had no idea what would happen. On the way down, we told them what we wanted to do. This was, I think, at the end of 1989, just before we went to Mexico. They each had their helmets and overalls and I remember Jochen Mass was there too. I remember that they planned to do some driving in the C9 and at the same time Schlesser did some work with the C11 and Jochen Mass did ten laps too in the C9, to check the car and make sure everything would be okay.

'We just sent them out and around on the first day and I think it was Frentzen who went first. When Schumacher went I could see he was very aggressive. Immediately. You could hear him as he went down the straight, crashing the gears. You could hear him coming! There were obvious differences. On the second day, we did some work on the set-up – just little things – to see if the drivers felt or said anything about the different settings. It was quite interesting. After that, of course, we went off to Mexico for the final race and then we came back and started again in Jerez.

'This time we did a simulation of a race distance. I think it was the first time. We gave them each a full tank, which I think was 100 litres in those sportscars, and they had to go and drive a distance like a race. We wanted them to learn about fuel consumption. Heinz-Harald was very impressive at this, I recall. He was fast and smooth and good on the fuel, right from the beginning. They were all three careful. We told them to adapt slowly and we tried not to put too much pressure on them. But some of the time it was like a qualifying session between the three of them!'

Reiss had other memories of Schumacher's formative months with Mercedes. 'I remember there was a big dinner in Stuttgart around the time of the preliminary test in France,' he said. 'A lot of people from Mercedes were there and so was Jochen Neerpasch and he told them what was going to happen. He told them Jochen Mass would be the teacher and they would be the pupils. This was in November 1989.'

For them all it was a dream, but the bigger dream was a fast ticket to Formula One. Gerhard Berger, who was a close supporter of Wendlinger, advised him to look carefully at Formula 3000 and to ignore sportscars, and Heinz-Harald had connections with Jordan, via some people in Germany, with Camel, for Formula 3000. They thought it was the way to go. 'I remember an interview with Gerhard Berger on television,' said Reiss. 'In it, he said it was all wrong. He said if you wanted to go into Formula One, it was stupid to go with sportscars. Frentzen had a chance to go and he took it. I think both the others would have done too if they had received the chance.'

As it worked out, Heinz-Harald's decision to drive for Jordan in Formula 3000 was not the best for him. Mercedes maintained their interest for a short while and then concentrated on their other two, allowing Frentzen to pursue his own interests. 'They really made progress with us,' said Reiss. 'Heinz-Harald had a strange manager and some bad advisers. We had no confidence in him. He was too confused. By doing a lot of testing, Schumacher soon caught up with him in lots of things like fuel consumption. It was very close. Karl could not push himself so fast and he needed more time with everything to gain his confidence. He had a little too much caution and he did not like to make any mistakes. He could not push himself to the limit easily.

'Michael was different. But in the beginning with us, he was no good at setting up the car. He learned it. Then, in the race at the Nurburgring in 1990, he took over from Jochen and he learned to overtake. After that, I think Michael realized he could do it and he pushed really hard and he made great progress. Sometimes he pushed too hard and he alarmed us, but it was typical of him. At Le Mans, I remember he pushed too hard and he had some problems with the alternator. Something to do with the water pump. Schumacher pushed so hard. He tried to go too fast and I felt there was a split in the team between the youngsters and the old guys. Schumacher pushed so hard and always the older guys stopped him and said 'Slower, slower, this race is for 24 hours.' But he was only 21 and he just could not think of a race going on for 24 hours. I think he pushed too hard and he pushed it over the edge . . . I remember we had to open the gearbox and we lost the alternator also. The other car ran on perfectly. They all said he pushed too hard.

'He wanted to win Le Mans and he thought he could do it in the first six hours. It was lack of experience, but it was also his mentality. I think that night at Le Mans is just about the only time I have seen him lose his self-control. It was not total, but it was close. Everyone wanted to stop him that night. But he wanted to win Le Mans and he wanted to do the last stint. And he wanted to do the qualifying. But Karl did the qualifying and we told him that, anyway, qualifying is so unimportant at Le Mans because of the race, but it did not matter to him . . .'

Jochen Mass was also there. 'We raced Le Mans in the night and I spoke to Michael and I said 'You guys are going too quick,' and he said "No, I am not going too fast. I do it easy. There is no problem." But for me, it wasn't the speed that was strange, it was that he got upset almost, temperamental, and he told me "Nonsense, I'm not going too quick . . . If you cannot go fast that is your problem." That is what came through to me so I just shut up and I laughed inside, to myself, and I thought he will learn his own way. He did learn. The car had a problem later and he came back and said "You were right, we were going too fast, sorry about that." I was pleased. He had an arrogant attitude, but he had learned too. It is necessary to be strong like that and to admit the mistakes.'

For Reiss, the race at Le Mans was the one where he saw Michael come closer to losing his famed self-control than any other. 'That was as close as I have seen him to losing it,' he said. 'He has so much strength of character. He enjoys food, for example, but he really controls his diet. He has worked very hard. And one of the other things with him is that physically he is the strongest of the three of the boys. I remember he lost 15 kilos of weight when he came to us at Mercedes. When he first came, he was nearly like me [well-rounded] and he did a lot of physical training, really seriously. He worked very hard at Dungl's in Austria and he found his own special way. He worked so hard at it that when he was told about diet, eating this and that, he did with 100 per cent commitment. Total dedication. If he saw anything that could help him, he would do everything he could for it. He would really give everything.

'When they went away together to do a week of fitness training, Schumacher would always do too much, or almost too much work. If they said "Do this, for this distance," Michael would always go back and do it twice. He always put too much pressure on himself that way. He wanted to win so much. He wanted to be the best. He is a Capricorn, you know, and maybe that is part of the reason why he is so determined, so ambitious and why he works so hard. He comes from a poor background and he knows that the only way to be able to have a good life is to work hard to be rich and successful. Like the Russians, you know. They grew up and all they wanted to do was to get out of Russia. They did everything to get out. Michael was a mechanic and, I think, that was not the life he wanted to follow. There are a lot of reasons for him being the way he is, but one of the big ones is his mentality.'

That mentality exhibited itself as visibly as Michael's skill at the wheel on many occasions, according to Reiss. 'I remember at Silverstone, in 1991, at the end he and Karl came in second in their sportscar. It was raining. Not heavy rain, just a fine drizzle. Typical English weather really. And Schumacher had never been to Silverstone before, but after 35 laps, he was eight seconds faster than Martin Brundle. The next lap, he was in the gravel. So, we had to repair the car for 45 minutes and at the end Brundle was still only just in front of Schumacher. It was just him.

'At that time, he made very little contribution to the car. He just trusted everything to us. He left it all to us. At first, he had very little mechanical understanding of the car, but by the end, he did. It was much better. At the beginning, he would just get into the car, get settled down and just go. Typically, with him, always flat. By the time we got to the Nurburgring the first year he was more interested and he was asking questions and talking to the engineers. In the beginning, it was too much for him.

'Away from the track, it was all a big thing for him personally. He was experiencing a lot of fairly big changes. He was from a very ordinary family, from a plain part of the country. When he joined Mercedes, his whole environment changed. Suddenly, he had his own flat, near Kerpen, he had a Mercedes car and a lot of people who wanted to be his friend. His father never came to the races, but Michael used to talk to me a lot about the personal side of his life. He talked about girlfriends and flats and he was really just normal, someone who needed someone to talk to. He was not very shy. He was quite open. He has not really changed.'

Another who grew to know Schumacher better during the Mercedes 'junior school' spell was Frentzen. They had grown up in the same karting environment and first raced against each other in karts at Kerpen when Frentzen was 14 and Schumacher 12. 'I had already been driving for two years in the junior kart championship and it was at Kerpen, so there was a great fight between us for first place,' remembered Frentzen, whose career so often interlocked with Schumacher's. 'Well, I came first! He was second on the grid but he won the start and then there was a small fight and then he made a little mistake. He came sideways and I overtook him and he finished second, but it was his first race in junior karting and I had more experience. You could see immediately that he was one of the best.

'The next year, I stepped up to senior karting, so we did not drive together any more. The next time we met was at Hockenheim in 1989 in Formula Three, the first race of the season. We split and did different things in that time.'

According to Frentzen, it was with the assistance of the organizing body, the ONS, who helped find sponsors for each of them to the tune of 250,000 Deutschmarks. 'It was half a budget for Formula Three in those days,' he said. 'Michael went to Willi Weber's team and I went to Schubel, so this was when our careers came back together again. Michael was successful immediately. He was third, third and always in the points, but I was eighth and then sixth and it was not so good.

'At the start we were using a Dallara chassis and it was not so good, so we changed to Reynard and suddenly we were on the pace. Michael was already the leader of the championship in 1989 before I managed my first win. I remember us at Zeltweg, battling in the rain. It was such a demanding circuit in that weather and we had a great fight. We came together in the Bosch corner and I lost the car and spun. I continued, but Michael won the race and I finished second. There were no problems. The next race was at Hockenheim and there I won my first race. Again it was a terrific battle. It carried on like that and it was a very close fight for the championship with Karl winning it in the end.

'Of course, we were close on the track and quite close off it too. I had a girlfriend, so I was very quiet and Michael was the same as he has always been. In 1989, when we were together in the junior team we became friends, travelling together a lot and spending evenings together. Sometimes we did sports together, but motor racing was the number one thing in our lives. It was nearly all we ever talked about. We had some fun and went out at night together once or twice. I remember too, our first test together at Mercedes. We were all a bit nervous. But we did not show this to each other at all. There was one car for us and we all wanted to show we were the best and the quickest at this test at Le Castellet.

'The team kept telling us not to go quick, we know you are quick, but don't destroy the car. Take it easy. We were saying "yes", but thinking "no", of course. I was thinking, well the other guys might be clever and maybe they are not saying what they want. They may want to ask afterwards about the details of the car, like the oil temperature, the water temperature, that sort of thing. So I was thinking about these details they might ask later and I was also worried about my first run with a 750 bhp car. I knew it was going to be demanding. I was the first one to sit in the car and I was very impressed with the power, the torque, the grip in the high-speed corners and I was still trying to check the instruments on the straight. It was difficult. I was pushing hard and trying to set up the car for the other guys. So, I pushed and then I waited while they set up the car for Michael.

'And you know, nobody asked me about the oil temperatures. I thought, "Oh hell, no," and Michael was driving. He was immediately pushing hard, really hard, so hard you could see it. He was five-tenths of a second quicker than me and then he came into the pits. And still nobody was asking me about the oil temperatures. I was so upset that he was quicker than me that I asked him about the oil temperatures and he said: "Oil temperatures? I haven't seen any of the oil temperatures. Or the water temperatures." So, again I said "hell" or worse, to myself and I didn't care about them next time. And that was how it all began.'

Frentzen's girlfriend at the time was Corinna Betsch, who was later to change camps and become Michael's girlfriend and fiancée. They had been a four-year fixture in and around the Stuttgart company's junior team in these years and for Frentzen it was not easy to accept as Michael, his fortunes soaring in late 1991, became Corinna's partner as well as the man with the Formula One drive for Jordan. This was ironic because Frentzen was attracted away from Mercedes by the prospect of a Camel-sponsored Formula 3000 programme with Jordan in 1990, a decision which blew up on him, as he explained.

'Well, my relationship with my girlfriend started in 1987. We were four and a half years together and it was good. At the end of 1991, it was not so good any more, the relationship we had, and later on we switched and changed partners. It is difficult to explain. It is just life. I cannot say exactly what happened. She found herself more happy with Michael at the end. It was generally a difficult time for me. I lost my sponsor Camel in 1991, I lost my chance to go into the European Formula 3000 Championship and Mercedes did not want to help me any more because I had gone away from them. It was a difficult year for me, 1991. And she chose then to go with Michael . . .'

Buessing remembered the surprise he felt the first time he saw Corinna with Schumacher, the Formula One driver, and not Frentzen, the Mercedes exile. 'When I saw them, I was surprised. I said "Hey what's going on here now?" and Michael just shrugged and smiled. I think really it was Corinna who made the decision. Heinz-Harald had problems at this time. He had bad advisers around him, professionally, including an ex-driver called Klaus Niedzwitz, who told him if he stayed in sportscars with Mercedes, he would never get to Formula One. He represented Camel and he was the one who took him to F3000 and Jordan. Look how it backfired! He had a split with Mercedes, with Corinna and with Michael who ended up with everything. Camel wanted to bring a German into F1. They approached Heinz-Harald and told him they would do it through F3000 for a year. But it did not work out that way. In the end, all the Camel money went to Benetton and Michael. What a business. It just happened in 1991 and at the end, for Heinz-Harald it was all over. He took a long time to recover. That is understandable. He sees Corinna with Michael now at all the races. He would be inhuman if he felt nothing.'

Frentzen remained calm and philosophical. 'It all happened around October or November 1991. I don't know if she was unhappy or happy with me. It was not a big problem. But since then I have not had any kind of special relationship with Michael. I talk to him and he talks to me, for sure, but we are not friends any more like we were before. It was not something that Michael did. I think we were separated, she and me, before . . . In any relationship, you need two people and I was always the last one, you know? She took a lot of care of her clothes and her appearance. Like me she had a similar problem when she was young and her parents separated. Her father was responsible for her, I think, but her mother was always saying to her that she had to get security from a driver. And I was in a situation where I had no money and I still had to pay a lot of money back to Formula Three because one of my sponsors had not paid. I also did not have a good relationship with my father in those days . . . In the end, I was left with zero.'

For Frentzen, however, the world went full circle. He ended up racing in Japan and then returned to drive for Sauber-Mercedes again, in Formula One. 'It was ironic after all that happened,' he said, 'that in the end Michael did not go into Formula One with Mercedes. He was not there to make the step. Now, I hope we can have some more good battles on the track. We are two different characters. I think I am more philosophical and he is more straight. He is very straight. He goes in one direction and concentrates on only one thing, but I want to know about a lot of other things along the way. I make mistakes and I do not think mistakes are wrong. But Michael is a person who does not like anyone to make mistakes.'

5 SILVERSTONE

WELCOME TO EDDIE'S GREEN AND PLEASANT LAND

> *I have to sign the contract, otherwise I cannot drive for Jordan.*
>
> Michael Schumacher talking to Jochen Neerpasch on the eve of his Formula One debut with Jordan, at Spa-Francorchamps, in 1991

IN THE HEART OF ENGLAND, surrounded by fields, trees, rolling countryside and a typical mixed agricultural landscape, lies Silverstone. It is a pleasant, but ordinary village, better known for things other than its shops or public houses. Nearby is a former wartime airfield which was transformed into the fastest racing circuit in the world until, in the early 1990s, modern safety requirements changed its layout. Still it remains one of the fastest and most historic places in motor racing. On a quiet winter's day, Silverstone can blend into the misty, rural landscape, but each summer, in the first half of July, it becomes a festival of noise and speed as the venue for the British Grand Prix.

Silverstone is also the home of Jordan Grand Prix, the jaunty, young and attractive outfit who joined the Formula One club in 1991. In the same year, Michael Schumacher made his transition from sportscar racing driver to Grand Prix racing driver, joining Jordan for just one race before being enticed away to Benetton Formula at the next race, the Italian Grand Prix at Monza. On the surface it seemed that Jordan had not finalized their contract with Michael for the rest of the year after his blistering Formula

One debut at Spa-Francorchamps and Benetton had capitalized on this opportunity with some *élan*. This was true. But below the surface, there was a trail of negotiations, manoeuvring and indignation, coupled with claims and counter-claims about honour and honesty, as well as several wild rumours of even more sinister affairs.

Schumacher was represented at this time both by his manager Willi Weber and the influential Jochen Neerpasch, who in turn represented both International Management Group (IMG), the international sports management company founded by Mark McCormack, and Mercedes Benz, for whom he was competitions chief. Between them, Weber and Neerpasch guided Schumacher's career through a chapter which was to provide furore in the Monza paddock and plenty of work for the lawyers of both Jordan and Benetton, and the Anglo-Italian team's Brazilian driver Roberto Moreno. It was a a tough weekend for Jordan and for all involved. For Michael, it was symbolic of the year, a turning point. It was a year of great change. It was also the last year of his normal life. Life before Formula One with its fame, fortune and intrigue.

For Michael, 1991 began with the prospect of another season of Group C racing with Mercedes and another year under the wing of Jochen Mass. It was likely to be the final year in the junior team, the final term in Mass's 'school-room' where he had learned so much. 'He did so much for all the juniors,' said Michael. 'Jochen's not a man who holds back on the important points. He has taught us a lot and not merely on the driving side. Also with the press. If we are talking in English, he helps out. If I don't know the words, I can ask him and if I make a mistake he will say "Stop, you must say this . . .". He is always there for us.'

At the start of the 1991 season, Schumacher was just 22, but already seasoned by his year with the Stuttgart giants. The junior school had given him confidence and knowledge. 'We worked together and that helped a lot. I learned so much. Mostly because I had to think more in the race because of the tyre and fuel situations. It was a big help for me in F3 as well, because now I can drive with really low wings and keep my tyres good for the whole race. I think that is why I was able to drive away from Otto

[Rensing] last year,' he explained. 'It wasn't that I could drive faster than him, as he is also very fast, but that I could do it for the whole distance. With Mercedes I have got another feel for driving. Before, I was driving a little bit like Senna. Now, I am more like . . .'. The final word remained unsaid, but was clearly meant to be Prost and to be delivered with a smile. Schumacher, in those days, was always a happy young man.

He looked ahead to the 1991 season with great enthusiasm, not knowing it was to include Le Mans, a foray into Formula 3000 in Japan and spectacular entry to Formula One. But, for Michael, as he looked ahead that January, Group C was all that mattered. He saw it as his route to the top and he relished the chance to throw off his 'L' plates from 1990, and team up with Karl Wendlinger. 'If we shared with Jean-Louis Schlesser, he would say "Okay, I will do it, but I'm the number one,"' said Michael. 'That meant I would always do the middle stint, never the qualifying. In this situation, with Karl, it is really good. We alternate starting and qualifying. Nobody is number one. We must show who is number one this season. We have the same equipment. We have made many tests now and we are really close in our times. I think we can go well.

'I think Jochen [Mass] is a little bit slower than Jean-Louis, just a couple of tenths. Karl and myself can do about the same time and I know I can do Jean-Louis' time so I think we have a chance to win. We must now find our own set-up, that's the only problem. We haven't got as much experience, so I think they will have a better set-up. I think we can maybe drive a little faster. Last year, we were the learners, the 'L' team. This year, we are the juniors. Maybe in one year . . . something else.'

In 1991 however, there were other changes, notably the introduction of a new 3.5 litre naturally-aspirated formula for the World Sportscar Championship. This meant a switch from the old turbo-powered V8s to new engines for Mercedes. It was a change which was not without problems. The new engines, in the new C291, were down on horsepower and lacked reliability, particularly at the start of the year. They were also a challenge for the mechanics for whom an engine-change meant nearly six hours hard graft. For Michael, this signalled a season of frustration. Nevertheless he put on some stirring performances in tandem with Karl Wendlinger, including a run to second place at Silverstone and a splendid win at Autopolis in Japan as well as a fast, if erratic, and ultimately doomed debut at Le Mans in the old turbo car.

Michael's solitary experience of Formula 3000 came in Japan, at Sugo, on 28 July 1991, roughly a month before his Formula One debut in Belgium. It was a one-off trip, designed to give him experience away from the spotlight in Europe. It was conceived and arranged by Neerpasch, who put together a good package: both car and circuit. Schumacher, driving a Suntory-sponsored Le Mans Company Ralt RT23-Mugen, as teammate to Johnny Herbert and Ross Cheever, adjusted quickly to the Sugo track as expected and finished second behind Cheever. Good preparation paid off. He had tested at Snetterton at the end of June in David Brabham's Ralt RT23, fitted with Bridgestone radials, and clocked a fast time. A week prior to that he had also sampled the German Touring Car Championship for the first time, making his bow at the Norisring when he took over the Zakspeed 190E 2.5 normally driven by Fabien Giroix. He also tested at Sugo, two weeks before the race and, so it is understood, benefited from special treatment from the team. Herbert, for example, had a terrible weekend with a badly-handling car, clutch problems, few of his regular mechanics and, unexpectedly, an older chassis. Michael had the best and the newest chassis and some new developments from Mugen.

Michael qualified his car second in his group and sixth overall, started from the second row of the grid, ran fourth and reached second place with four laps remaining. He finished two seconds behind Cheever. 'Sugo was an important experience,' admitted Schumacher. 'The competition was incredibly fierce. There were many people who have been driving in Japan for a long time, who were familiar with the proportions, the ratios, the cars, the tyres. The level of competition was very high, much higher than I had expected it to be . . . I never expected to finish second. But I gained a lot more experience for the future. In Group C, the qualifying tyre is maybe half a second quicker than the race tyres, but the Bridgestone qualifier was nearly three seconds faster. It was fantastic. A really good experience for qualifiers. The difference taught me a lot. More than F1. You need more power from yourself to hold the steering. The tyres have so much grip and you really feel it. Also, F3000 is quick. Nearly as quick as F1 in cornering speeds and so on. It helped me a lot.'

The Sugo trip was expected to be part of the preparation for a later entry to Formula One. Instead, it was a prelude, as both Footwork-Arrows and Tyrrell began overtures for his services which preceded his entry with Jordan at Spa. Michael, who took it all in his stride, learned his lessons. 'His learning curve was amazing,' said Jochen Mass. 'In 1991, he was extremely fast. He drove a lot. The year before he had listened, watched and learned. He quietly absorbed everything so well and never made any excuses. He was always working. When I was faster than him in the C9, for example, because I could muscle the car, he would accept it. He knew he would be faster eventually. In 1991, though, you could see him developing as a character too. In a way that you could not explain to anyone really. You could not do anything with him. I would say to him "do this" or "do that" and he would always say "why?" Then when I explained it, he would say I was wrong and his way was better. It was good to see this. He learned. He just watched me. I didn't really teach him anything. I probably did in a subtle way, but he took it all in. I am sure he didn't idolize me at all. I was a good driver, but he probably only respected that and knew he had a good chance in the team if he learned and behaved properly. He had to focus properly. He needed to if he wanted to succeed.'

Mass, who still lives within close reach of Schumacher in Monte Carlo, was the guiding light to his career at that time and in 1991 saw the maturing Michael move from youngster, with eyes agog, into his new role of future Grand Prix star. He took his lessons on board. 'We used to talk to him about how to handle certain situations. I liked him. He listened to me, I think, because I was German and it was easy to get through to him. I had no particular notion to teach him all the time, but I didn't want him to do foolish things. I don't think he is inclined that way anyway. He is focused. He knows what he wants. Now [1994] he impresses me more and more. He makes decisions which are good in Formula One. He can say this is right and that is wrong and he also admits his own mistakes. That is one of his strong points and it was there then back in 1991. You could see he would succeed in the long run.'

Mass was fully qualified to guide the young Schumacher. He drove in 105 Grands Prix, winning one, in a career with the Surtees, McLaren, ATS, Arrows and March teams. Never a champion and only rarely a truly convincing front runner, he was nonetheless much respected by his contemporaries and particularly in Germany. He also has a mastery of the English language which added to his list of qualities as Schumacher's unofficial teacher and mentor through 1990 and 1991. 'Language-wise, he came along very nicely,' said Mass. 'His school record was not very good, so the way he speaks English now, when compared to someone like Gerhard Berger for example, who has been using it for many years, is impressive. He is articulate. I don't know the family well and I didn't then. I have seen his father twice, I think. But judging from the way Michael is, I think they must have been a good influence. He was brought up well.

'I think the Schumachers are sincere people. A lot of the credit for his success should rest with his family. Sometimes you get very pushy, extrovert parents, particularly with racing drivers. But his father was never there. Never in the way. He never came to the races. He knew he would only be in the way. So he stayed out of it. He just let his son get on with it because, I think, he knew his son had surpassed him anyway. There was nothing his father could do or say at all. All of his races were good. But the last one in 1991 at Autopolis was very good, when he won with Karl [Wendlinger]. The two were flying so fast. Very quick. It was refreshing to know him at that time. We were also driving, Schlesser and I, and we were doing good times. But they were two seconds quicker. Their motivation was stronger. We still enjoyed it, but we couldn't pretend that it was the same . . . Michael was in the right place at the right time in 1991. He was lucky and he was lucky to be able to see it, because I think Frentzen had the same opportunity, but he listened to the wrong people. He was like a mad dog. I could have whacked him. But I did not do it. My input on him was not very strong. He was under the influence of a lot of managers. But Michael was not and he was there when it mattered for him.'

In 1991, Michael drove in eight sportscar races for Mercedes, including Le Mans where his temperament for a marathon proved to be suspect and he retired. He was second at Silverstone with Wendlinger and together they won in Autopolis, Japan. Schumacher finished ninth in the championship with 43 points. Teo Fabi won with 86, while Derek Warwick was second with 79. In Formula One, he raced in six Grands Prix, one with Jordan and five with Benetton, after the famous clandestine transfer between the two on the eve of the Italian Grand Prix. In the World Drivers' Championship, he finished with four points and 13th place. All the Formula One points were scored for Benetton, although it was Eddie Jordan who took the risk to give him a car to test, at Silverstone's south circuit, on Tuesday, 20 August 1991, and who then ran him in the Belgian Grand Prix. The test, as we know, was a successful demonstration of his speed and promise, a typical Schumacher arrival show.

Willi Weber, Schumacher's manager, recalled it all clearly. 'I had been so scared to see him move through the formulae, going up to a bigger car with more horsepower, but by the time he got to Sauber-Mercedes, it had become unbelievable the way he could handle a car. How he drove on the limit. How he could save the gasoline . . . He was so effective and so smooth. Normally, you need a year to learn it all. But Michael was very quick. He did the same thing in F1. It was like a gift to him. It still is. But it was amazing how he switched from one to the other.

'I remember we were at the Nurburgring, for a Group C race, and one of the journalists stopped me and asked if I had heard the latest news. He told me that the Jordan driver, Bertrand Gachot, had been put in jail. Five minutes later, I was on the phone to Eddie from my hotel. Eddie was in Spain and I asked him to give us a chance to drive for him. He said "Are you crazy? Who do you want to put in my car?" I said "Schumacher" and he said "Who the hell is he?" I told him about Macau and then he remembered me. We were actually good friends, quite close, through Formula Three. We met very often in racing and he was a good, honest guy. A good friend. It cost me 1,200 Deutschmarks in phone calls and faxes. Eddie told me he needed £80,000 for a test drive and I said I would guarantee the money. Just put him in the car and let me know how he gets on after the test.

'Then I had to get the OK from Jochen Neerpasch because he wanted to win the championship in Group C with him. When I spoke to him, he was not too friendly towards me, but eventually he backed down and things moved very quickly after that. Mercedes backed us in a fantastic way and Michael was very impressive in the test. The team manager Trevor Foster fell in love with Michael immediately. He called Eddie in Spain and said "Maybe we have a racing man in the car or a superstar – I am not quite sure which," and, after another hour, he was sure they had a superstar. We agreed to race on Eddie's terms and then Mercedes came up and said they would pay for Michael and they saved me a lot of money which was fantastic.'

The race in Belgium followed and, after it, the backroom moves which took Schumacher from Jordan to Benetton after just one race. 'For me, it was a good move,' said Weber. 'The package was better, the engine was better. Before we jumped in the car at Spa, we signed a letter of intent for Jordan, but not a contract, because the deal was not acceptable. I like Eddie very much and I know Michael was a fantastic driver in the car and everyone in the team were so lovely . . . But Eddie overpushed things and then it was finished. We just couldn't work with him on a long-term basis. So I called Flavio and suggested we sit together the next morning at eight and that's what we did. And there we are.'

These were tense times for Michael and for all around him. The move to Jordan was a swift one. The move to Benetton even swifter. Trevor Foster remembered his arrival. 'We had spoken to Willi Weber before about Michael and there was some talk of him running in Eddie's F3000 operation. But it did not happen. Then, quite suddenly, we had to replace Bertrand. Obviously people realized the car was quite good, so there was a queue of people after it, including Keke Rosberg. I think it was virtually a contest between Keke, Michael and Gary Anderson and I just felt it was better to go for a young team. The Jordan tradition was to go for young drivers, virtual unknowns. Gary and I voted for that and Eddie went along with us. Then he came over for his test and the rest, as they say, is history.'

Eddie Jordan was excited. He rang his sponsors and he prepared a contract. Gachot failed to get out of jail and, very quickly, Schumacher was a Jordan driver. It was the start of one of the most exciting weeks of his life and one of the most disappointing episodes in the development of the Jordan team. 'We had to rush to get a letter of agreement to Schumacher. We supplied him with a contract in English, but he wanted it translated into German,' Jordan recalled. 'He signed it and a letter came through from Sauber to agree to how much they would pay and we went ahead. It was for the remainder of that year and for three years after that, 1992, 1993 and 1994. It was always said and agreed that in the fourth year an official Mercedes team would have priority over my contract. All the terms were agreed in advance and we issued him with a contract. He said he needed time and so we said we'd better have a letter of intent to say that he would sign the contract.'

For Jordan, this was the beginning of his problems. At this stage, he did not know that he was signing the hottest property to have arrived in Formula One since Ayrton Senna. He knew he was signing a promising, talented driver, but not a star of the future. In Germany they did. Schumacher had Weber, his manager, and Jochen Neerpasch, then representing the International Management Group, to advise him. Their advice was to delay, take time, stall and to ensure that the future remained open. They guaranteed backing from Mercedes, through Sauber, and then from TicTac and Dekra, but only for the one race. Their advice was to prove decisive and led to an unprecedented struggle for Michael's services.

'When the signed agreement came back to us,' said Jordan, 'he had changed one word in it. His adviser [Neerpasch] had told him to change one word from "the" to "a" . . . But he had signed the agreement in German and it was witnessed. He signed and that in itself is binding!'

Jordan's recollections, jumbled with passion and hurt, included remembering Schumacher arriving at Spa-Francorchamps on the Thursday before his debut race to be confronted with confusion. 'He didn't want to sign anything when he got there, so I just said

"Fair enough, forget it" and I told him I would ring Stefan Johansson. I was ready to say "Stef, come here immediately. I need you to drive tomorrow." I was ready to do this, I'd already spoken to him about why I didn't take him for the drive. I would have rung him. I said to Michael "If you don't sign this I'm not taking all the risk of putting you in a car and giving you your chance of Formula One if there is nothing in it for the company or the team." That was how it went on. Right through the weekend.'

For Michael it was a day of anguish. No chance to drive on the track. Squabbling over his contract. Neerpasch recalled: 'On that Thursday night, Jordan wanted Michael to sign a contract. I wasn't there. Michael phoned me and I said "Don't sign any contract" and he told me "I have to sign, otherwise I cannot drive." Then, I got the contract faxed and we changed a paragraph which made sure that he did not sign a contract. Then he signed this letter of intent to discuss a contract after Spa. The real problem was that we wanted to continue that season, but not the following season, with Eddie. Michael was interested in this. We all wanted this, but there were other problems. When we discussed the contract for the rest of the season, after Spa, Eddie was not prepared to give us the space on the car. My understanding was that we had it for the year, but he said it was only for Spa. So then, the whole thing started. After this we contacted Benetton . . .'

Ian Phillips, who was closer to the day-to-day dealings, remembered that Neerpasch, although entrusted by Mercedes Benz to authorize a cheque for £150,000 per race, was not authorized to permit Schumacher to sign any contracts. 'I gave Willi [Weber] the contract, prior to Spa, when they came over to test,' he recalled. 'He said "No problem, I'll take it back and give it to Neerpasch and it will all be done." Then Neerpasch said no. Although he could consent to the money, the contract would need to go to the Mercedes lawyers and he couldn't do that until the following week. That is why we asked Michael to sign a piece of paper, undertaking that he was going to sign the contract. He said something in German, that we were not entirely satisfied with, so we drafted out a four-line thing which said "I undertake to sign the contract prior to the next race." '

Against this background, at Spa-Francorchamps, Michael delivered an explosive debut performance as a Formula One driver, delighted the large German contingent who made the short trip across the border and confirmed he would be back at Silverstone for another test with Jordan, prior to the Italian Grand Prix two weeks later. 'That upset me the most,' said Jordan. 'He came back and tested here at Silverstone the following week, on the Thursday. We were sure everything would be fine. We even booked hotels for him and his manager, Weber, which had to be confirmed for Japan and Australia. That meant the rest of the season. But they knew what was going on and what they were doing and, obviously, IMG were heavily involved behind the scenes. The Thursday that he tested here, they spoke to Trevor and they booked a hotel which still niggles me. The deposits which we never got back . . . I find all that the lowest of the lows. He [Weber] never paid them off. He owed me. He still tries to talk to me but he is the only guy in the paddock I cannot talk to. He lied to me because he honestly thought we were not going to survive.'

During the weekend of the Belgian Grand Prix, Weber had become aware, through information supplied by Benetton's Tom Walkinshaw, that Jordan were considering switching from Ford Cosworth engines to Yamaha for 1992. He was adamant that this was bad for the team and for Michael's prospects, if he remained a Jordan driver. Weber made this clear to Phillips and Jordan. 'I suppose the buzz was that we were going to go with Yamaha,' said Phillips. 'But we were also talking to Porsche, who had a new engine, and we had made no commitment to Yamaha. The one person who really knew that we were going to go was Tom Walkinshaw because he had told us that we weren't going to have a deal with Cosworth, when we were in Hungary, earlier in August. We weren't to know at that time, but Weber had been approached by Walkinshaw and this information was one of his levers. It came out many months later that this was the crux of the problem.'

Walkinshaw, of course, as head of the Jaguar sportscar racing team operation, knew about Schumacher's potential as well as anyone in Formula One, if not more. It is pretty clear too, that he was in contact with Michael and his advisers at this time, having

identified Schumacher as a driver he wanted at Benetton soon
after joining them in July as Engineering Director. His
impressions were confirmed in Belgium when initial contacts
were reinforced and Jordan found it increasingly difficult to pin
their new young driver down to a contract. 'Neerpasch went on
about how he couldn't do the contract,' said Phillips. 'Michael
signed the piece of paper modifying one word from signing "the"
contract to signing "a" contract. So, we did the race and then it
was the following week, about Wednesday, when I was speaking
to Neerpasch and asking if everything was all right. He said it
was fine and asked if we had ever thought of taking Karl
Wendlinger. He said he was as quick as Michael but just took a
little time to get up to speed. I just thought he was trying to get
both his drivers in the team for next year.

'On the Friday, he said everything was all right with the
contract. He said he was having one or two things amended and
having it typed up and would bring it up on Monday. In the
afternoon, I got a call from Weber, when I think Eddie was in
Japan, and warned me to be careful of Neerpasch. I said "He's
told me the contract is all right, what's the problem? Michael's
money?" He said "Yeah."'

By this time, Phillips knew there were problems, but still felt
they were not insurmountable. When Jordan returned from Japan,
he called Weber and Neerpasch and arranged for them to come to
Silverstone to meet him and to sign a contract at 10 am on Monday
morning, 2 September. Clearly this was to be a decisive and
important meeting. Understandably, the Jordan management
were anxious to complete their deal with Schumacher and they
were filled with nervous apprehension. It does not take a great
deal of imagination to picture the mood when no-one arrived at
the appointed hour. 'It got to about lunchtime and I couldn't find
them anywhere,' said Phillips. 'EJ tried to contact them. He
decided to contact IMG because they were advising them on the
contract. I cannot remember exactly what the response was, but it
was evident that they were with IMG and they told us not to
worry, saying they would be with us around 4.40 pm.'

Jordan was livid. 'I remember we had about five different faxes
overall from Mercedes through all this and we were continually

told that their main legal adviser was reading the contract. But that wasn't the case,' he said. 'We were lied to. What surprised me, and what I couldn't cope with, was that good friends of our team realized that it was such an underhand thing and they were told to give them the benefit of the doubt . . .'

Ultimately, Neerpasch arrived later that day at Silverstone together with Julian Jakobi of IMG. Phillips and Jordan were aghast at the implications. 'We said we don't want any IMG royalties. We want Michael. Where is he?' recounted Phillips. And he was told Michael 'was not feeling well, or something like that.' The meeting was unproductive for Phillips who took control as Eddie was, by then, doing something else. 'They had totally disrupted our day,' said Phillips. And, he went on, they produced a contract which was nothing like the one he and Jordan were prepared for. Neerpasch later said this was because Jordan had attempted to vary the terms of their original outline agreement. In retaliation, he delivered that afternoon a contract which had been prepared by IMG. Fred Rodgers, who was then acting as Jordan's solicitor, said: 'This was a re-worked version of the one I had compiled originally. It contained things which on the face of it were not acceptable and they were obviously put in in the knowledge that they would not be acceptable.' In Jordan's opinion, later, this was seen as very abnormal since he believed it was usual for it to be a contract produced by the team and not the driver's representatives which formed the basis of any such agreement. 'Their contract and ours were nothing alike,' said Phillips. 'They were at opposite ends in terms of space on the car they were going to have, the money they were going to pay, the duration of the contract, everything. Nothing was correct. We said that we couldn't sign it. And we agreed to work on it overnight and to meet again at ten in the morning, with Michael present.'

That Monday evening, Neerpasch travelled to Benetton where later he signed a deal for Schumacher to drive for the team. At the same time, Phillips and his Jordan colleagues were working through the night to produce a contract which was, they hoped, acceptable for all parties involved. The following morning, at 9.55 am, a fax arrived from Michael Schumacher which said he was sorry, but he was not able to go through with the contract and would not be driving again for Jordan. This was the signal for much undignified, but quite understandable, anger at Silverstone. 'We found out that on Sunday, he had been at Benetton for a seat fitting,' said Phillips. 'And that day he was testing for Benetton at Silverstone too. There was all sorts of yelling and screaming going on. We decided to go for an injunction, but it took us all day that Tuesday to really find out what was going on. Tom [Walkinshaw] sent over his helicopter to pick Eddie up and there was total chaos. By then we had already nominated our drivers to the FIA [Federation Internationale de l'Automobile]. It just went on and on and eventually we arrived in Monza in this chaos, trying to get injunctions heard that day [Thursday] and without a driver.'

Rodgers recalled that Walkinshaw, on his flying visit to Jordan, had offered money as compensation for losing Schumacher. 'Walkinshaw offered a sum and it was turned down,' said Rogers. 'I don't remember how much it was, but it was turned down. After that, the team had a meeting and it was agreed that they wanted Michael Schumacher to drive and they would do all they could to achieve that.'

The Jordan team applied to the High Court in London for its injunction, which was heard on the Thursday they flew to Milan for the Italian race at Monza. Eddie Jordan himself was the picture of abject nervous confusion and anger as he stalked through Heathrow and onto the flight for Linate. Even as he boarded the British Airways plane, he was talking on his mobile phone, delivering further instructions. There were many oaths too. He was outraged. He wanted an injunction in place to prevent Schumacher driving for any other team but Jordan, on the basis that he had already signed a binding agreement. But this was not granted, a decision which meant Schumacher was in that court's view free to drive for Benetton in Monza. There were, however, other obstructions for Flavio Briatore and his team to overcome first.

•••

In all that happened between his first test with Jordan prior to the Belgian Grand Prix through to his 'transfer' to Benetton 17 days later, Michael remained a passive accessory to the financial and legal dealings which surrounded him and his future. Indeed, in the course of the 21 days from the race at the Nurburgring, where Derek Warwick was victorious, to his racing debut with Benetton, alongside three-times world champion Nelson Piquet, his world was tipped upside down around him, but he never once lost his composure. The chronological order of events may have seemed chaotic, but Michael remained focused on one thing only: his racing, his talent and his future. He displayed an uncanny ability to concentrate his mind on his own interests at the expense of all else around him. This was manifested more than ever at Monza, where he qualified seventh and finished fifth in the Italian Grand Prix on his debut for Benetton. It was to be repeated later, again and again, when controversy descended upon him, no more so than in 1994 when successive events left Formula One rocking, some with shock, others with mirth.

6 MONZA

AN OVERNIGHT MOVE TO THE FAMILY

I'm sorry. I didn't want it to be like this.

Michael Schumacher talking to Ian Phillips on the eve
of his Benetton debut at Monza, 1991.

To THE NORTH-EAST OF MILAN, in the grounds of the
old royal palace of Monza, where the Italian royal family once
spent its summers, is the Autodromo Nazionale di Monza. It is an
historic and atmospheric place, one of the great cathedrals of
motor racing. The royal park is beautiful, a walled garden of
woodlands and fields with views of the peaks of the Italian Alps
in the distance and the derelict banking of the old circuit still
standing among the trees. Every September it is filled with the
tifosi, the passionate Italian fans, who generate an unequalled
atmosphere, lending it frenzy, colour, noise and tradition,
bringing back the ghosts of past legends and, by squeezing up
close to the high, wire fences, turning the modern paddock of the
television era into a zoo-like maelstrom of wheeling and dealing
and politics each year as the season draws to its climax. In 1991 it
was no different and on the eve of opening qualifying for the
Italian Grand Prix, the biggest story of the day was the row over
Schumacher's contract and the sacking of Roberto Moreno by
Benetton. Even by Formula One's Machiavellian standards, this
was a high-octane start to the most exhausting weekend of the
European summer season on the Formula One calendar.

Michael arrived in Monza to find himself, not unexpectedly, at
the centre of a major row. He could not claim it was a surprise to
him, as he knew what was happening, though he had not played

an active part in it at all. His performance at Spa-Francorchamps had impressed many people, not least the Benetton hierarchy of Flavio Briatore and Tom Walkinshaw. Within minutes they knew they wanted him to replace Roberto Moreno who, by a quirk of fate, happened to finish fourth in the second Benetton, behind his team leader Nelson Piquet, in that Belgian Grand Prix. Moreno also scored fastest lap that day, but it was not enough to save his seat with Benetton. He had been unwell at an earlier race, at the Hungaroring, Budapest, when he finished behind Andrea de Cesaris's Jordan-Ford, in eighth position for Benetton. That result, which disappointed the Benetton decision-makers, led to his dismissal and the pursuit of Schumacher after the Belgian race, which was the first time Benetton's managing director Flavio Briatore set eyes on him.

'The first time I saw Michael was in Spa. The first time I spoke to him was in London, a few days afterwards, in my house,' he said. 'He was with me and Neerpasch and we discussed Michael's position with Jordan and it was confirmed to me that there was no contract. It was only a one-race deal. I told Michael I was ready to put him in the car and that we didn't need any money from personal sponsorship, and that was how we did the deal. It was very important for him to get into the car immediately. For me, that was no problem. I felt it was important to find someone for the future of the team. We all felt very strongly that he was our driver for the future.

'My only worry was that he would not have enough laps, but we did not expect instant miracles. We knew too that we did not have the best car, but we were working on it and we wanted a driver for the future. I knew my situation at the time was not a winning one, but we were looking ahead and Michael was the first really important step. Nelson [Piquet] and Moreno were our other drivers at the time. I had already decided what to do and two weeks before I met with Michael. I had told Moreno what I wanted to do in the future. That he would not be driving with us any more and that it was not our intention to renew his contract.

'I knew a little about Michael from Group C. If you saw the times he was doing on his laps on the same circuit in the same car as other people, it was obvious there was a very big difference and the guy was talented. But it was a big risk too for Benetton and also for the sponsors. But it was the kind of risk you have to take if you want to make the difference. Michael had no real experience in Formula One and it would have been quite easy to blow up. But we went ahead with it all. We did the contracts because we believed in it all. For the future.'

On the assumption that he had signed Michael, Briatore flew to Milan for the Italian Grand Prix as a happy and satisfied man. Schumacher was to replace Moreno, who had been released from his contract. He did not know what was to hit him. 'When I got there, I really did not understand all the stuff going on because it was nothing to do with the Benetton team. Jordan never sued Benetton. Moreno took an action, but this was quite normal . . . We paid his salary to the end of the season anyway. I thought we had to do this because I could see it was difficult for him. But this was never an issue. None of it was ever really a big problem for Benetton.'

Briatore recognized, however, that it was a problem for Michael and for Jordan. A big problem. 'It was a very big weekend,' he said. 'It was very difficult for Michael. There were a lot of negotiations going on on all sides. I had the situation with Moreno, because he did not accept my first proposal on the Thursday night, and I am sure Michael knew all about this and what was going on, but he still went and did a superb job anyway. There was pressure on him from all sides: from Jordan, from IMG, from Mercedes, Neerpasch and Moreno. But Michael handled it all very well. As soon as he got into the car, he forgot it all. It was fantastic. He was immediately quick in qualifying and gave a good race performance. It was his first time at Monza and how he did it was just fantastic. Nelson was very close to him and in the beginning he was a little bit upset because he had seen what happened and he was friends with Moreno and he missed him in the team. But then, I believe, Nelson realized that Michael was something special and, after that race and during the final races he worked with him and there was a very good relationship between them.'

The calm, this time, came after the storm. At Monza, between 5 and 8 September 1991, hardly a minute could pass without discussion of what came to be termed the 'Schumacher Affair'. It was a complex weekend. Preceded by the events in England, which saw Michael's talents transferred from Jordan to Benetton by Neerpasch and Weber, those which followed at Monza were, if anything, even more bizarre. Moreno, having been dismissed by Benetton, took advice (he rang Jordan's solicitor Fred Rodgers and, after initially asking if he might have the Jordan drive, was persuaded to take action) and chose to act independently through the local Italian courts in pursuit of his full and proper rights and compensation. Unlike Jordan, he was successful, thanks to a local court in Milan, in obtaining an injunction which prevented anybody but himself from driving the second Benetton.

Moreno's move meant that, as Phillips so succinctly put it, 'Benetton were in trouble – they sacked Moreno, he applied for his injunction in an Italian court and he won. They could not run that car for anyone but him. Then it got a bit, well, messy.' Jordan had attempted to block Schumacher's move to Benetton. They had lost. But the news of Moreno's success gave them some hope of rescuing something from this situation. 'To be honest, we were in a right state,' said Phillips, candidly admitting that for a new Formula One team all these events had built up into a mountain of pressure under which they could barely cope. 'We had Moreno lurking in our motor home in the afternoon, when his court case against Benetton was going ahead. By then, he had been sacked anyway. I wondered then if he might end up getting a drive for us. He was worried that afternoon, though, and he didn't want to go outside.

'About 7 pm, we got a call in the motor home from Mr Ecclestone. He said "Get up to the Villa d'Este, we'd better sort this out." We also had a representation around then that we should run Alessandro Zanardi, the runaway leader of the Formula 3000 championship . . .'

According to Jordan, his hand was strong. 'To begin with, when Bernie advised me to see Flavio, we were not moving. At that stage, our position was strengthened by Moreno. He said he was driving and Piquet said he was driving. He had a legitimate case. We were happy to discuss Schumacher driving for us for the rest of the season. But then the whole thing became unreasonable and fell apart. We wouldn't move. We are not a team which is going to be bought. We were not going to prostitute ourselves on an issue we felt so strongly about. In the end, though, we went.'

'We went up to the Villa,' said Phillips. 'We had no idea where we were staying that night because we hadn't been to our hotel. We got there, to Villa d'Este, about 9 pm. There was Eddie and myself and there were Moreno's two lawyers, one that went to court and the other that briefed him. We said to Moreno's people "Absolutely no way, you can forget it, he's not going to drive for us. Not at all." And they were arguing, bartering and so on. There were arguments all around us and there was Flavio, with Tom and Bernie. We sat in the foyer of the Villa d'Este and we shuffled our way around it in little clusters. It was some scene.

'It is an imperial foyer. Really beautiful. There was Flavio promising to send us smoked salmon sandwiches. Tom was pretending to be a wine waiter and wandering around the room with some incredibly fine carafe which he had found in the dining-room. It was getting pretty silly. All these meetings in clusters were getting nowhere at all. There were IMG people there too, Hample and Jakobi. Michael was there and came to apologize. Neerpasch wasn't there.

'Eventually, Bernie called me and Eddie to one side and said Moreno wasn't going to get anything out of Benetton. "Absolutely nothing. They don't have to pay him one penny and he's not going to drive the car." We said we were not going to run him. Then we told Bernie to remind Flavio and Tom that under the terms of the injunction they could not run that car for anyone else and they could not claim *force majeure* for that car not running that weekend. It would be thrown out of the world championship.

'Then Bernie went back to report to Tom and Flavio. Moreno's people were called into the meeting and they agreed a settlement of $500,000 for him not to drive. "Don't accept it," I advised, "Make them sweat. They can't run the car for anybody else. Leave it until tomorrow night because if they can't run on Saturday, they haven't taken part in the meeting – and believe me, there is nobody prepared to agree with them claiming *force majeure*. You can take it right up to 1.55 on Saturday afternoon, if you like . . .". They really shouldn't have agreed to those terms there and then, but they phoned up Moreno and eventually they agreed. Their instructions from Moreno were to agree that and do a deal with Jordan.'

Jordan did not really want to do a deal, but in the end had little or no choice. 'There was a lot of shouting and roaring,' he recalled. 'There was a problem between the lawyers representing Moreno, and Benetton. Something silly was said that was interpreted by the lawyer as something quite unethical. The meeting went on for hours. They would speak to Moreno and then they would speak to me. Michael had clearly been told not to speak to us. But he did. He was terribly embarrassed and confused by the whole thing.'

Phillips continued: 'By this stage, it was 1.30 am. We told Flavio that he had to book us a room because we didn't know where our hotel was and the man from Marlboro Italy kept saying "Zanardi, Zanardi". Walkinshaw told us then that he had got Zanardi under contract because he had had a seat-fitting that afternoon. Under that contract, he said, he could not drive for anyone. So, there we were: we were told we couldn't have Zanardi, Moreno had done a deal so we lost Schumacher, or Schumacher might not have been driving for anybody . . . Eddie put a price to Moreno's people, I think at $65,000 a race. There and then. And then at about 2.30 am, one of my greatest ambitions, to spend a night in the Villa d'Este, came true. But I never expected to share a bed with Eddie Jordan!

'I phoned Trevor Foster at 2.30 am to tell him "It's Moreno and he'll be there at 7 am for a seat-fitting. Make sure you get the letter to the FIA, nominating the drivers." Eddie and I didn't really sleep, we left the hotel at 6 am and at the traffic lights the man from Marlboro Italy pulled up alongside us. "What happened? What happened?" he demanded. "Moreno." "What about Zanardi?" "Walkinshaw said he had a contract with Benetton." "No, not true." And later, at about 8.30 am, Zanardi came to the motor home in a flood of tears. "I would have driven for you. No problem. Walkinshaw has no contract with me." What they'd done, thinking they might lose Schumacher, was to give Zanardi a seat-fitting on Thursday afternoon.

'Bernie, when he had taken me and Eddie into the corner by the porcelain cabinet at the side of the stairs, had said "These people are going to do a deal. They're ruthless people. Forget these injunctions." That was the only hint of things happening there then. It was like a train station for very rich people and there were all sorts of people coming up to Eddie and saying that no end of nasty things could happen . . .

'We had seen Michael quite early on in the proceedings and he was on his way to bed. "I'm sorry, I didn't want it to be like this," and off he went to bed. I don't remember seeing him again that year. It was one of those things. Weber tried to be friendly, but he knew all along what was happening. Neerpasch was the one who masterminded the whole thing. But Weber knew all about it. None of us have a problem with Michael. He was an innocent pawn in the whole thing.

'It was an administrative error that gave them a loophole. What we didn't realize was that we were being manipulated by Neerpasch from day one. He is a man that no-one in this company will ever speak to again. He has to be the most slimey character. And, of course, you have to remember Walkinshaw was running the Jaguars against the Mercedes in sportscars. He was aware of Schumacher's abilities. So the moment he saw Michael in a Formula One car and looking good, he was ready. But Neerpasch wasn't there on the Friday in Spa. But he was on Saturday and I reckon Walkinshaw went in there pretty quickly and asked what the deal was . . . They'd been pretty unhappy with Moreno for some time and Tom had been brought in as a trouble-shooter three or four races before. He is the one who would have put the boot in for us because he knew of our situation with Ford and Yamaha. I can see it all now, with the benfit of hindsight.

'The whole of that Sunday in Spa, Weber was going round asking "Are you going with Yamaha?" and we weren't admitting we were. We were just about to face a legal battle with Cosworth over broken contracts, so it was pretty delicate. We couldn't really say anything – even though on the Monday night after Spa, Eddie went to Japan to do the deal and the only person who really knew was Walkinshaw. We'd put a proposal for Ford, first

of all after Canada, then after the British Grand Prix, about what
our position would be for 1992. Yamaha were unhappy with
Brabham and we were getting no response from Ford . . .

'Eddie went to see Walkinshaw at Hungary and said "What is
going to be our deal for next year?" "No deal. With the engines
you've got at the moment, you're an embarrassment to Benetton.
You can't have any increase in specification. At best, you'll have
what you've got now." "In that case," said Eddie, "we are not
interested in the deal." At that time, there was an embryonic
Reynard Yamaha team with all the ex-Benetton guys like Rory
Byrne and Pat Symonds, and Tom wanted them back at Benetton.
But he could only do that if he spiked Reynard's project. And he
gave Eddie the tip-off on how to get the Yamaha. "You aren't
going to get a deal out of Ford, but why don't you go and get the
Yamaha? They're not sure if Reynard is going racing, they are
unhappy at Brabham. Go and see Bernie and you can have the
Yamaha deal; and if you get the Yamaha deal I can get Rory
back." Tom was the only person who knew about the Yamaha
thing and of course he would have used that with his approach to
Weber . . .

'Michael was extremely humble through the whole thing. But
in hindsight it was the best thing that could have happened. It was
a shame. Even if we couldn't have held on to him for the
following year, we could have won a race with him in that car. At
Suzuka, the thing was blindingly quick. And at Adelaide. I think
he had a chance of podium finishes in both of those. That guy's
car control is everything. Zanardi has the speed. He hasn't got the
control. Michael just never raised a sweat. Never. I suppose this is
synonymous with all good sportsmen in any sport.

'The thing they have above anybody else is time. He was
thinking two corners in front. Not where the front wheel is on the
road. It is like the batsman (in cricket) who has time; he sees the
bowler's wrist and that's why he knows what is coming. He's not
trying to watch it coming towards him and then "Christ, it's
landed there." No, the guy has got time and anticipation and that
is what Michael has in everything he does. He's relaxed and just
totally in control. Nothing comes as a surprise to him. The guy's
probably got a heart rate of about 36; he just doesn't fluster. He's

just like Senna, probably a little better because he combined speed and control at an early age. It wasn't until 1991 that Senna had everything right. He had the speed before, but he was prone to do daft things. I don't think I've ever seen Michael do anything daft. Never. He's been fast. You don't think that there's 50 per cent of his game that he has still got to improve. He has 98 per cent of everything together now.'

Phillips recalled all the action and the emotions calmly, but the pain remained for Jordan even three years later. 'You know, Michael was crying out "I really want to be with you" and it kills me. Not because he has done so well but because I started him. I helped him. He knew that. He could quite easily have been rolled into oblivion. His chance – and it was a chance – came from me. What other team in Formula One would ever have taken that chance?

'No-one can take it away from Jordan. Michael's a smashing boy. He's always nice to me. We know his girlfriend well because she was Frentzen's girlfriend and she was with us for a year in Formula 3000 . . . There is no reason why Schumacher could not have done with the Jordan team what he has done with Benetton. Growing up with them and lifting them. We could have done that together.'

These were reflective words, later, much later. At the time, there was little reflection in Jordan's instant reactions as he stormed around the Monza paddock. 'We intend to initiate a compensation campaign to recover the potential sponsorship we have lost by losing Schumacher's services. We plan to claim against Michael, IMG, Neerpasch, Mercedes-Benz, Sauber and Benetton. And I can promise you that if Mercedes-Benz or anybody else says anything critical about us, I will make public our dossier to the press on an international basis. We will open our books completely and make public all our evidence.'

Walkinshaw was confident he was beyond reproach for his part in the dealings. 'Neerpasch had been canvassing several teams to see if they were interested in Michael and of course I had been impressed with his performances in the Mercedes sportscar and was keeping an eye on him,' he said. 'I said I was interested in running him, but understood he had a prior commitment to

Jordan and was only interested if the Mercedes lawyers could give me clear legal advice that he was not committed elsewhere. I would want my head examined if I didn't go after a driver of his obvious calibre.

'I had no problem with Eddie applying to the court. He tried on several counts and the judge dismissed every one. I think there's been a lot of nonsense on this. The fact is that Schumacher, for whatever reason, had no contract with Jordan. He was a free agent. How anyone can allow a talent like that to be walking around the paddock, I don't know. That's their business. When we were informed of that we went about the proper way of securing him.'

Walkinshaw's first telephone call to Neerpasch caught the German in his bath. He answered and the pair, to Walkinshaw's mirth, had a sensible business conversation. 'I wasn't happy with Moreno because I wanted someone in the second car to liven things up a bit,' he recalled. 'Jochen agreed to come over to London to discuss the possibility of Michael coming to Benetton for the next race at Monza. They came over with their lawyers and a contract and we examined it and satisfied ourselves that indeed, there was no agreement with Jordan. The only thing was that there was a block in the contract that if Mercedes Benz came back into F1 racing in the following three years then they would have the right to take him back. I thought it was worth taking that risk and we signed him for Monza.'

Neerpasch also felt he had dealt with the matter in a straightforward way. 'Michael Schumacher signed an agreement with Eddie Jordan on the Thursday before Spa,' he said the following week. 'It was an agreement to talk about an agreement. What he signed was a letter of intent. Eddie Jordan offered him the drive, but he needed money. Mercedes-Benz agreed that money and asked for sponsor space. We talked with Eddie about the rest of the season and also the future, but only on the condition that our money would guarantee a certain space on the car.

'I went to see Eddie Jordan on the Monday and we could not agree. A number of teams were interested in Michael and we went to Benetton. They wanted him and it was a straightforward deal.

He is paid as a driver. I think the Jordan is a very good car for this year. There was no need to change. Michael wanted to stay with Jordan, but Eddie would not agree with our requirements for sponsor space and wasn't prepared to discuss our contract. He wanted Michael to sign before Monza. Michael is still a Mercedes-Benz driver, but we have released him for F1. At the end of it all, I think it is very important for Germany to have a competitive driver in F1. Sooner or later, we [Mercedes] may want to have him back . . .'

Michael may not have taken an active role in all these dealings, but he was aware of their taking place. He also knew that, as Neerpasch said, he remained a Mercedes-Benz-trained driver and owed them much. Indeed, throughout his years with Benetton he often, when asked about Mercedes, stressed how important the company had been to him and alluded, by comparison to Italian drivers and Ferrari, to a secret ambition to return and win the Formula One World Championship with the silver arrows from Stuttgart.

'The first deal with Benetton was for a number of years, but I cannot recall the details,' said Neerpasch. 'Benetton offered Michael money to drive, too. It was not a lot, but it was enough. He was paid by Sauber anyway when he raced for Benetton. The Sauber contract was for three years, with an option. So, he had a long-term commitment to them . . . But later we had a problem with this at the start of 1992, when we, Sauber, wanted him back. Benetton said "No" because in the contract he could only return if Mercedes were the team involved. We had made a press announcement that Sauber was coming to F1, with Mercedes support, but not as Sauber-Mercedes. It said that the drivers would be Karl and Michael. It was our opinion then, and still is now in 1994, that he was contracted to Sauber. But Flavio and Benetton took their chance. They made a big thing of it. Sauber were in a difficult position because they were not financed completely and, for Michael, it was a big risk to come back to a team which he did not know, when he was already being successful. It was difficult. But this showed his character. He did not want to come back. He knew exactly where he was going.'

Neerpasch explained further. 'The Mercedes decision not to go into Formula One came at the end of 1991. Before that, however, we wanted our drivers to gain F1 experience for Mercedes in the future. I was, at that time, responsible for Mercedes' motor sport and also on the board at Sauber. I was responsible, at Sauber, for the drivers. When the chance came, at Spa, for Michael, it was Sauber's decision to spend the money for his Jordan drive. On top of that, we supplied the guarantees and found a sponsor. We also looked very closely at the contract to make sure Michael did not sign anything in contradiction with his Sauber-Mercedes deal. I made sure he signed a contract for one race, which in the end was actually only a letter of intent.

'It would have been against our strategy to release him. We built up the drivers and we wanted them for our own team. It was senational, of course, for the F1 people to see Michael at Spa. Everyone was interested in him. We discussed a lot of things. In the end though, Eddie said he was using Yamaha engines and we discussed this and decided that Yamaha were not going to be reliable or victorious. We wanted Michael to have a season in F1 and we wanted to finance the season for him. We wanted him ready for the following year for the new Mercedes team for 1993.

'At that time, we saw 1992 as a preparation year. We wanted both Michael and Karl to get F1 experience. We discussed this with Michael and he decided to stay at Jordan. They were a very nice team and made him feel welcome. He did not want to change. But we discussed it for a long time and finally decided to change.'

By the time that Friday morning's qualifying session at Monza began, it seemed the worst excesses of the 'Schumacher Affair' were over. Michael climbed into a yellow Benetton and Roberto into a green Jordan. But the talking went on. Ayrton Senna, who was staying at the Villa d'Este, revealed his own personal disgust at the murky manoeuvres and strongly defended Moreno's position. At the hotel, he told Briatore that he felt it was 'disgusting' the way he and his team had treated Moreno. On Saturday afternoon, after claiming pole position, he said: 'It's difficult to comment in a clean and fair manner, without knowing all the clauses in the contracts. But, as you know, even the best contract in the world, drawn up by the best lawyers, is only worth anything if both sides are really working for it . . . What has happened was not correct. It's always the people in the top teams who are written about the most, so I feel that unless one of us speaks about it, something like this just goes by and people get away with it.

'Moreno is a good driver. He's dedicated. He's a professional. And he had a contract for the whole season. But people just push others who are maybe not in such a strong position and they threaten, use their apparently strong position to get a driver to change his mind and accept things. As a principle, I don't think this was a good move. There were commercial interests involved and future prospects which made certain people do these things.'

Moreno himself was the fall guy. 'I think everyone in the paddock was surprised by what happened,' he said. 'Unluckily for me, I was alone at the time I was told, as my wife and daughter were in Brazil. I didn't even tell my wife afterwards because I thought it would hurt her too much. It is very difficult for a person to go through all that alone. Fortunately, I am a religious person. I believe in God. I opened the Bible and asked God to put me in the right direction and it opened at a good page. That gave me self-confidence and I kept myself together. It was very stressful.

'My only problem was that I caught a virus before the race in France in July. I went to the doctor and took some penicillin. It upset my stomach and I was not recovered for the race. I think it is the only problem I had this year. I took legal action because I just wanted to defend myself. I had to defend my rights on the contract I had for this year. On the Thursday night, I slept for only two hours and had my seat fitting at seven in the morning. I got in the car, concentrated and tried to do my best.

Ironically, Moreno and Schumacher qualified in exactly the same positions at Monza as they had at Spa. Michael was seventh and Roberto was eighth. Michael behaved all weekend as if there was no pressure on him at all, but he felt it. 'Yes, there was a lot of pressure,' he said. 'But you have to live with it, don't you? I had pressure in Formula Three, when I became the German champion. I had pressure in sportscars. If you cannot deal with pressure, you won't last in the sport. That's all there is to say about it.'

Michael's move to Benetton meant also a move to the bright yellow colours of the team's primary sponsor, Camel, and a renewal of his brief acquaintance with Richard Grundy. 'It was almost like he came in F1 fully-formed,' said Grundy. 'He made a couple of mistakes early on in his career, but by and large he has made very few errors. He was on the pace and effective almost immediately. I asked him if he remembered me from Macau and he did. He gave me his address, because he wanted some Camel merchandise. I saw him after the race and he finished fifth and Piquet finished sixth and he was not out of breath. He was not even tired. That is why I said that, from Macau, he had not changed at all.

'I don't recall any arguments, but Piquet certainly upped his game a little bit. I even remember at Monza, in one of the qualifying sessions, Nelson spinning off in trying to keep up with Michael. Interestingly though, in qualifying Nelson was the closest driver in the team I've ever seen to Michael. He was only three or four-tenths adrift. And in the final race of the year, in Australia, Nelson actually out-qualified him. And that's never happened in Michael's career in F1 really. But for Benetton, he was marvellous. The whole level of competitiveness of the team increased when he joined. Points were scored on a regular basis. Qualifying was a lot better. Before Michael arrived, they were struggling to make the top eight. When he came, they moved into the top six.

'He settled in very quickly and well. There were a few comments from some of the engineers that he tried to set up the F1 car like an F3 car, but he's a very intelligent guy, a quick learner and he developed all the time. Now [1994], his detail and analysis of what is going on in the car is incredible. His recall of a lap, his description of the car and how it is behaving in every corner. His feedback is as good as anybody's around.'

Once he had put the Monza weekend and its dramas behind him, Michael proved his quality with points again in Portugal, where he finished sixth (Piquet was fifth), and in Spain, where he was sixth again and Piquet was out of the points. Then he had a big accident in qualifying for the Japanese Grand Prix at Suzuka, before completing his year by taking an unscheduled excursion out of the rain-hit Australian race with electrical problems. The Japanese accident was another remarkable example of Michael's single-minded pursuit of his personal goals. He lost control of the car on a 170 mph left-hand curve, the rear of the car drifting fractionally out of line. Almost immediately, the car was out of his control, spinning wildly before slamming into a metal crash barrier behind him. It was a violent collision. The car was destroyed. Michael's shoulders, back and neck took the first brunt of the convulsion of energy. Yet, after a brief massage from Josef Leberer (a surreptitious job, as Josef, a friendly Austrian, was assigned to the McLaren drivers) who deputized for the absent Harry Hawelka, Michael's personal dietician and masseur, he was back on the track in the spare car. Not only that, but he was able to lap just as fast as if this massive accident had not happened at all. The outcome, by the end of the year, was five races for four points and a respectable start to life in the drivers' championship. He earned plaudits for that from the team and from the sponsors. Camel loved him, especially because he was prepared to work hard for them too.

'He was absolutely first-rate,' said Grundy. 'Like a dream. He is one of the generation of drivers who have come into F1 when the sport is at a stage where it is fully commercialized and drivers know what is expected of them. Piquet came in during an era when F1 was not as professional. Michael saw it as part of his job. He was always on time. Always willing to put the Camel shirt on. Always very polite with people. He gave forthright answers.'

Grundy was very much a Schumacher admirer and prepared to defend him against those critics and cynics who sneered that he was over-Teutonic, too synthetic and lacked the humour and humanity of a true Grand Prix star. 'He's like a lot of modern sportsmen,' said Grundy. 'I think tennis players are particularly accused of this. They have done nothing all their lives except play tennis since the age of six. Michael had driven a car, or a kart, since the age of four.

'To get to the top of your profession, you've got to be very good and very disciplined about one goal. That often means excluding things that other people include in their lives. It can end up with a rather one-dimensional personality. It is not a criticism. I think he did just what was required to get to the top. It is a very demanding business and he was very focused and concentrated on achieving success. You have to remember that he is also very young. He has come from a small village near Cologne and you could not expect him to be world-wise from the outset . . .

'He was still something of a home boy. He used to come to the motor home and eat apple-strudel. He liked pancakes as well. He was not sophisticated. He was down to earth. You could see that in his clothes. I suspect he missed out on some of the other things that young Germans experienced when growing up. I never saw him drinking, for example, at least not in any large quantities. There were a couple of occasions when he let go a little – when he won at Macau and at Fuji. But then again, he is a sportsman, an athlete and you just don't get legless every weekend with the lads like normal people do. Also, he never said anything silly or stupid. He was in control.'

But Michael's year was not only about the single-seater outings at Sugo, in F3000, and in Formula One. It should not be forgotten that he drove impressively with Wendlinger in the World Sportscar Championship, helping transform early frustration into triumph for Mercedes-Benz. This was the year when Tom Walkinshaw, later to be such an influential part of Michael's F1 career at Benetton, introduced the Silk Cut Jaguar XJR 14, a super-fast prototype sportscar, designed by Ross Brawn (who followed Walkinshaw to Benetton), which was a class above the rest from the opening race in Suzuka in April. The C291, Michael's new Mercedes entry, had endured a troubled winter testing programme. Engine installation was only one of the problems, as Michael was to discover.

Wendlinger had qualified the overweight and under-powered car third in the wet on Saturday, but the real drama came for Michael the following day. An engine fire during the warm-up, while Wendlinger was at the wheel, should have been a warning of things to come. In the race, Wendlinger enjoyed an entertaining scrap with Keke Rosberg in the Peugeot 905 through the opening 21 laps before pitting, his speed through the corners compensating for lack of straightline speed. As Michael prepared to rejoin, aboard the C291, a fuel filler valve failed to close. Fuel spilt on to the hot engine and caused a flash-fire just as the car pulled out of the pits. It was a spectacular sight and a foretaste of what lay ahead for Benetton at Hockenheim in 1994. Urged over the radio to pull up, Michael pulled off and retired after helping the marshals to aim their fire extinguishers at the flames. It was the end for the new junior team's first race together (Schlesser and Mass won in the old C11), but not the only story of the weekend. Michael, who was push-started in the pit-lane during practice, was embroiled again in a minor controversy as his team appealed against a $5,000 fine for breaking the regulations. According to Neerpasch, representing the Sauber team, it had never been a problem in the past. Nevertheless, it was typical of the way things such as this happened around Michael throughout his career.

Frustration and disappointment followed at Monza in the next 'sprint' sportscar race of 430 kilometres, but only after Michael had thrilled the spectators with his handling of the C291 chassis, trimmed in weight by 10 kilos for this race, in almost incessant rainfall. Almost, but not quite. Unfortunately, although it was Michael's turn to qualify, he was actually spectating when the only worthwhile spell of dry weather coincided with Wendlinger being in the car. The result was sixth place on the grid, a position which proved academic anyway when Michael failed to start the C291's flat-12 engine on the button for the race. As the cars pulled away at the start of the formation lap, Michael flung open the door of his C291 and waved frantically. He was pushed back to the pits for urgent repairs to the engine control unit. By the time he was away, leader Teo Fabi, in the XJR14, was a lap ahead. Michael chased hard, sometimes almost touching the Italian's Jaguar. It was a fearless drive, full of potential from Michael, but unrewarded. When he came in after 22 laps, to be replaced by Wendlinger, the starter motor ring failed again.

And so to Silverstone where a near-faultless weekend, in contrast to Michael's experience the previous year, took him to second place and helped the Mercedes team take the the leadership in the teams' championship. This time the starter ring had been made of different materials and five kilos taken off the weight of the car with a reconstructed gearbox and the introduction of an acrylic screen. By now, Michael was relishing driving this car, and in practice he gave it everything, spinning in both morning sessions. Alas, in qualifying, his efforts were hampered by a faulty gearbox which required 43 minutes to repair. It meant there was not time to do better than accept fifth on the grid. Both Karl and Michael fulfilled their talent in the race, during which the Austrian seemed particularly to enjoy lapping the fourth-placed Schlesser, in the old C11 Mercedes, near the end. It was the juniors' first finish of the year and signalled more than ever that both were destined for much greater things.

By the time of the next sportscar race at the Nurburgring, this was clearer than ever, especially for Michael. Rumours had been rife for several weeks that he was talking to Formula One teams and his second place in his Japanese F3000 outing at Sugo had only added to this intrigue. Furthermore, Michael added to his reputation that weekend in one way or another. He began by topping the times on Friday morning and then, in the afternoon qualifying session, became embroiled in his altercation with Warwick, who at that time was perceived widely to be one of the top men in a Jaguar. Once again, it was Michael's turn to qualify, but he was let down by the reliability of the new engines supplied by Mercedes and finished up fifth. During all this, of course, other matters were occupying the mind of Willi Weber, who did his best to keep information about Michael's impending Formula One opportunity away from his driver.

As a result, Michael went into the race with only another blown engine – during the warm-up – to worry about. That meant using the spare car, with an old engine, for the race. An early and vain attempt to find a way past Mauro Baldi's Peugeot required a pit-stop for the removal of Esso lubricants from the screen of his car before, after rejoining, another engine failure ended Michael's race. Warwick won, emotionally, and the following weekend Schumacher was in Belgium and Formula One.

It was a similar story at Magny-Cours in September. A

transmission problem followed by an oil pump failure spoiling practice and qualifying – though he still took third place on the grid. Then, in the race, Michael collided with Jesus Pareja's Porsche after eight laps, pitted for repairs, rejoined at the back and then retired again, after 23 laps, with a water leak.

Another month later, in Mexico City, where he had been proclaimed a victor the previous year, another oil pump failure ended what had looked like being a sensational individual effort. With Karl Wendlinger struggling against illness and only one car to share between four men in opening qualifying (after both Wendlinger and Mass had parked their cars during the untimed session), it needed a dash of brilliance to salvage the situation for Mercedes, and Michael duly provided it on the second day. Karl, still unwell, had secured fifth place, but, because the second car had only a restricted amount of running because of wheel damage, two sets of soft tyres remained available. These were given to Michael to make the most of and he did so by claiming second place for the juniors. It might have been even better too, but for the obstruction provided by Fabi's stranded Jaguar on his second run.

In the race, Wendlinger started but fell away into the pack and Michael took over after 23 laps. He then launched a memorable charge, recorded fastest lap, worked his way up to third and, with a pit-stop when rain fell, retired. It seemed bad luck was always to dog him and Karl, but their fortunes were to change dramatically at the futuristic Autopolis circuit, on the southern island of Kyushu, in Japan, three weeks later. It was, for Michael, just a week after his big accident in qualifying for the Japanese Grand Prix at Suzuka with Benetton where Karl, driving for Leyton House, had also raced and made his own Formula One debut.

At this time Mercedes were beseiged by speculation about their future in motor racing and it was vitally important for them and for Sauber to deliver a strong performance. Once again, however, their efforts in qualifying were upset by engine problems. Michael finished up sixth on the grid, one place ahead of Schlesser, and no-one expected what followed. Thick fog delayed the warm-up by three hours and the race started 90 minutes late, but when it did Michael enjoyed a near-perfect start. He was inside Warwick's Jaguar for third at the first corner, after starting on the third row of the grid, and involved in the scrap for the lead by lap nine. Michael passed Fabi on the outside at the first corner and then took the lead when Yannick Dalmas, in a Peugeot, succumbed to an engine failure. Once ahead, Schumacher pulled away at two seconds a lap to give Wendlinger a 21 second lead at their handover. Karl held the lead and gave an 11 second advantage to Michael when he resumed on lap 61, ahead of Warwick.

The Englishman did all he could, but found the track conditions (there was much spilled oil around) hampered his progress. As a result, he was left hoping that yet another engine failure would bring Michael's silver streak to a halt. He hoped in vain. The gap went up to 30 seconds, heavy fog gradually began to descend again and only the elements appeared to be a threat before Michael crossed the line to win. 'I heard so many noises, he said. 'I just did not believe we could finish the race – we had killed so many engines in practice and one of them had not even done 500 miles. It was amazing.' Warwick, who drove the full 430 kilometres by himself, finished second and Fabi, who was third with David Brabham, won the drivers' title.

As usual, Michael enjoyed the post-race celebrations, though at this time it was unclear what his future held. Rumour had it that Mercedes were preparing to sever their interests in sportscar racing in readiness for a full-blooded and totally committed assault on Formula One in 1993. According to that theory, Michael and Karl were to be the drivers. None of this was confirmed or clarified, least of all by statements from Mercedes officials that 'The board has not yet made its decision' and 'We are continuing to develop the C292 for next year.' What did this mean? For Michael Schumacher, it was not a worry as he looked back on a roller-coaster year of progress and success before embarking on his winter programme. The prospects looked auspicious as he surveyed the Benetton test schedule, planned his holidays in Austria, Germany and the Seychelles and determined to be fitter than ever for whatever his first full year of Formula One was to bring.

7 WITNEY

LEARNING FROM MARTIN, FIGHTING WITH AYRTON

I was much quicker than him. And even though he had some kind of problem, he chose to play around. I really don't know what sort of game he thought he was playing. He seemed to brake in the slow corners and then accelerate away. I got past him and thought that was it. If we had been having a serious fight, I would not have left him room at the next corner, but he came late-braking down the inside. It was not the thing to do because I had to let him through and that could have given others a chance to pass me as well. I was upset about it afterwards because, really, I was surprised by his behaviour. It was not what I expected of a three times world champion.

Michael Schumacher on his tussle with Ayrton Senna
at the 1992 Brazilian Grand Prix.

DEEP IN THE TRADITIONAL SHEEP-FARMING country of central England, on the edge of the Cotswold hills, lies Witney. It is a pretty place, built mostly from Cotswold stone and it is a town whose light-industrial history has for centuries been associated with weaving and blankets. The Domesday Book records that there were two mills in Witney in 1085 and the town's unobtrusive blend of well-designed modern factories and historic buildings give a sense of continuity and prosperity.

To many people, Witney may always signal bedding and

woollen covers, but for motor racing folk, it is better-known as the base for the Benetton Formula One racing team, formerly known as Toleman. The Benetton family, having been a primary sponsor of Toleman, bought the team outright in 1986 and re-named it Benetton Formula. It enabled the hugely successful Italian clothing company to market its image profitably around the world and it linked two knitwear interests by totally unexpected means.

But Benetton Formula was not content with a quiet life in the slow lane at Witney and wanted to expand, build an impressive and modern Formula One facility and become one of the front-runners in Grand Prix racing. Michael Schumacher was to be part of that plan.

In the summer of 1991, Tom Walkinshaw joined Benetton, closely followed by Ross Brawn and Rory Byrne. Flavio Briatore, the team's managing director, was reorganizing for technical and engineering strength. Briatore, an ambitious Italian, was the driving force, but his background was in marketing and sales. A long-time friend of the Benetton family, he brought a new dimension to Formula One and to Michael Schumacher's career in the winter of 1991–1992. At the same time, Luciano Benetton's company became more and more aggressive, expanding fast and rapidly becoming one of Europe's and the world's most extraordinary success stories.

The Benetton Group had been set up in Treviso, in north east Italy, in 1965. The first shops opened in France and Italy in the late 1960s, exports boomed through the late 1970s and 1980s together with international expansion, and stock exchange listings followed in the late 1980s in Milan, Frankfurt, New York, Toronto and London. Links with the United States, China, Latin America, India and Central America followed and by 1992, Benetton was arguably the best known name in international leisurewear. All this was the background to the Benetton Formula team which Michael joined in 1991, signing a contract which paid him only a basic 300,000 Deutschmarks (£100,000) for the 1992 season (plus bonuses of $5,000 (£3,333) per point), with options which were to keep him there under contract until 1995. That, at least, was how it seemed as the new Benetton regime began its long-term planning in the cold early days of 1992.

The planning meant, among other things, the dismantling of the existing technical set-up for the team which had been created by former technical director John Barnard. This had involved a design, engineering and research centre at Godalming in Surrey, away from the race team headquarters in Witney. For Briatore, Walkinshaw and Brawn, it was not satisfactory and as 1992 unfolded so the team went ahead with its plans for a totally new base away from the crowded Thames corridor of outer west London. This was to be the Whiteways Technical Centre at Enstone, in rural Oxfordshire. The new team was being built around new plans and new people, including Englishman Martin Brundle who, at 32, was nearly 10 years older than Michael. Brundle had been recruited the previous autumn to replace Nelson Piquet and provide the experience and race-craft from which his younger partner was to learn so much.

For Brundle, a dedicated professional who had six full years of Formula One behind him with Tyrrell, Zakspeed, Williams and Brabham, it was the best opportunity of his career. Brundle had won the sportscar world championship with Walkinshaw and Jaguar, but had always been among the extras in Formula One. Now he wanted to prove he could perform at the highest level. In January he and Michael went testing with the team in the familiar surroundings of the Paul Ricard circuit in France, the same track at which Schumacher's Mercedes career had started at the end of 1989. It went well, but Brundle learned that Michael was no ordinary young driver filled with hope.

'I'm a very levelheaded guy,' said Brundle, deliberately turning his situation into a positive opportunity. 'Schumacher is the perfect guy for me to be with this year and we are the perfect line-up for Benetton. He is going to bring out the best in me. No teammate has regularly blown me off, particularly on a race day. I'm at my best on a Sunday afternoon, and I know qualifying is not my forte. Everyone thinks that Schumacher is going to blow me into the weeds. That basically, I will be history. But that's not going to be the case. He's the guy who has got the reputation and he is going to beat the world . . . He thinks he is going to blow me off. That's quite apparent from his manner and that's just fine by me. We'll see. Let's count them up at the end of the year.'

They were prophetic words from Brundle. For, though he accumulated 38 points for sixth place in the drivers' championship and delivered unrivalled consistency through the second half of the season, he was to find it was not enough to retain his seat alongside the 23-year-old Schumacher for the following year. Michael scored 53 points and finished third. As a pairing, however, they worked happily together. Brundle, who was not known to be among the fittest of drivers, learned from Michael about athleticism and conditioning, shared time with him in Austria at Willi Dungl's fitness clinic and enjoyed teaching the youngster some of the tricks of the trade. It was clear that Michael was hot property as Brundle and the Formula One world at large very quickly learned when the next in the series of controversies which were to punctuate his career erupted.

Enough had been said, it seemed, the previous August and September at Spa and Monza, but more was to follow on Wednesday, 5 February 1992, when Peter Sauber issued an unexpected press release through Mercedes-Benz. This statement claimed not only that Sauber was to enter Formula One in 1993 with Ilmor V10 engines, but with a driver line-up consisting of Karl Wendlinger and Michael Schumacher. In effect, as Neerpasch had warned, the Sauber team were calling him in . . .

Sauber, a pleasant and educated man, had lost the support of Mercedes-Benz for both the Sportscar and Formula One projects the previous autumn, but had been promised continuing technical support. He had been associated with the Stuttgart company since the late 1980s and had been a catalyst for their decision to return to sportscar racing, with him as their entrant, in 1989. It was widely recognized however, that this decision was a risky one, a gamble that should he find success in Formula One, then Mercedes would follow in the future. And part of the gamble was Schumacher and THAT contract. 'I know Tom too well from sportscar racing to know that he will not free Michael without fighting,' said Sauber. 'But I'm not quite sure that the Benetton people have full knowledge of our contract. We have a signed deal with Schumacher which allows us to use him as a driver if we enter Formula One, with or without Mercedes. It is a contract with Sauber. Not with Sauber-Mercedes or Sauber-Ilmor. If necessary, we will fight to get him – and I am sure we will win.'

Benetton, having signed the man they were planning to build their future around, were briefly nonplussed. A full legal review of the situation was initiated and a statement issued. This made it clear that Benetton Formula had 'an exclusive Formula One driver agreement with Michael Schumacher which gives Benetton Formula the option on his driving services for Formula One racing up to and including the 1995 Grand Prix racing season. The only condition under which Michael may terminate the agreement within this timescale is on receipt of written notification from Mercedes that they intend to enter Mercedes cars in the FIA F1 world championship the following year. Michael Schumacher has confirmed to us that he has not received notification from Mercedes that they wish to enter Grand Prix racing which is consistent with the public statement issued by Mercedes in 1991. Michael Schumacher has also confirmed to us that he intends to honour fully his driver agreement with Benetton Formula. The only rights contained in the agreement between Benetton Formula and Michael Schumacher in favour of PP Sauber Ltd. are specifically for non-F1 events. With this in mind, Benetton Formula take a very dim view of the irresponsible statements contained in the press release by PP Sauber Ltd., and have given PP Sauber Ltd. written notice to retract the claims made.'

Within a few weeks it was over, a private settlement ending the argument, but it was not forgotten. Stories surrounding Michael's future and his contracts were to punctuate his career. Indeed, not long after he had finished fourth in the season-opening South African Grand Prix at Kyalami on 1 March, in a race run in scorching heat and won comfortably by Nigel Mansell in a Williams-Renault, Michael was being linked with Ferrari. Again, it was all denied. By then, however, Michael had other things on his mind – and not only motor racing.

His romance with Corinna Betsch had blossomed over the winter and they had settled into a comfortable relationship. She was not Michael's first girlfriend – he had several during his schooldays and while working as an apprentice mechanic afterwards – but she was the first to form a serious and lasting partnership with him. Like Michael, Corinna was also planning ahead. Michael knew he was likely to run into tax problems. He knew, too, that it was better for him to train and live in a warm Mediterranean climate than the colder climate of his Kerpen homelands in northern Germany. A move of home to Monte Carlo began to circulate in his mind. His life had changed dramatically in less than a year and his pre-season schedule included a trip to Dungl's fitness clinic at Gars-am-Kamp in Austria, as well as a holiday in the Seychelles before flying to Johannesburg for the opening race of the year. The holiday came first and with his liking for good food, Michael found he put on four kilos, going up from his favourite fighting weight of 67 kilos to 71 kilos.

'It had to come off and that is why I went to Dungl's,' he said. 'And there is no better place than Dungl's, not only to lose weight but also to make sure that you are in peak fitness for another Grand Prix season. I felt really good after that. I was convinced about my fitness after all my winter work. I was ready.' Typically, Michael's final preparations included a few days of playing around like a young pup beside his hotel swimming pool in South Africa. He and Brundle trained and played together, with the Englishman suffering a soaking into the bargain.

Brundle recalled those early days with the young Schumacher. 'I'd met him for the first time at a test at Estoril the previous October when I was almost crippled by Piquet's seat in the car and he, Schuey, was flying,' said Brundle, speaking with some affection. 'He had a lot of arrogance and a bit of immaturity, but he was gifted with speed. He had the ability to question anything that anybody else tried to do, which at times was amusing to watch and to listen to, but at the same time it was impressive that such a young guy with so little experience would sit and argue with an extremely experienced engineer or designer and never give in.

'I respected his ability and his approach. But I didn't warm to him as a person, privately, for six months or more. He had little respect for other people's experience or advice, and that is actually a quality in a Grand Prix driver – if you have that kind of personal self-confidence. I like to work with my teammate and I think we worked well together. In the early days, he gave me stick for being old and I gave him stick for being young and inexperienced, but we got over that period. It was like two boxers jostling for positions.'

Schumacher, at 23, was in perfect condition for the rigours of a full Formula One season. His mind was open, his appetite good, his body honed, his career moving in a perfect upward trajectory. 'I loved South Africa and Kyalami,' he said, in typically positive style. 'It reminded me very much of Australia with its countryside and its climate and I felt happy to be there.' A familiarization day on Thursday, followed by an evening of Zulu dancing at the Heia Safari Ranch, preceded a serious first day's qualifying which ended with Michael fifth on the provisional grid. On Saturday he qualified sixth and on Sunday he finished fourth in the race.

'After Kyalami, I was happy,' said Michael. 'It felt great to fly home to Frankfurt that night with that result. I met Corinna and we went out to celebrate, with a bit of shopping. Nothing too glamorous. Just the usual things for a young guy who lives on his own. It was such a good feeling. But even that was surpassed after my first podium finish in the next race in Mexico City. For me, that was a fantastic result. I was so happy to finish third. I had not expected it. I was hoping for a podium finish, but did not expect it to happen so early in the season. It took a while for it to sink in.'

Another reason Michael was surprised at his own success in Mexico City was that his preparations for the race were far from ideal. Having spent much of the previous week in discussions with his tax advisers, he was looking forward to a smooth trip to Central America. Unfortunately, to begin with, Willi Weber was late and they were forced to switch to a later Lufthansa flight, arriving in Mexico City on Wednesday night. By then, Michael had picked up a slight cold, for him a typical reaction to the air-conditioning on a plane. In Mexico, he stayed at the vast and impersonal Fiesta Americana hotel at the airport, popular with regular travellers because it is within a short walk of the terminal building. 'When I arrived, I was given a room with the runways on one side and loud music on the other,' said Michael. 'So, I had to change straight away. Luckily, I was given a quiet one. It makes all the difference to get a good night's sleep.'

Michael was third on the grid for the race, behind the two dominant Williams–Renaults of Mansell and Riccardo Patrese, but sharing the second row with his teammate Brundle. 'At the beginning of the race, I was aware that there were going to be a lot of fast cars around me,' said Michael. 'Both Gerhard Berger [fifth on the grid] and Ayrton Senna [sixth] were quick in the warm-up. Martin pushed me hard at the start, but then he disappeared and I began to have trouble with my right front tyre. Then when Berger started pushing, I found I was able to go quick enough to control his pace. And that meant I went on to take third place. It was a terrific feeling. I really felt we had a good package and that everyone in the team was giving 100 per cent.'

Overheating accounted for Brundle's departure this time, a typical mechanical failure for him in the early part of 1992 before he fell into the groove which was to make him the most consistent points-scorer in the championship in the second half of the season. This was the year in which the so-called high-technology driver aids were introduced in force for the first time in Formula One, computerized devices like active suspension, traction control and automatic or semi-automatic transmissions, and Brundle made the most of the realiability of his conventional Benetton, *sans* techniques, once he had settled in. The driver aids were helpful, but not completely reliable at that time and not entirely popular. Senna, as he stated in Mexico (where he crashed heavily in qualifying), did not approve and nor did many other top drivers. They may have made the leading cars faster and safer, but they removed the driver's instinctive touch and control over his car. Michael was among those drivers who began that year without any driver aids, but he still made the most of his opportunities.

'There are some of these things I agree with and some I don't,' said Michael. 'What Williams have introduced with their 'reactive' suspension system is fantastic. I have to admit that. But I do worry that the role of the driver is being reduced too much and that is why I am not in favour of traction control. At the end of the day, it is the driver who should control his car, not the technology and the computers. I am suspicious of the Williams' traction control system, but I am also worried by the electronic control of the throttle and the transmission in the McLaren. Controlling the car, driving it and racing it is the responsibility of the driver and not a technological system . . . Traction control is one of the things I particularly dislike and I feel strongly about it because when I go into a corner I want it to be me in control, my throttle, my backside and my sensitivity.'

Michael's sensitivity was tested in Brazil, but not by his car. Instead, both he and Brundle were angered by the antics of rival drivers Senna and Jean Alesi respectively. For each it was the start of a problematic relationship. Michael finished third behind the two Williams' again while Brundle's race was ended after his collision with the Frenchman after 31 laps. 'I am sure we would have claimed even more points than the four I won in third place if Martin had not had such bad luck,' he said. 'His collision with Alesi left him very angry, I know, but he was not the only one.'

Indeed, he was not. Schumacher, in a blast of invective which signalled what lay ahead, accused the defending world champion of 'playing dangerous games' on the track. 'I really felt upset and angry and my anger was directed at Ayrton Senna,' he said. 'I made a really good start and got ahead of him. If we had been having a serious fight, I would not have left him room at the next corner, but he came late-braking down the inside. It was not the thing to do because I had to let him through and that could have given others the chance to pass me as well. I was upset about that, but it was his behaviour which really surprised me the most. It was not what I expected from a three-times world champion.'

Senna, who retired after 18 laps with electrical problems, was not around in the Interlagos media centre after the race to hear Michael's comments for himself, so he was not aware of these remarks until later. Nor did he know how upset Michael felt. Between Mexico and Brazil, Michael had been to Acapulco to recover his health and his weight. But, after racing in Sao Paulo, he flew straight home to Germany via an overnight flight to Paris. Even the next day, in a coffee shop at Charles de Gaulle airport, he was still seething with anger at the Senna clashes during the previous day's race. It was a rivalry that was to intensify dramatically, especially after Michael had begun testing the Benetton team's new B192 a week after the Brazilian race. The new car gave him much-improved grip and even greater confidence, two factors which were to help propel him to his best result to date when he finished second in the Spanish Grand Prix at Barcelona on 3 May in near-torrential rain.

This race, more than any other, established Michael as a genuine champion of the future, at the same time earning him the 'new Senna' headlines he did not want. 'I am Michael Schumacher, not the second Senna,' he often said. Any doubts about his talent were dispelled, however, by a courageous, skilful and invigorating performance which brought him home behind Nigel Mansell with a broad smile across his face. 'The weather was obviously a big factor, but I could not blame it on Friday when I had a real accident,' he said. 'I had been trying different set-ups on my race and T-car in the morning and in the end I chose the spare. I preferred it. But the problem arose when I tried to do one lap too many on the first set of tyres. One of my rear tyres, on the left, blistered. We changed them over, but it happened again, I lost the car and it spun. I hit the wall really hard . . . At least I walked away unhurt – which is a tribute to how safe the new car is. Second on the grid was not bad, though, especially as Saturday was a washout.' Just as impressive as his grid position that weekend, however, was his bravery in climbing from his shattered car, after the accident, to run back to the pits in pursuit of more action. It was the stuff of which sports features are written and Michael was soon to become as big a name outside Germany as he had been inside since his debut at Spa the previous year. Fearless was the adjective most freely used.

Sunday was a washout too, but they raced. 'During the last 10 laps, I was trying to wave to get the race stopped,' said Michael. 'But it was no good. It was just a battle to stay on the track. I had made a poor start, the track was so slippery, I just could not find any grip or get going in the early stages. But once I got some speed up, I was able to pass Alesi and chase hard. I did not notice how near I was to Mansell until it was down to below five seconds. I thought he must have spun or something, but then he

Michael (third left), was one of several promising young German drivers racing at Zweltweg in 1989.

At Macau in 1989, his first trip to the far-eastern track.

Michael always enjoyed his victories. Here he celebrates his win for WTS Racing at the Formula Three race at Le Mans in 1990.

Always at home in the wet, Michael relishes the action during the German F3 race at the Nurburgring in 1990.

The way we were – the juniors arrive for their first Mercedes test. Heinz
Harald Frentzen, Michael and Karl Wendlinger all turned up in their
Formula Three overalls.

In action at his Formula One debut with Jordan at the Belgian Grand Prix in 1991.

Michael and Corinna, a partnership which has survived and blossomed as his Formula One career has taken off.

Michael and Ayrton Senna meet to discuss their relationship and the state of Formula One during a break at the 1994 Pacific Grand Prix.

Shaking hands with Damon Hill after a press-orchestrated quarrel on the eve of the 1994 European Grand Prix.

Victory at Jerez in the European Grand Prix 1994.

Michael masterfully powers his way from 16th on the grid to victory in atrocious conditions at the Belgian Grand Prix.

A winning partnership – Michael and Flavio Briatore share a joke in the pits.

Michael cruises to victory in front of 128,000 passionate fans at Hockenheim.

Michael ecstatically celebrates both a Grand Prix victory and retaining the championship at Aida.

just pulled away again and there was nothing I could do.'

Second at Barcelona in the B192 suggested an even better performance to come at Imola with the introduction of the Series VII Ford engine, but it did not work out that way. For the first time, Michael was outraced by Brundle who until then had endured a miserable sequence of misfortunes and had failed to score a point. Brundle admitted, before Imola, that he had been required to reassess himself and his job because of Michael's speed. 'It's made me change my thinking,' he said. 'Over the years, I've had some pretty formidable teammates in Formula One and sportscars, guys like Stefan Bellof, Eddie Cheever and Stefano Modena, and I've been able to handle them. But I have to say that Michael Schumacher has been a bit of a shock. When a guy gets in the same car as you and goes quicker, it's hard to take. I've also seen him operate during debriefing and he's impressive there too. He has an old head on young shoulders. He's someone special. A man of the future.'

By this stage of the 1992 season, the boy-man from Kerpen was emerging as a new and irresistible force in Formula One, accumulating admirers all the time and multiplying the media interest in him and the Benetton team. 'He is snowballing,' said Willi Weber. 'I'm not sure he can take it you know. The pressure is so great. He did more than 30 interviews in Barcelona and it takes a certain mentality to be able to concentrate like he does. He needs someone like me to take the pressure off. I take care of everything so that he can keep his head clear for driving.'

Weber did just that in Italy for the San Marino Grand Prix, organizing all of Michael's appointments with the precision of a chef timing saucepans and ovens. And all around was the ever-constant passion of the Italian fans, the frenzy of the media, the determination of Brundle to match his teammate's speed and Michael's own impending planned move to Monte Carlo. Was Michael's head turning? 'I made a mistake in the Imola race and I had to pay for it,' he admitted after his four uninterrupted successes had ended. 'It was my fault. Nobody else's. That was all there was to it. But it bears out what I have been saying for a long time now. I am only 23, I have driven in less than a dozen Grands Prix and I am still learning the business. I am bound to make some mistakes.'

In all, it was a difficult weekend for Michael. He had a new Ford Series VII engine, a circuit he did not know particularly well and a series of small problems. It was a difficult one for Brundle too, but he rose to the occasion and overcame his problems. 'I had had four terrible races and on Friday I had a coming together with Alesi,' he recalled. 'I went flying through the air and hurt my back. I qualified badly. That night was the turning point. I had total depression and I just came out the other side of it. The next day, I went to the circuit, relaxed and just did the job as I knew how to do it. I was actually quicker that afternoon than Schumacher. It was my best work of the year and, all credit to him, he came and congratulated me on that. I think it is one of the few times he's had a teammate quicker than him on any given date and from that time I think he began to respect me more. I just wasn't some old guy who had lucked into the other drive! He began to realize his inexperience in certain situations and my experience, and he realized that maybe there was something to learn from this guy after all. At the same time, I accepted that this guy was gifted with speed in a way I wasn't. I knew I could not out-qualify him – he out-qualified me 16 out of 16 times – but I knew that if I applied myself and all my experience and all my determination, I could race with him and sometimes outrace him.'

Michael's first racing visit to Monaco two weeks later was a happier one. He qualified sixth on the grid and came home fourth, having learned the circuit as he went during the course of the weekend. 'I had a spin at the Loews hairpin in the Thursday morning session and slightly damaged the front suspension,' said Michael. 'But you find me a driver who can drive this track on the limit and not have any spins.

'It's that sort of place. I knew what to expect and that is why I came early and spent a lot of time going around on a motorbike. I like to learn a circuit carefully, doing it my own way. I am quite quick at doing this. I break the track down and learn it in different sections. I think it is quicker that way. For Monaco, for example, I had five different parts to learn and I felt I did a good job with them. I felt it was another lesson in my Formula One education.'

The race saw Michael finish fourth behind Senna, who took full advantage of Mansell's suspected puncture to keep ahead of Mansell and Patrese at the end. Two weeks later, he was in Canada and finished second at Montreal behind Berger's McLaren after another impressive outing on a new circuit. Again, Michael had researched the job well in a road car, set up his B192 perfectly and exploited his own physical fitness which had been honed back to near-perfection by a committed training programme at home in Germany before the trip to Montreal. This included an average of more than 35 miles of cycling each day. 'This gave me back my edge and my strength, mentally and physically,' said Michael after a straightforward race during which various mechanical ailments saw off his main rivals.

After Montreal, Michael's growing celebrity status was endorsed when he was introduced to the great Juan–Manuel Fangio at a special Mercedes Benz day at the Norisring, where he drove a W154 and Fangio a W196 alongside him, before taking a few days off in Spain before the French Grand Prix. Recharged again, he was keen to impress, but instead produced his least impressive performance of the season. Fifth on the grid, Michael tangled with Senna again on the first lap. 'I tried to pass Senna, I tried to go by him in the last part of the braking area,' he said. 'But he came in and I just could not stop my car in time. We were very close and, almost inevitably, we touched. It was my fault. There was nothing I could do.'

Michael pitted for repairs, Senna retired and then came heavy rain which halted the race, forcing a re-start. 'When the race stopped, I thought I might have a bit more luck after the re-start,' said Michael. 'But it did not work out that way for me. It was so tight when we got off again. I tried to pass [Stefano] Modena on the outside, because I thought he was going to the inside. But he didn't. He just came across. We touched wheels and that was it.' The bare result was another Schumacher retirement, another Mansell-Patrese one-two for Williams and Brundle's best result to date, a well-deserved third. But that was not all; this race also saw the second flashpoint in the growing feud between Schumacher and Senna. It came after their collision, which

Michael admitted was his own fault, when Ayrton, changed already into his casual clothes, confronted his young rival on the new grid, protesting vehemently, waving his arms, remonstrating with great force, all only minutes before the race was to resume. The issue was not so much their latest collision, but their relationship. 'At the beginning of my career, I also made mistakes like that,' Senna told Michael. 'Look, I am coming to you first, to talk about what happened between us. I am talking first to you and not to the press. You should have done that in Brazil, also. You should have talked to me if you thought there was a problem . . .'

Little wonder then that Michael made another costly error. It was a situation he did not want in the final minutes and seconds before the re-start of a Grand Prix. 'I simply told him that I didn't think this was the right place to have such a discussion. If he wanted something more, he should come back after the race,' said Michael, for whom that French race marked a decline in his initial good relationship with the German media. 'If I had succeeded, if I had managed to pass him [Senna] there, I would have been a big hero. Now everyone is putting me down. I get praised to the skies and then I get dropped . . .'

A few weeks earlier, Senna had given interviews, during the Magny Cours testing, in which he severely criticized Michael and described him as 'only a stupid boy' and explained his part in their contretemps in Brazil. 'I would explain everything to him and he can look at Honda's computer records,' said Senna. 'Then he could see what really happened with my engine, if he wanted. But if he wants something, he has to come to me. I don't care what he goes on about . . . he's only a stupid boy.' It was a throwaway line from the Brazilian, an indiscretion. But it found its way into the headlines after the French Grand Prix, leaving both drivers with much to think about.

Seven days later, Michael was preceded at Silverstone by his growing reputation as a future champion and a character of sufficient substance to make Senna feel unsettled. 'Even if it is someone like Senna or Mansell, it doesn't matter,' said Michael. 'If somebody is making a mistake, in my eyes, I have to tell it the way I see it. I still have the same opinion. If someone is wrong, I say so. I don't just shut up because I think I should. They all know what I think about them and that is the important thing for me. They cannot just do what they want with me.'

Michael's superconfident approach began to bridle with some of his rivals, but it did not bother Brundle who remained fair and accurate in his comments on his younger teammate throughout the year. 'Not many people envy me the task of having him as a teammate,' said Martin. 'It was a problem early on, no doubt about it. But in the last couple of races, I've been within a couple of tenths. I'd like to outqualify him of course, but he is a seriously fast young man with no apparent fear and great guidance behind him. He is a serious racing driver and a great star of the future. I would not want to take anything away from him at all. I'm very impressed . . . Michael has been in circuit racing for only three or four years and he's obviously a natural. It's been a pleasure to work with him.'

By this stage of the season, Martin was settling into his own groove and he had adjusted to the exceptional talent he recognized in the driver of the other Benetton. This weekend too, was a special one for Martin, as it was at Silverstone, and without argument he delivered his best race performance of the year to beat Michael, taking third place again to his fourth. For Michael, it was an unusual experience and not one he wanted to have too often in the future.

Within days, however, he was plunged into a new and, this time, far more sensational, confrontation with Senna. If he needed any reason to forget the disappointment of the British Grand Prix quickly, this was it. It came at Hockenheim during testing in advance of the German Grand Prix when Senna, angered at being brake-tested by Michael after a misunderstanding on the track, marched down to the Benetton pit and grabbed him by the throat. A crowd of reporters and photographers saw the incident which was broken up almost instantaneously by several McLaren mechanics, who had followed their driver in fear of his actions. Michael was clearly shaken, but took the confrontation in his stride, almost implacably. 'I guess we had a little misunderstanding on the track,' he joked. 'He came down to the pit and grabbed me by the collar – probably to give me a little massage.' The comment may have been light-hearted, but it did not hide the animosity that existed between the two at that time. Nor did it help to discredit the notion that Michael, almost by instinct, was already destabilizing the man everyone had always regarded as the champion of his generation, in advance of his first appearance at his home German Grand Prix. The hype was already building up for the Hockenheim race and Michael's fame and success was such that tickets were selling faster than they had in living memory, the fans all hoping to celebrate the arrival of another wunderkind to succeed the late Stefan Bellof.

When it came, however, the German race was less explosive than the test session, watched by nearly 40,000 fans, had been. Michael made an effort to play it down and explained that a meeting between the two, after their Hockenheim 'fight' had solved many of the problems. 'In my heart and in my mind, there is no problem between us any more,' said Michael, who finished third behind the victorious Mansell, then Senna, in the race thanks to a Patrese error in the closing laps. 'People have suggested all sorts of things about my relationship with Ayrton, simply because he made an impression on me when I was much younger,' he explained. 'That was when I went to a kart race in Belgium. I saw him karting and he was very impressive. But it is not true in any way that I then said I wanted to follow his career or emulate him. I never made him my idol or anything like that. That is not true.' Third place at Hockenheim was still something to celebrate as Michael became the first German on the podium on home soil since Hans-Joachim Stuck in 1977, albeit after a weekend of spectacular off-track excursions in qualifying and several incidents, including a run over the kerbs which damaged a radiator, during the race.

In Hungary, in early August, Michael retired after a collision involving Brundle in a race which was won by Senna, but remembered as the coronation of second-placed Mansell as champion. He did not enjoy the weekend. Michael could have been excused if he had other things on his mind in Budapest. Not only was it the race which completed his first full year in Formula One, but it was also his first since moving his home to Monte Carlo and becoming one of the Mediterranean principality's new residents. In many ways, that Hungarian race also marked the end of his innocence in Grand Prix racing. He could no longer joke about his little Yorkshire Terrier, called Jenn, being the only girl in his life after spending virtually a full 12 months with Corinna. Nor could he hide the fact that his new wealth was changing his lifestyle. In public, he denied the move out of Germany was for tax reasons, blaming encroachment of his privacy. 'With my income, it's not a necessity, yet. But I should have a quieter life, with much less recognition. I do everything I can for the public, whenever possible. But there are limits and when I have a barbecue at home and 100 fans climb into my garden, that is when I have to draw the line.'

None of those who may have felt rejected by Michael's change of address that August could complain at his performance in the rain at Spa-Francorchamps on the final Sunday of the month. By knowing exactly when to switch tyres in the changing conditions on his favourite track in the Belgian Grand Prix and by enjoying the luck that had always favoured his career, he recorded his first Formula One victory on the circuit where he made his debut, with Jordan, a year earlier. The dry-wet-dry race win, abetted by electronics-induced engine problems for Mansell's Williams–Renault, was also the first by a German driver since his friend Jochen Mass won the 1975 Spanish Grand Prix at Barcelona and it made him one of the three youngest winners of a race in Formula One history in only his 18th Grand Prix. 'I had a funny sort of feeling about this race when I arrived at Spa,' admitted Michael later. 'It was strange, but I had a strong impression it might be one of those weekends for me.'

Third on the grid behind Mansell and Senna, with Patrese alongside, Michael knew he had a chance of victory. He could smell it. 'It was dry and then wet and then dry again and the race was full of incidents and decisions,' he said. 'It was tactical and it was a challenge to the drivers and the teams. My car was perfect. It had been good in qualifying, but on Sunday it seemed better than ever. The changing conditions were lucky for me. I would say it was my decision to come in for dry tyres at the end when the track was drying on the racing line. That was the most important decision of the afternoon. It was just perfect timing and, of course, came after my only mistake really when I went wide and off at Stavelot. I just ran wide and missed the apex and when I turned in, it was too late and so I turned wide. I was really lucky then not to have an accident and go into the barrier. That was when Martin passed me.

'As soon as he got by, I could see his tyres were blistered and that was my bit of luck really as it helped me make my decision to go in immediately for new tyres. What a difference they made. After that I felt sure I was going quick enough to win and the car just got better and better. It was a great race and my only regret was that my mother was not there to see me win, but back at home in Germany. It was a very emotional win for me. I could hardly believe it.'

The tears of celebration on the podium had barely dried before Michael was involved in more unexpected drama that evening when his parents were involved in a road accident on the way to meet him for dinner. 'No-one was hurt, luckily,' said Michael. 'But it took the gloss off the evening and, as it happened just a few hours after the race, it was a salutary lesson on keeping my feet on the ground.'

A first full week in Monaco followed before Monza and the Italian Grand Prix, by when Michael had learned that Brundle's reward for a year of consistency was to be replaced by Riccardo Patrese. It was also the anniversary of Michael's first race with Benetton and the weekend which saw Mansell announce his departure from Williams and Formula One. Ironically, Michael was to finish third behind Senna and Brundle whose strong showing for second place reflected his input into the team. Michael's race included a poor start, a first lap collision with Thierry Boutsen's Ligier which required an early stop for a new nose and then a storming charge through the field. It was a stirring spectacle and one that was to be repeated in similar fashion in Estoril.

The Portuguese Grand Prix, however, also saw Michael suffer a braking problem on Friday and a major 'off' on Saturday when the front wing on his B192 split. 'I was completely sideways and went over the kerbs,' he said. 'To be honest, I was very lucky to recover the car without touching anything.' On Sunday afternoon, his engine cut out at the start of the formation lap and forced him to start the race from the back of the field. He climbed, in scintillating fashion, to seventh, but then ran across the debris from a spectacular accident involving Riccardo Patrese and Gerhard Berger, collecting a puncture and a damaged nose-wing which effectively prevented any improvement for a finish in the points.

Before Estoril, Michael had returned home briefly to Kerpen to enjoy a day's karting. Afterwards, he stayed on in Portugal for testing, followed by some public relations and television appointments, a further week's testing at Silverstone and then the long flight to Japan. This was typical of his schedule at the time, giving him little opportunity to unwind or to meditate on the rapid changes in his life in less than a year. After landing in Tokyo, Michael was involved immediately in promotional work for Camel; Japan. As he travelled by car towards the function, Richard Grundy remembered 'he insisted we played track seven of Michael Jackson's CD which was "Heal the World" . . . something a 14-year-old schoolgirl might listen to in England. But then sportsmen are not that geared up on culture anyway . . .' After further sponsor-related functions for the team, Michael was embroiled in a weekend of struggles which ended with an early retirement with gearbox troubles and much envy of the technological aids carried by the Williams cars. These aids had been particularly noticeable in wet conditions on Saturday, leaving Michael looking ahead to 1993 when Benetton's own 'driver aids' were expected to be ready. 'We have shown this year what we can do with a conventional package,' he said. 'With all the new technology, we will have a really exceptional package next year.' Without any driver aids, Mr Consistency (Brundle) finished third, after emerging from his sickbed. It was his eighth successive points-scoring finish and set up a grand finale in Adelaide.

For Michael, it was a remarkable end-of-season. But not because of the holiday he promised himself between the two final races. Instead of a trip to the Barrier Reef, he found himself back in Italy for testing at Imola in the week after Suzuka. The previous year, his first in Formula One of course, he had been required in Autopolis on sportscar duties between the final two events. All in all, it left him cursing his luck and catching up on his sleep when the holidaymakers arrived in South Australia for the final race of the year. 'I left Germany on Sunday night, had two nights in Singapore and then left for Adelaide, arriving on Wednesday,' he recalled. 'I felt very short of sleep but by race day I was fine and I enjoyed the whole Grand Prix.' The result was another refulgent drive, particularly after a collision had removed both Mansell and Senna from the race, which saw Schumacher finish less than a second behind Berger's McLaren, with Brundle third in his final race in the second Benetton. Benetton had scored points in every race of the year.

It was a satisfying ending to a highly eventful and progressive year, as Benetton's technical director Ross Brawn confirmed. 'Michael's speed was just incredible,' he exclaimed. 'He has such fantastic car control, yet he is still very young. People forget that. We forget it often because he has such a mature attitude in the car. For his age and experience, he had an exceptional year. When he joined us, he would come in and say "I want different springs on the front, different roll bars" and so on. He had to learn to have confidence in his engineer. The biggest problem was him telling us what he wanted to change rather than discussing the car's behaviour. But a lot of the time he was absolutely right. There was no issue about whether we should make the changes, but the way we work is that we have to know why something needs changing otherwise we won't make any progress. So, we eventually overcame that hurdle from a technical point of view.

'Michael seems to be able to extract time out of various set-ups. When you have a driver like that, it is sometimes a little bit more difficult to find the optimum. He can drive round a problem, but what we have to find is the set-up which is best for the race. Michael, because of his ability, will not have a problem if the car oversteers a lot – even in the fast corners . . .'

8 ENSTONE

A TECHNICAL YEAR
WITH RICCARDO

I have been in Formula One for just two and a half years. I think that I have learned a lot and I think I have done well, but there are a lot of things that I still need to learn. When you look at the history books, you find that those drivers who have won the world championship did so with at least five years experience behind them.

Michael Schumacher talking about his career prospects in 1993.

By THE START OF 1993, Benetton Formula were 'at home' in a new factory, a futuristic building of 85,000 square feet, designed to hide itself in 17 acres of rolling rural Cotswold landscape at Enstone in Oxfordshire. The new facility, built into an excavated area of rock and soil to prevent its gleaming architecture from breaking the skyline, was completed in August, 1992. Indeed, the Whiteways Technical Centre, as it is known, was so cleverly designed and integrated into the countryside, it is almost impossible to find without a carefully-studied map. It would also be difficult to guess, from the outside, that it was the home of a Grand Prix racing team, including research and development, technical offices, race preparation departments, machine shops, composites, stores, dust extractors, two vast fridges, two 'clean' rooms, administration offices, drawing offices, a restaurant, three autoclaves, a massive generator, soccer and cricket pitches and every other conceivable need for a team of 200 people dedicated to ensuring Michael Schumacher and Benetton came home first as often as possible.

After years of being scattered around on different projects within the same team, the Benetton staff were under one gleaming white roof. Following the moderate success of 1992, in which they had ultimately finished third in the championship with 91 points, behind Williams on 164 and McLaren on 99, like Michael, the team were looking forward to a more progressive and, they hoped, rewarding 1993 with 'technik' as Michael liked to describe it. He had finished third in the title race with 53 points to Mansell's 108 and Patrese's 56 and now found himself partnered by the veteran Italian, who was heading towards his 39th birthday. Michael also found himself in increasing demand from all quarters: the team, the sponsors, the engine-suppliers, the media and his personal sponsors in Germany, not to mention Corinna, who had moved with him to Monte Carlo, his family and his friends. And he was only just 24.

'The pressure has now become much bigger,' he acknowledged freely. 'I've got less and less leisure time and that's not an easy situation for someone of my age. I am a normal guy and I want to live a normal life. But I want to drive in Formula One too, so I have to deal with it somehow. This means sometimes I have to be rude to people a little and this is something I don't like. But it does not seem to work otherwise. Sometimes you just have to be tough and hard with your decisions otherwise you have no life of your own left at all.'

By now Michael's once-simple life in Kerpen-Mannheim had gone. He adhered to a strict diet, slept at pre-scheduled hours and worked to a prepared diary of appointments, which were organized down to every half an hour. As a result he had little time left to himself. But he accepted this because he wanted to become a winner and, eventually, a Formula One champion. 'If you want to reach the top,' he said. 'You have to have the ambition and then you have to do the work. But you can relax and have some fun along the way too. I like to enjoy my life and I don't want to just work and work without ever smiling. It is important to be happy.'

Happiness, of course, had been synonymous with Michael's appearances on the podium in Formula One in 1992 and was to remain a Schumacher feature throughout 1993 when he was dubbed 'the happiest man in Formula One.' It had always been thus, of course, right from those 10 wins out of 11 in Formula Konig, to Macau, to Mercedes-Benz and to Jordan. 'The world has so many problems,' he said, 'if I think I can do something to help, I feel I should try. But the thing is that with the press, there is always so much concentration on how bad things are and it makes you feel so bad. It makes me wonder about the politicians and why they don't do anything. It is not my job. I am just a driver, not a politician.'

Asked about his long-term ambitions at this time, Michael was wary. 'My ambitions are not big ones,' he said. 'I am careful about this. I suppose my ultimate ambition is to enjoy being in Formula One now and to be successful. For the future, beyond that, I don't know. I want to stay like I am as long as possible, but maybe I'll go back to karting afterwards. Really, I don't know. If I try to imagine what I am going to be doing when I am 50, it will be a quiet life. I don't really want to be in this kind of environment, this sport; but if I am, then in the background only.' His short-term dreams were easier to articulate. 'If Mercedes-Benz were to return with a team to Formula One, as a truly competitive force, I would love to be their first driver,' he said. 'To lead that team would be fantastic. As a German, I would be very happy, if I were free, to join them and to work on a serious challenge with them. Nothing could be better for me. A German driver, leading a famous German comeback . . . it would be like a dream. But, right now, I am with Camel Benetton Ford and I am very happy, so perhaps I should not tempt providence so much.' The comment was a typical one from Michael and was to become a recurrent theme of his Benetton career.

When the 1993 season began in South Africa, after a winter of intensive testing in Estoril, Le Castellet and Silverstone, Michael found himself billed as the young threat to the old establishment of Alain Prost, back after a year's sabbatical with Williams, and Ayrton Senna. At the same time he was set to work against an agenda of political powerplay, as his own Benetton team began crusading for reduced costs and technology, using a clerical error at Williams, whose entry for the championship had gone in late, as leverage for change. On top of that, Prost was in trouble with the ruling body for some published comments. In all, it was a tense and grisly scenario. On the track, however, the Williams-Renaults were expected to sweep all before them again, though not with quite the ease of 1992, and it was suggested that Damon Hill, Prost's teammate, might find it difficult in the early races. If Michael, in his Benetton with a Ford Cosworth V8, could beat Senna, in a McLaren powered by a Ford Cosworth V8, not a Honda V12, he could be the man to mount a challenge. So it was assumed. 'I believe we can establish ourselves in the first two and have a chance of a real run at the championship,' said Tom Walkinshaw. 'I think it will be very close.' It was a situation filled with tension even before Michael and Ayrton arrived in Kyalami just a few days after the Brazilian's impressive late test with McLaren at Silverstone and his agreement to drive for them on a race-by-race basis.

Michael felt the stress building, but did not often show it. His confidence, fuelled by his pre-season billing and his successes of 1992, not to mention his wealthy new lifestyle in Monaco, gave him, at times, a gross sense of self-importance. It was understandable. The boy-man from Kerpen-Mannheim found himself devoured by a new world in which a different order of values held sway. He seemed to be heavily influenced by people whose sense of taste was at best questionable, and at worst garish. Michael, it was apparent, was by nature a modest and thoughtful young man with little worldly experience, and was therefore easily led by others' less considered behaviour. This was revealed by one incident at the Lost City Hotel at Johannesburg. According to one eye-witness, Michael, wearing only a bikini-sized pair of swimming trunks and a gold medallion on a chain, offended the hotel staff by crossing the lobby towards the pool. When asked to obey the house rules and wear more garments, he declined and told the staff 'Hey, don't you know, I am staying in this hotel!' It was all delivered with a swagger which he later learned to recognize, understand and control.

For seasoned Michael-watchers, it was clear that the gilded world of Formula One was having a negative effect which had to be curtailed. 'Sometimes, it is difficult to know just who you really are,' said Michael later in the year, after a significant change of appearance, the purchase of Italian clothes, the introduction of a shorter hairstyle. 'Basically, you are still the same person of course, but you do have to make some adjustments and adaptations and those change you . . .' And asked about his role as a celebrity, he said: 'You'd think that this job would be mainly racing, training and working on, and with, the cars, plus a little bit of publicity work. But actually, it is just the opposite. It is a little racing and a lot of PR.' Michael was aware of his new status, but not yet comfortable with it. He was learning about the media, its ability to manipulate and his power to manipulate it back in return. It was not a part of the Formula One business he liked, but one he came to accept. 'Last year [1992] was a difficult year for me,' he said. 'So much happened so quickly and I took notice of what was being said in the newspapers and on television. Now, I don't read the papers. I believe only what I know to be true. This way there is not so much pressure. I don't feel it and I won't accept it. It is a question of attitude and because of this I am much more self-confident this year. Last season, I was not so much myself as I am now. You have to come back to yourself. I have realized this. A little experience helps, of course, and I feel more mature.'

Changed or not, Michael found 1993 less straightforward than 1992. He had a more technologically-advanced car, more experience, an older, but slower, teammate, a new lifestyle and a team focusing its challenge around him. The season, however, did not unfold quite as consistently as the team had hoped. This is partly due to the staggered introduction of new technology features and the delayed introduction of the definitive 1993 car, the B193B, designed for the use of active suspension and traction control. In the end, though active suspension and semi-automatic transmission were available with the B193A from the opening race, the wet weather in Brazil and at Donington Park in particular, exposed the team's lack of traction control in those contests. By the time it was introduced in Monaco, there was a deficit to be recovered. Senna had performed wonders in the rain and the Williams had run in a class of their own. But Michael was not too disappointed, having set himself apart from any claims of impending glory by declaring his ambitions as nothing more than another learning year, in pursuit of second place in the constructors' championship. 'I always believed we could win some races in 1992,' he said. 'But I also felt that the championship was something else, beyond us.'

Instead of seeing his total of four non-finishes reduce, Michael saw it increase to seven. He scored points steadily: with three thirds, in Brazil after a brilliant recovery from a harsh stop-and-go penalty for overtaking Luca Badoer under yellow flags, Spain and France; five seconds, in San Marino, Canada, Britain, Germany and Belgium; and one beautiful win, Portugal. But the outcome was a slip back to fourth in the drivers' championship with 52 points, behind Prost, on 99, Senna, 73, and Hill, 69. Not a bad year, but not a sensational one. The impression left behind was that it was the last year of preparation and change, a final season of fine-tuning in readiness for a serious assault on the title.

The Brazilian race might have been a win, but for a stop-and-go penalty in a wet pitlane; Donington should have been a triumphant entry for the new B193B, but was wrecked by wet weather. Apart from the win in Estoril, it was a year of 'might-have-beens' and plans for improved showings in the future. It was also a complicated year off the track as the sport reshaped for the future and Michael overcame fitness problems, reorganized his own life and established himself as the outstanding driver of his age and generation. Patrese recognized that before he joined Benetton as his teammate, but had the impression confirmed many times during a disappointing year personally, his last in Grand Prix racing after 16 years. 'It was not so much his speed as his maturity which surprised me,' he said. 'He always talked a lot of sense. He was in control. I never heard him say any stupid things, the sort of things you might expect from a 24-year-old. I thought that maybe he had to improve on the politics. It seems to me that if you want to be world champion, you must play politics and be a little on the bad side, otherwise you find this world is very tough.

'I thought Michael was a real champion of the future. I knew he was very good. I could see it in 1992. Any driver who comes into Formula One and after his first full season has a win and finishes third in the championship has to be good. And you have to remember he did not have the best car that year. He was ahead of both Senna and Berger when they had better cars. He is improving all the time and when I was with him he had confidence, he knew he was strong and he had tremendous motivation. In my career, I always had the philosophy that it is better to build up a nice relationship with a teammate because it is in my interest, in his interest and in the team's interest if there is a good atmosphere and no problem between us. I didn't play politics and nor did Michael.'

In South Africa, Michael's hopes ended with an early tangle with Senna. It was just what the German tabloids wanted – Senna closing the door on a Schumacher attack, the young German's car hitting the back of Senna's and suffering damage which forced him into retirement. Immediately, he rushed to the stewards to protest, only to be told that any protest had to come from the team. Michael cooled down later. 'I should have waited for a better chance. I had time. I could have finished second,' he complained. 'I really did feel I had the right opportunity to make a move at that time as I was running a lot faster than Ayrton.' Senna saw both sides. 'He was faster than me, no question. But not quick enough at that place to pass. I was having problems with my car and he would surely have passed me easily later on.'

For both men, it was a marker for the season. Ron Dennis of McLaren and Flavio Briatore led a struggle between two teams fighting to prove they deserved the best Ford engines. But that was not all. They were also fighting for second place behind the dominant Williams team in the championship. Senna and Schumacher, the champion and the challenger, were understandably affected. Each used the other as a sounding-board, to monitor his own performance. Each had disappointing support on the track from his respective teammate, Michael Andretti and Riccardo Patrese. And each, as the year went by, resorted to forms of kidology to try and gain the upper hand in a private duel.

One example of this psychological rivalry came in Budapest where Briatore, latching on to an opportunity to promote his team, suggested Senna might sign for Benetton for 1994. The

Brazilian accepted the idea without rancour. He even massaged it a little himself, since he knew it could only help him in his advanced negotiations with Williams. 'Anything is possible,' he said. 'There are no concrete negotiations, but I could imagine it. I would have no problems with driving for the same team as Michael. He is young, fast and talented. But I am a three-times world champion and I have won almost 40 Grands Prix . . . and he only one. For me, it would be no problem.'

These remarks upset Michael and caused him to drive erratically in the Hungarian Grand Prix. Later, questioned about his relationship with Senna and the prospects of them racing together at Benetton, he was typically outspoken. 'If Ayrton drove alongside me, I think it would just upset the happy atmosphere that has been built up at Benetton. Senna seems to think he can do things to me on the track which he wouldn't do to others. He has done several things which I have not been happy with. If that's the way he wants to race, it is up to him. Formula One is very competitive and you just have to deal with these things. Maybe he feels I am the only guy capable of fighting him and getting the best out of him.'

At Spa-Francorchamps, worse was to follow for Michael. On his second lap, he claimed Senna forced him off the track. Senna knew nothing of it. 'If he thinks something like that, it's his problem,' he said. It was clear by now that there was no love lost between them and that Michael, if he wished to prove himself as a leading driver and the equal of the great Brazilian, would have to do it the hard way.

To succeed in that, Michael knew he had to return to his best physical shape. In 1993, he found it a struggle to train to his previous standards, owing to knee problems. Years of strenuous work, building up muscle, lifting weights, running and cycling had taken their toll. The first admitted signs of this had come at Monaco, where his car was equipped with traction control for the first time and led until lap 32 before being hit by gearbox hydraulics failure. 'I practised a tremendous amount when I was a boy,' he said. 'I did hundreds of crunches, hundreds of knee bends and I often went jogging. Today, I am paying the price for this over-exertion. There are signs of wear and tear, the meniscus is worn down and it is causing me pain. It may not just be from my training, it may be partly inherited too as my father had some knee troubles.'

For Michael, his slight loss of peak fitness was an extra area of stress in 1993, a year of evolution in which he had to take on the role of outright team leader – despite Patrese's seniority in age and experience – at Benetton for the first time. Harry Hawelka, friend, confidant, dietician, guru, quasi-brother and fitness coach, a former Dungl man, played a vital role. He had to keep Michael's morale high, his fitness as high as he could. 'When I have my body under control,' Michael said, 'then I feel mentally better.' His fitness was to become a subject of amazement in 1993 as he finished races looking cool and fresh while other drivers were being helped from their cars. On the podium, as Prost or Hill struggled for smiles and energy, Michael was the embodiment of exuberance. 'An advantage of being completely fit is that you can suppress a cold or a stomach problem,' said Michael. 'That way I can give 100 per cent even if I have a problem like that.'

The knees, however, were a chronic problem. At Hockenheim, where he raced home second in front of a huge and vociferous crowd, he was racked with pain and it got worse as the season wore on. In Germany, however, the sheer adrenalin pumped through his body by the excitement of the event enabled him to survive intact. 'I knew the big crowd was there to see a German driver do well and I did my best,' said Michael. 'I felt mentally matured. I enjoyed it all differently. I feel my mental self, my physical self and my driver self were all together in harmony.'

By the time he arrived in Australia and finally enjoyed a week's holiday at the Sheraton Mirage Hotel at Port Douglas, he was determined to change his training methods drastically. Instead of jogging, he went swimming, but he still enjoyed kick-about games of football with Richard Grundy, the former Camel marketing man who had joined Benetton, and photographer Steven Tee. 'With the football, he was very undemanding,' said Grundy. 'He didn't want to win and he was quite happy to put a couple of jumpers down for goal posts as if he was in the park. There were only five of us playing, but he got stuck in. He had good skills and incredible fitness. Steve and I actually beat him and Harry [Hawelka], but we were absolutely on the floor!'

A few weeks later on 10 November, just three days after the Adelaide race, both of Michael's knees were operated on by Dr Runzheimer at the Meingau Hospital, in Frankfurt. Afterwards, he went to a rehabilitation clinic in Bad Witesse and restarted his fitness campaign in preparation for 1994. In Monaco, when Michael returned, he was soon back in the gym and adhering again to the Hawelka diets. 'Michael is a pasta fan,' said Harry, 'so he is quite easy to work with . . . he eats vegetables, fresh salads, fruit, a little fish or poultry, especially in the evenings. But no red meat at all.' It is a typical motor racing driver's diet, usually preceded by muesli and fruit tea for breakfast and followed, for Michael, in the evenings, by a full plate of spinach. Michael was particularly fond of spinach and became known as 'Popeye'.

The fact that diets, knees and fitness routines were uppermost in much of Michael's thinking by the year's end reflected both his new status as one of the sport's leading personalities, a role in which every detail of his life was to be examined, and his position with Benetton as team leader and future championship challenger. His car and his performance were taken for granted, particularly as it was clear following the introduction of the team's traction control system on the B193B at Monaco that, as a combination, they had the potential to win.

The new chassis, introduced at Donington in downpour conditions for the European Grand Prix on Easter Sunday, 11 April 1993, showed its potential, in vain, at that race. Michael lost control and retired after only 23 laps, blaming himself after crashing out while running at the limit on slick tyres in wet conditions. 'It is virtually a completely new car,' said Ross Brawn at the time. 'Last year's was a passive car in which we were able to fit active suspension, but this car has been conceived as an active car and to accommodate the new – narrower – tyres. Although it appears to be the same, it is quite a lot different.' That difference showed more clearly for the team and for Michael at the San Marino Grand Prix two weeks later. It was another wet race, but in dry qualifying conditions, Michael took third place on the grid before Sunday's rain intervened. This time the clouds were in Michael's favour and he drove a finely-judged race, changing from wets to slicks with good judgement, to finish second behind Prost. Senna and Hill retired ahead of him on the road. 'I knew I had to wait for the car to be really competitive,' said Michael, adding some evidence of patience to his natural instinct for outright speed. 'The wing settings we chose meant I was able to pull away on the straight, but the corners were a bit of a sruggle. In the second half of the race however, the car worked perfectly. I did not push 100 per cent because I knew I already had a place on the podium. I just took care to finish.'

The next race was in Spain where Michael had shone in the rain the previous year. Again, Michael was disappointed because there was no traction control and on the opening day he collected a minute piece of carbon fibre in his eye. He qualified only seventh, completing just 11 of his 23 laps, before visiting an eye specialist at a clinic in Barcelona. 'It happened before I went off in the gravel,' he said with typical honesty. 'It did not hurt, but it was uncomfortable. I was glad when it was gone.' On Saturday, he claimed fourth place on the grid – behind the two Williams and, inevitably, Senna – and on Sunday he finished third. Prost won, again, with Senna second, but only after the Brazilian resisted a determined attack by Michael who nearly crashed on oil dumped on the circuit by Alessandro Zanardi's Lotus Ford. 'I could hardly see for the smoke and oil,' said Michael. 'I knew he was still on the line, so I pulled out wide to pass him, but when I turned the wheel, the car went straight on.' It left Michael struggling to keep his car on the track as it arrowed off across the grass. He succeeded and wrestled it back under control before later berating the team for not having introduced traction control.

'I have been asking for this since the end of last year, ever since we knew which direction we were going with the car,' said Michael in his official Camel column. 'I thought we would have had it some time ago, but we are still being told to wait. This is very frustrating. One of the main reasons for this delay is that we have developed a specific type of traction control which does not work through the ignition or fuel systems, but through the throttle. It is more complicated but the team feel it will save engines and that is important to us and Ford. But the effect of not having traction control has been clear for everyone to see in the wet races. If we don't have it now for Monte Carlo, we will not be totally competitive. For me that means beating McLaren, a realistic target.'

The target came into focus at Monte Carlo where, finally, the throttle-intervention traction control system made its racing debut. On a damp opening Thursday morning, Senna crashed, damaging his left hand, at Sainte Devote; Michael went off twice at Mirabeau, but finished the day third on the provisional grid behind Hill and Prost. 'The control worked fantastically well,' he announced. After a leisurely Friday, including some sponsors' tennis, Michael was attuned perfectly for the final session and took second on the grid alongside Prost. Given his personal crusade for traction control, he felt justified in praising it and explaining why. 'The car has more mechanical grip with the active system and now the traction control adds to it. In the morning I tried it on and off and realized the gain was 1.2 seconds,' he said. 'That's a big difference here. It gives you so much more confidence. I am looking forward to this race.'

After a sensational start, when Prost crept clear before the lights blinked from red to green, the race turned into a thriller. Prost, called in for a 10 seconds stop-and-go penalty, conceded the leadership to Michael on lap 12, and then stalled twice in the pit-lane as he attempted to restart. Michael, in supercharged mood and form, led for 21 laps before being forced to retire with hydraulic problems on his car's active suspension system. 'To have led like that at Monaco, and to have pulled away, was a wonderful sensation,' he said. 'It just did not last long enough.'

After a five-day break in Nassau, during which he consumed two John Grisham thrillers, before a brief holiday at Florida's Disney World, Michael arrived fresh for Montreal's Canadian Grand Prix where he confirmed the widespread belief that he was ready to be one of the real threats for future successes by finishing second behind Prost. Lack of traction control may have been a disadvantage for Michael in the wet, early-season races at Interlagos, in the Brazilian Grand Prix, and at Donington Park, for the European Grand Prix, but he had put those disappointments behind him.

By mid-season, Michael was comfortable with the Benetton and its high-technology 'driver aids' such as traction control, active suspension and semi-automatic transmission. By then too, Formula One was learning that these aids were to be banned – at first, it seemed, with immediate effect, but later, it transpired, only for 1994 – with the sport reverting to a more conventional style of racing car together with the proposed re-introduction of refuelling. 'I cannot agree that it makes sense now to ban semi-automatic gearboxes,' said Michael at the time. 'They make life better for the driver and they are good for the future of the automotive industry as a whole. All the research which goes into the development of F1 is important in this way. I do think, however, that traction control takes too much away from the driver and so too does ABS. It used to be part of the fun of racing to try and challenge yourself to drive into a corner and to drift the car and to hold it and handle it well.'

Montreal, where the technological 'driver-aids' were unexpectedly announced illegal by the ruling body, delivered another third spot on a grid led by a Williams front row and, as was becoming more and more usual, and appalling start. 'I wanted to overtake at least one of the Williams at the start,' he said afterwards. 'But instead it went all wrong. There was a problem with the traction control adjustment. I nearly stalled . . .' The outcome was a scrap from seventh place through to second – as Patrese retired after a spin and a bout of leg-cramp – after a close battle with Senna. The pair traded fastest laps before Michael squeezed through as the McLaren suffered an alternator failure. 'I was lucky to get by,' Michael admitted. 'Lucky not to hit the wall – maybe he didn't see me. He seemed to slow down just as I caught him.'

Michael's battle with Senna continued in France where he qualified seventh, after a disappointing gamble on hard-compound tyres in the final session, but finished third behind the Williams after spearing ahead of Senna in traffic on the closing laps. At the British Grand Prix, a week later in July, Michael spun off at Copse in qualifying, ran back to take Patrese's car and then qualified third; a phenomenal effort. Another emphatic drive earned second position in a race remembered for Prost's 59th victory, after Hill's engine blew while he was leading, and a welcome third place for Patrese, after Senna ran out of fuel. It was the Italian's first podium finish for Benetton in a race which saw the McLarens vanquished. For both Benetton and Michael, it signalled a greater potential.

A home race at Hockenheim came next. On a circuit famed as a 'power track', the race was not expected to be an easy one. For Michael however, this meant nothing since he was to be backed by the emotional support of a vast 150,000 crowd again. The background of political moves, which resulted in the teams retaining their technological driver aids to the end of the year and the acceptance of refuelling for 1994, also had little direct effect. 'Seeing all the fans as excited as they were there, was an experience I had never known before,' admitted Michael. 'I could hardly believe it. I am sure they helped me find the extra four-tenths of a second I needed to take third place.' As always, Michael coped with the media demands, with Willi Weber's planning and schedules, as attention focused inevitably on him and his hopes of victory. It was also interesting to note that at this race McLaren received the latest specification Ford engines from Cosworth, in tandem with Benetton. It meant there was parity in power for Michael and Senna; a parity which meant nothing as Michael, in his spare car, romped home second, via two pit-stops, behind Prost – after a puncture robbed Hill of his first win – with Mark Blundell third and Senna fourth.

Budapest left Schumacher unsettled. Third on the grid on a circuit where he expected better was followed by a race to forget: a poor start, fifth at the first corner, a spin, a charge and another spin off with an auxiliary drive belt failure. Hill won, Patrese was second and rumours about Senna moving to Enstone for 1994 were, as we know, stealing attention. By now, too, the season was shaped and Michael was among the also-rans for what was destined to be Prost's fourth title – second in Belgium, an engine failure at Monza, before that win at Portugal and two more non-finishes in Japan and Australia. At Spa-Francorchamps, another disastrous start preceded a storming drive only interrupted by a near-miss with Senna at La Source as the Brazilian exited the pits. Optimism, raised by the performance of the new Series VIII engine, was literally blown away at Monza after 22 laps when Michael was running second.

In the Portuguese Grand Prix, at Estoril, Michael's luck changed dramatically as he claimed his first victory of the season and the second of his career, after he had started from a disappointing sixth place on the grid. During qualifying for this race, the team had been puzzled by problems. Hill and Prost, in the two Williams, dominated the front row, Prost racing for the championship. 'I thought we would be good here,' said Briatore, before the race. 'But we are not . . . But it's the first time we've gone backwards in a long time . . . With a little luck, we'd have won four races this year – Brazil, Monaco, Hungary and Belgium. But I am confident for the future . . .'

Michael also admitted that he had never expected to win in Estoril that weekend. 'I went to bed on the Saturday night with data swimming before my eyes,' he said. 'I had no idea that we would be able to solve the problems which upset everything during practice and qualifying at all – and everything seemed just as bad the next day during the morning. I ended up 12th in the warm up and I had understeer, oversteer and bumping. It was the worst I had known for our car. That is why I chose to race the T-car and, luckily for me, it worked.

'It was one of those races where everyone was close from the start. You had to be careful and you had to conserve the car well and the tyres. I was running fifth early on, but found it difficult to pass Alain Prost. That is when I decided to make an early pit-stop for fresh tyres. It worked. When the others made their first pit-stops, I was out in front and had to work very hard to stay there. Alain pushed me and he was definitely quicker at the end of the race, but I was able to hang on to win.'

Unfortunately, for Michael, Estoril was to be his last points-scoring finish in 1993 alongside Patrese, a teammate he respected and liked, but never feared. 'For anyone in this business to drive in 250 Grands Prix is amazing,' he said. 'But for me, it seems even more extraordinary because I had driven in only 32 races then, at the time of the German Grand Prix, and when Riccardo started his career, at Monaco in 1977, I was only eight years old. My hero was the Cologne and Germany goalkeeper Toni Schumacher!

Riccardo was always a very honest and friendly teammate with me. I liked him very much and we had a great working relationship.' The feelings were mutual. Patrese, though he endured a terribly difficult opening spell with Benetton, never allowed his own poor form to affect his attitude to Michael. He did his best to compete professionally, but the sheer pace of his younger teammate destroyed him in terms of recovering as a front-line driver.

By the end of the year, in Adelaide, Michael was the hottest and most sought-after driver in the business. At the Camel end-of-year and end-of-era party on Sunday night, after the Australian Grand Prix, he was pursued by Ron Dennis, the managing director of Marlboro McLaren. There was no attempt by Dennis to disguise his approach and, after a brief meeting inside the crowded room of dancing and drinking F1 people, he escorted him outside onto the pavement for further talks. Michael was aware too that it was the right time to re-negotiate with Benetton. He was no longer the unproven newcomer with little experience he had been the previous year. As a result, with the combined efforts of Willi Weber and the International Management Group (IMG) on his side, Michael concluded talks on a new deal by the first week of December and re-signed with Benetton in a new three-year contract, taking him from 1994 to 1996.

In 1993, Michael had manifestly matured. Rory Bryne, one of Benetton's most experienced and senior engineers, recognized the changes. Byrne had been with the Benetton team since its earliest Toleman days and had worked, in 1984, with Senna. 'Michael is very cool and methodical, exceptionally so for a driver of 24,' he said. 'He's an exceptional driver in every aspect. His speed, his fitness and his stamina are remarkable. He won a cycle race round Silverstone at a canter before the Grand Prix, against people who cycle on a regular basis. When I see that, I look at him and I think there's someone a bit special. It's very difficult to make comparisons, but Ayrton drove for us in his first year and Michael has all the same attributes. He is going to be a world champion one day. I've got no doubt about that.'

9 MONTE CARLO

A NEW LIFE, A NEW CHALLENGE

My chief aim this year is to help establish Benetton as the number two team – or even number one if we can . . . My motivation will be to beat Senna and Hill at Williams. For me, they are the main contenders and the favourites. But we have not been asleep this winter at Benetton.

Michael Schumacher talking before the start of the 1994 season.

IT IS THE QUINTESSENTIAL PICTURE OF Formula One racing: bright sun, blue skies, yachts anchored in the harbour and the glitterati posing on their decks for the Monaco Grand Prix. But Monte Carlo, with the Grimaldi palace and its Mediterranean royal family, is not only the home of the world's most famous street circuit race. It is also home for dozens of leading sportsmen, including several of the world's top Grand Prix drivers.

Michael Schumacher moved to Monte Carlo in 1992. By the end of 1993 he had become accustomed to the sun-tanned lifestyle and a new image as one of the principality's immigrant gold-chained celebrity community. For Michael, however, it was a far cry from Kerpen and his schoolfriends, his family and his old kart track. He missed them, but he learned to live without them. The switch of cultures and climates was not easy, but he and Corinna adjusted, made new friends and settled into a different way of life with successively bigger and more comfortable apartments in the Fontvieille district.

Early on in his career, Michael had said he would not waste his money, not spend it on millionaires' toys like yachts, motor bikes or expensive cars, but after his first full year in Monte Carlo he began to find the temptations irresistible. In early 1993, not more than six months after moving to Monaco, he and Corinna had their Mini stolen. The theft left Michael with only two vehicles to park; a Ford Escort and a scooter. But once he moved to a bigger rented flat in Fontvieille in June 1993, things changed quickly and by early 1994, he was purchasing a big 1400 cc 'chopper' Harley from Jochen Mass and adding further luxury accessories to his collection. These included a Mercedes 500 SL and a Ferrari F40. A Bugatti followed in the spring. Michael and Corinna also, for contrast, enjoyed taking their West Highland Terrier, Jenny, out for walks. They had become a homogenized Monte Carlo couple.

'Things have changed very quickly for me in the last two years,' said Michael. 'I feel I am getting to the time now when I can relax a little more. Enjoy things more. Feel more confident. I know how much time is taken up by the job in Formula One, so when I get the chance now, I make sure I enjoy myself more.' This was a new Michael. More mature, more self-assured and with a greater sense of responsibility. He was aware he would be team leader for Benetton Ford – now sponsored by Japanese Tobacco's Mild Seven brand instead of the American Camel – in 1994, and while enjoying the early sense of responsibility, he did not lose his boyishness, and still relished noisy motor-bike rides up and down the Cote d'Azur, with Corinna riding pillion, or shopping trips to San Remo for his favourite Italian clothes. His knees, operated on in November, had healed quickly, helped by wearing shoes with special inlays, and he had set his ambitions for 1994. 'My chief aim this year is to help establish Benetton as the number two team – or even number one if we can . . . My motivation will be to beat Senna and Hill at Williams. For me, they are the main contenders and the favourites. But we have not been asleep this winter at Benetton.'

Indeed, Benetton had been wide awake. A new chassis, the Benetton B194, a completely new engine from Ford-Cosworth, the Zetec-R, and two new teammates in J.J. Lehto and Jos Verstappen indicated that they were determined to mount a serious challenge. The team had also warded off an approach from Ron Dennis, who wanted to recruit Michael for Marlboro

McLaren. 'We just danced together for a while,' said Michael, with a laugh, as he recollected Dennis's approach in Adelaide. 'That is all. There was nothing else to it.' Michael was equally happy to talk freely about the new car. 'It has outstanding mechanical traction, the new engine gives at least four per cent more power and it has been tested and tested. I am delighted with it.'

The laugh and the smiles of those early winter months of 1994, when he spent eight days in Kenya with Briatore, were infectious. Michael relished the prospect of leading Benetton's challenge to Senna and Williams in cars stripped of the high-technology of the previous year. Gone was active suspension, traction control and four-wheel steering, as used in the closing stages of 1993 by Benetton. Only the semi-automatic transmission remained, though events later in 1994 were to raise questions about other alleged computerized software devices which may have been left behind. 'I'm happy that we are running with the technical situation as it is now,' said Michael. 'It's going to make the competition more even. Hopefully, anyway.'

Michael had such confidence in his ability to drive fast and to perform both reliably and quickly in his car that he knew he would be among the front-runners. But he was not one to tempt providence and, knowing both the scale of Senna's great talent which had earned three drivers' championship titles and how difficult it had been to beat a Williams in 1993, he felt the new year was likely to be another learning and chasing experience. 'Hopefully, we can push the Williams,' he told Richard Williams of the *Independent on Sunday*. 'Sometimes to stay close. Sometimes to win a race. But, as for the championship, I think we are one more step away from that.'

Senna and Hill were identified as the main contenders, the Brazilian seeking a fourth title, the Englishman a first to add to the two won by his father Graham in the 1960s. 'They have the best package,' said Michael. 'But there will nevertheless be races where they don't find the right set-up and we might find the right set-up and then it will be very close. We will fight together and then by strategies or stuff, we will win some races. But, too many bad things would need to happen to other teams for us really to have the chance to win the championship. Drivers like Senna or

Hill, a team like Williams, they don't make mistakes . . .'

No-one, not then, could have foreseen what lay in store for the Williams team in 1994.

•••

There had been other changes over the winter. Weber was no longer in control of Michael's media schedule, the Benetton team having decided the time was right for them to exercise their power over his diary and his utterances. The announcement had been made at a Benetton press conference in December, 1993, at the Arabella Grand Hotel in Frankfurt. Rumours about Weber's past were hinted at by certain sections of the media, but Michael, loyally, supported his manager. "We have always worked fabulously together and Benetton is only now taking charge because, perhaps, they have more experience in this area."

A former driver himself, Weber had maintained a tight grip on his young client until that day. But he had still found time to work on other projects including his own WTS team for which Verstappen drove in 1993, and also a chain of restaurants and hotels. But as the pressures of Schumacher's success grew, he had concentrated more and more time on him. He sought endorsement deals, promotional and advertising opportunities, but he was not always successful. One German company, Sonax, signed up Ayrton Senna rather than their own man. Some of the highly-critical German media suggested this was not due to Michael's image at all; it was due to Weber's somewhat exaggerated sense of self-importance, his rather flash style of dress and appearance. The Germans, according to Karin Sturm in her profile 'Michael Schumacher "Superstar"' dubbed him 'Mother Willi' and 'Important Willi'. None of the criticism had any effect on him or Michael however, and, as the start of the season approached, the new Michael Schumacher collection – of jackets, toys and souvenirs, ranging from hats to telephone cards – was launched with great success to an eager German market. Whatever the critics were saying, Weber and Schumacher remained a solid and well-organized combination.

Michael, satisfied with his new contract, was the fastest man in the final pre-season test at Imola, a test which was interpreted as signalling the initial shape of the opening races. He was clearly happy too. 'The offer from McLaren was unsettling and it was a good offer,' Michael remarked on the eve of the opening race at Interlagos. 'But I felt it was correct for me to stay at Benetton. I have grown up with them. I don't want to move on and be expected to win the world championship straight away. I prefer it the way it is. There is no political manoeuvring. I have the team's full support. They give me real warmth and I feel like one of the family. For me, the other point was that I had a contract until 1995 and I am not a person just to get rid of contracts and ignore them because I have another offer. They had a very cheap driver and they knew they could not keep paying me that amount, so they made changes for me. I am a different driver now from the one who raced for the first time at Spa.'

There was no doubting Michael's value to the team. 'If we had a choice, which is the acid test, I don't think we would change him for anyone,' said Walkinshaw. 'That's how good I think he is. He's incredibly fast, he's very mature and, the more he races, the more experience he gets and the better he can apply himself. So he'll get quicker and quicker.' Walkinshaw was right, but not even he, with his well-founded confidence in Michael's ability, could have foreseen how his young driver would perform in the opening races of the year. No-one, least of all Michael himself, expected to beat Senna on his own circuit in Brazil on 27 March, let alone repeat the achievement on 17 April in Japan, the new Pacific Grand Prix at Aida. It was a devastating start.

Before the season began, Benetton's preparations had been interrupted by an accident, in testing at Silverstone in late January, in which Lehto fractured two vertebrae in his neck. This had meant thrusting the young Verstappen straight into the opening race at Interlagos, in his first season after one year of Formula Three in Germany. It meant he had to face up to the physical and mental rigours of Formula One without much notice and with the unknown new factors of pit strategy and refuelling to take into consideration. On top of that, Michael was repairing his relationship with Senna in the run-in to the opening race, both men hoping to avoid any of the scenes of open conflict which had characterized their rivalry in the previous two years. 'We don't have a close relationship,' said Michael, in Sao Paulo, on the eve of the opening race. 'We have different interests, but we don't have personal problems. We may have done in the past, but they have disappeared. Every time we see each other, we talk. We don't have problems. And, as Senna said, journalists who don't have much to write about try to make our rivalry on the track more "salty" by turning it into a personal thing. It is not. I have said before that I did not have an F1 idol when I was younger, but I do recognize Ayrton as certainly one of the very best drivers, if not *the* best, we have. For that reason, I feel good to be in Brazil. I feel welcome here and that gives me confidence.'

Like many other drivers and members of the Formula One circus, Michael was suffering from a cold when he arrived at Interlagos for opening free practice. Damon Hill was also feeling under the weather and, it seemed, the fates were again to smile on Senna, giving him an ideal opportunity for another emotional home triumph on his debut with his new employers, Rothmans Williams Renault. His car, however, was not as easy to drive, not as grippy, not as tried-and-tested and not as driveable as Michael's B194, a fact which had been demonstrated at Imola in testing. Senna, inspired, claimed pole position, and made a good start. Michael, who started second, was beaten off the grid by Jean Alesi, in his Ferrari, and needed a couple of laps to recover his position. Alesi's lighter fuel load, compared to 1993, made the job more difficult than expected, but by lap 10, Michael was only two seconds behind the three-times world champion and following him with reasonable ease, monitoring his gap and planning a well-timed pit-stop. Michael knew what he was doing.

'It was very exciting in the early stages and I just concentrated on staying as near as I could to Ayrton's car, keeping in touch. When we chose to come in for the first pit-stop after 21 laps, we were running very close and I knew that if everything went perfectly, I had a chance of going ahead of him,' he said. 'It worked perfectly, like a dream, and from then on, I never honestly felt threatened. I knew I had to drive confidently and fast and make no mistakes and that is what I did. Once I was in the lead, I felt I could control the gap on Ayrton by pushing harder just when I needed to and then, of course, I was told that he had spun out and I felt much more relaxed. It just felt so tremendous to win for the team that day.'

By the time they came in together for their pit-stops, Senna's lead was only two-tenths of a second. Benetton's pit crew, having practised hundreds of pit-stops before the season started, having honed themselves into peak physical condition for the job and created a good team spirit, effectively won the race with their excellence. For Michael, it was a case thereafter of driving on to victory, avoiding any trouble, keeping well away from any debris left by a four-car collision triggered by Eddie Irvine's Sasol Jordan Hart swerving into Verstappen's Benetton, which cartwheeled off Martin Brundle's Marlboro McLaren-Peugeot. Eric Bernard's Ligier-Renault was also involved, but Michael stayed clear of it all and, with only one further pit-stop to interrupt his progress, he came home a lap clear of Hill's Williams. Senna, fighting his car to deliver, spun off after 56 of the 71 laps, long before Michael laughed and danced in celebration of his third victory with the team. It was also a triumphant day for Ford and Cosworth as their Zetec-R ran faultlessly to win on its racing debut and, as many observers noted afterwards, set up a perfect rivalry, like a new dawn, between the legendary and experienced Senna and the youthful, charging Schumacher. Few, especially Schumacher, could wait, for their next confrontation, particularly as Michael led the title race with 10 points to zero. 'We knew Benetton were going to be close, but we did not want them to be that close,' said Frank Williams at the time. 'They blew us away. We did not need geeing up, but this shows us what we have to do.'

Flavio Briatore enjoyed the victory. Michael had beaten Senna on his home track in his home city. 'If he can win here,' he said, before the dash for the midnight flight back to Europe, 'he can win anywhere.' His feelings were understandable but not shared by Michael who, recognizing that Williams were in need of some work on their car and that they would be far more competitive later in the year, predicted that Senna and his team would remain the favourites. With his cold for company, he too flew quickly back to Europe to rest at home, with a few breaks for promotional duties, in preparation for the next long-haul, to Japan for the Pacific Grand Prix three weeks later.

'It took me a while to shake off my cold, but I did it and then I knew it was important to prepare properly for Aida,' said Michael. 'Acclimatization is always a problem after long flights so I worked on my fitness, did a lot of swimming at home in Monte Carlo and left Jos and JJ, who recovered early after his bad accident at Silverstone, to do most of the work on setting up the cars. I kept in close contact with the team by telephone, but we knew so little about Aida that it was difficult to plan ahead in detail.'

Williams worked feverishly. Michael's 10-point lead was 10 points more than they had hoped to concede to anyone. They went to Jerez in Spain to try and find their answers, but travelled to Japan with hope more than conviction that they had their car developed enough to prevent a second Benetton triumph. At the same time, prompted by Formula One's ever present rumour machine, whispers began to circulate about the presence on some cars of illegal software and, in particular, of traction control. They were heard by everyone within the picturesque, mountain-side paddock at Aida, including Senna. The Brazilian, privately, had indicated he could not believe Michael's performances owed everything to his stunning natural talent and these asides, which swept like an invisible bushfire later that spring, were, to instigate a much more serious investigation than the rap across the knuckles with which Ferrari, metaphorically at least, had escaped. Sooner than expected, the Federation Internationale de l'Automobile (FIA), the sport's ruling body, was to make its own moves to police the rules which Ron Dennis, among others, had said were un-enforceable.

Aida, where it had been snowing a month earlier, turned out to be a tight, technical circuit, a place which Michael described as somewhere like a kart track for Formula One cars. It was very different from the power-orientated track at Suzuka, used for the Japanese Grand Prix, surrounded by green mountains instead of concrete amusement parks. It was also more favourable to the Benetton chassis.

Michael had been to the tropical island of Okinawa to help acclimatize before the race, but instead of sunshine and relaxation, he had experienced miserable weather in an unattractive resort. It made no difference to his performance on the track, however, as he and Senna, as expected, dominated the opening day. Senna was again the quickest, Michael second and Hill third. More significantly, that first afternoon Senna and Schumacher met, close to the toilets inside the paddock and, deliberately, stood chatting in public for five minutes. It was the first time they had been seen together talking without rancour. 'Just a chat,' said Michael later. 'He wanted to congratulate me on my win in Brazil, as he had not seen me since and we said some nice things . . . That is all there was to it.' But it was not the words, so much as the obvious demonstration of their new accord, in public, that mattered. The old ruler was accepting the young pretender in his court, as Michael made clear later that afternoon during his routine Friday press conference, when he vehemently denied that there were any difficulties in his relationship with Senna.

The following day, Michael was fastest in the morning, but in the afternoon, when both Williams men spun, he was unable to improve his time, because of higher temperatures and changed track conditions, and again accepted second place, alongside Senna on the grid. 'I did go out late in the session, but only to have a look, and as the track was very oily and slippery, I decided it was not worth doing more than one lap,' said Michael. 'It made more sense to conserve the tyres and to concentrate on making a good start.' It was a tactic to be repeated many times as the year unfolded.

'I did some work on trying to make sure the track was as clean as possible on my side of the grid,'' said Michael. ''I did a lot of preparation for the start and I concentrated hard on reaching the first corner first . . . When I pulled away, I managed to outbrake Ayrton going into the first corner. Then, when I looked in my mirror, I could see he was off the road. For a few minutes, I was worried they would stop the race and I must admit to being relieved when I saw no red flags at the end of the first lap . . . From then on, I knew we had a very good chance of winning.'

Michael's confidence was not misplaced. Two perfectly executed pit-stops, and 83 laps later, he crossed the line for an emphatic victory. Senna, meanwhile, had been to see the stewards and to protest at Mika Hakkinen's part in the accident that had put him out of the race. He had also stood at the first corner and studied Michael's car, learning something, it was said, that convinced him it required deeper investigation and that he may have been racing at a disadvantage. He did not know. Michael did not know. Nor did either of them know it was to be the last time they would leave a circuit locked as one in their new racing rivalry, planning and scheming their next qualifying battle, their next race and their next confrontation. This was to come another fortnight later, in the European spring, at Imola, in the San Marino Grand Prix. There, both men knew, the shape of the championship might be moulded for real; but Michael, who still felt he was unlikely to win the title, had the initial advantage as they flew home from Osaka on Monday, 18 April. The championship showed it clearly: Schumacher 20 points, Senna 0.

10 IMOLA

DEATH, DISASTER AND LEADERSHIP

*We have to learn from what happened this weekend.
We are all of the same opinion and perhaps today the
drivers are closer than they were in the past. We can
talk and discuss and, if we stay together, we can get
things done.*

Michael Schumacher, talking after winning the 1994
San Marino Grand Prix, unaware of the extent of
Ayrton Senna's injuries.

IT WAS ALWAYS A HAPPY PLACE to go in the spring: a
hopeful time of new beginnings. The sun shone on the rolling
hillside vineyards of Emilia Romagna and early-season optimism
filled the air at the excited and exciting Autodromo Enzo e Dino
Ferrari. Every year, it was the same: the intoxicating scents, fresh
pasta and rich, full-bodied Italian wine. The Formula One season
always felt as if it really began with the first European race. But on
the weekend of the 1994 San Marino Grand Prix, it felt as if it had
reached a sickening end. Two deaths, the first in the sport for 12
years, turned a time of seasonal celebration into one of mourning
for the losses of Roland Ratzenberger and Ayrton Senna.

Both deaths deeply affected Michael Schumacher. They
brought to a shattering and abrupt conclusion his brief period
of apprenticeship as a great Formula One star-in-waiting, they
ended his protected period of living in the slipstream left by
Senna's dazzling accumulation of three drivers' championship
titles, they deprived him of insulation against the ultimate risk all
Grand Prix drivers accepted and they left him thrust forward,

alone, as the natural heir to the Formula One throne. Almost overnight, Michael had to adapt from challenger to leader. From hunter to hunted. Tragically, Imola would always be remembered as that watershed in his racing life.

Michael had arrived at Imola that weekend on the crest of a wave, happy to have taken delivery of his new Bugatti, enjoying a big lead in the championship and relishing a chance to race hard against Senna's Williams-Renault on a track which would give a realistic signal of both cars' true potential for the season ahead. On Thursday and Friday (when Rubens Barrichello survived a high-speed accident which shocked many drivers) the media were intrigued by the behaviour of both Senna and Schumacher in the paddock. Ayrton seemed more withdrawn than usual, pensive, distracted and serious. But Michael was confident and talked freely of how he was adapting to the new pressures he felt from being a leading German sports star, his national media having developed an increasingly strong interest in their boy-man from Kerpen.

'I cannot compare my fame to that of Becker or Graf,' he said. 'It is too difficult. Certainly, I am getting more and more fame with each success I have. That is normal. I don't think I am more famous than them or have more success than them. But with these things, it is down to success and someone like Steffi is still having a lot of success. . . . As for me, it is sometimes a problem to do the things I like most, like driving go-karts. Just going to the circuit, driving and enjoying myself. It is becoming more and more difficult. It is nearly impossible. . . . Sometimes, when I stop and I think about it, I feel I'd really like to have the old times back again. But that is the price you have to pay for success.'

As so often happened in 1994, Michael was again being linked with Mercedes-Benz. And, as so often throughout the year, he explained that whilst he would love the opportunity to win a world championship, as a German driver, with Mercedes, he knew that Mercedes understood that he currently had his best opportunity to win a title with Benetton. It was to be a recurrent theme.

On that Friday, at Imola, on 29 April, Senna and Williams were in blistering form. Senna was fastest in both sessions, but the afternoon qualifying was entirely overshadowed by Barrichello's flying accident, his Jordan car clearing a tyre-barrier at the Variante Bassa before slamming into a fence amid a cloud of debris. Barrichello's life was saved by Professor Watkins who prevented him drowning in his own blood after breaking his nose. The following day, he was well enough to walk back into the paddock and talk about it all. 'I saw Rubens' accident on television and it was a shock to see,' admitted Michael. 'I was surprised. It was a very hard shunt. There is a bump at the entrance to that corner which also made me spin off as well . . . it is a very difficult corner.'

Speaking that Friday afternoon, as he did at every race, Michael had no idea of what lay ahead. He was in confident mood, lying second on the overnight grid with a time of one minute and 22.015 seconds, half a second slower than Senna's best for Williams. Asked about Senna, he revealed strong views. 'He knows that he has the best package to win the championship and if there is any pressure it is on him. Let's see how he copes with it. He has come into a new team with big pressures. It's all new. I think this is good for him.'

Michael was buoyed up, of course, by his two successive wins, but even this flood of confidence could not help him remove Senna from the 65th and ultimate pole position of his career in the final qualifying on Saturday, a session blackened by the death of Ratzenberger whose Simtek car crashed into the wall at the right-handed Villeneuve corner before Tosa. It was a sickening and frightening accident and one that had a profound and devastating effect on the paddock as drivers, Michael included, fought with the brutal and unpalatable fact that their popular Austrian friend had died. To make it worse for Michael, his Benetton teammate J.J. Lehto, back in the team after recovering from his serious neck injury, was a close friend of Ratzenberger's. He was devastated and the entire Benetton team was stunned in disbelief, horror and fear. It was almost too much for Michael to bear.

But there was more to come. After a difficult night of coming to terms with the risks of his work as a racing driver, Michael was back at the circuit on Sunday morning preparing for the warm-up and the race, the Benetton team, together with Williams and others, having withdrawn from what remained of the previous day's qualifying session out of respect for Ratzenberger. It had been a joyless night. A joyless morning. And it was to be an even more joyless and tragic day. Michael, aware of the hazards of certain of the circuits he had raced on, had been in contact with the Federation Internationale de l'Automobile (FIA) safety delegate, Roland Bruynseraede, to push for improvements, and on that Sunday morning, after an emotionally charged drivers' briefing, he talked to Senna, Berger and Michele Alboreto about ways of resolving various safety issues which confronted them. They all agreed to meet again at Monaco – not one of them imagining that anything as bad as Ratzenberger's accident could ever happen again.

But it did. That afternoon, Ayrton Senna crashed at Tamburello and was killed. Michael, unaware of the extent of Senna's injuries and not informed of the tragedy until long after the race was over, had followed him through the corner. He went on and won the race. It was, without doubt, the least satisfying, grimmest and most unwanted victory of his career. The race had started with an accident, involving J.J. Lehto and Pedro Lamy, the young Portuguese driver's Lotus crashing into the Benetton and sending debris into the crowd. After the previous two days of carnage, it was unreal. The race was stopped and the safety car sent out to pace the field – led by Senna, with Michael close behind – through the next three laps. When the race resumed, it was with tragic results as Ayrton's Williams car speared off into the concrete wall where the impact was catastrophic. This time the race was red-flagged to a halt. It should have been cancelled, but in Formula One the show goes on. When it did, from another start, Michael drove to victory, 10 more points and a stony-faced podium filled with anxiety and grief.

'We have to learn from what happened this weekend,' said Michael. 'We are all of the same opinion and perhaps today the drivers are closer than they were in the past. We can talk and discuss and, if we stay together, we can get things done. There are some good ideas which should be discussed with the right people. The weak point is the driver because we sit there with the car around us to cope with an incident. But the head is free and it cannot take a heavy impact.'

The catastrophic weekend in the garden of Italy left Michael reeling with problems of his own. Could he continue? Did he want to continue? What did it matter? What should he do? In his mind, he knew it was right to go on to Monaco, to race again, to fulfil his obligations and in the process to honour Roland and Ayrton. But could he? Did he have the heart? On top of the two deaths, there had been the earlier crashes of Lehto and Jean Alesi, in a Ferrari in testing after the Brazilian Grand Prix, both of which had resulted in serious neck and head injuries. Was it Imola? Was it the cars? What next?

To help him resolve his dilemmas, Michael spent some time at home in Monte Carlo, talking to Corinna, considering his position, discussing it with Willi Weber, and then some time on the Benetton yacht with Flavio Briatore before he flew to England for a make-or-break test session at Silverstone. He knew how much it meant, this test, and he was also aware that Gerhard Berger, a senior statesman of the sport, was seriously considering retirement. Gerhard, after all, had lost not only a fellow Austrian in Ratzenburger, but also a former teammate and a close friend in Senna. After all the years of apparently impregnable cars, seemingly guaranteed to save lives, no-one could digest the recent chain of events or make sense of them.

Monaco was the next race. Michael's home town, the beautiful, glittering picture postcard, but an archaic street circuit where the dangers were so obvious it was a wonder that racing had not been banned there many years before. The FIA immediately announced it was reducing speeds in the pit-lane at Monaco (this in response to a bad accident in the pit-lane at Imola in the closing stages). Michael's mind was made up, however, not by announcements or politics, but by the sheer thrill of driving again. 'It was so difficult for me, before the Monaco weekend, to focus my mind,' he recalled. 'In the aftermath of Imola, I found I could not focus my mind properly like a racing driver. I have to admit this. I did have some serious problems. I knew too that if I could not do the job the right way in my own mind, I would have to stop racing. But all these problems were resolved when I went testing at Silverstone the week before Monaco.

'I was able to get my mind right. To sort things out. And that helped me take my decision to accept one of the leading roles in the Grand Prix Drivers' Association when we formed it again on the Friday rest day at Monaco. I could focus on my job again. But I was still, like everyone, desperately unhappy at the deaths of Roland and Ayrton. I measured myself against Ayrton, he was the fastest driver in Formula One and nothing would have meant more to me than to have won my first pole position at Monte Carlo against him.'

To many observers, it seemed extraordinary that Michael had driven virtually as normal in the hollow race which followed Senna's fatal accident at Imola. But Michael, like all the drivers, had no real idea of the severity of Ayrton's injuries. 'There are two points to make about this,' he said later, in Montreal. 'The first is that nobody, apart from Eric, who passed it, knew what had happened. I saw the crash and I knew it was a big crash, but I have seen worse crashes, like Zanardi or others. And they had stepped out and they were okay. These were the only experiences I had in Formula One. All the crashes I had seen up to then, the drivers had been okay. There is no way I could have known that the crash was so serious. I wasn't even thinking "Is that serious?". I was only thinking that he might have a problem at Monte Carlo at the most, that he would not be able to drive there. I didn't think it was that serious. That was the first reason.

'Secondly, we didn't know anything about the spectator accident at that time and we didn't know anything about the accident in the pits. It was not until three or four hours after the race that I found out that the Senna accident was so serious. When I was on the podium, and in the press conference, all I knew was that Senna was in a coma. A coma though could be like Karl's at Monaco. You just don't know about these things. The thing is that we didn't have any feeling then that somebody could die in a Formula One car the way it happened to Ayrton. We all knew that if you had an accident like a broken suspension, or suddenly no brakes, if something crazy like that happened, you could have a heavy accident and there was a danger of dying. We knew about that risk. But myself, personally, I did not know that Senna's accident was that serious.'

Michael's reference to Karl at Monaco was to the terrible accident which his former Mercedes-Benz teammate Karl Wendlinger suffered during the opening free practice session on Thursday morning, 12 May. His Sauber-Mercedes car crashed into a barrier at the chicane after the tunnel, impacting at an awkward angle which left his head unprotected. He suffered severe brain contusions and swelling and was airlifted from the Princess Grace Hospital in Monaco to the Saint Roc Clinic in Nice where he lay in a coma for nearly three weeks before, eventually, making a full recovery. Karl, one of the three boys called up to be Mercedes juniors in 1989, was Michael's friend, lived near him in Monte Carlo and had known him since he was a teenager. Yet, as in so many other circumstances of severe pressure, Michael was able to block it from his mind. He had found that secret again at Silverstone.

'When I went round Silverstone in my road car, at that test, I saw so many points where I felt, "Shit, if you go off here, you're probably going to have the same results". I felt really unsure and different. But when I stepped into the car the next day and started testing in the dry, I immediately didn't have those feelings. I didn't think I might go off here or I might go off there. I just drove completely in the old way. It has always been like that for me in a car. I just do the job. I don't need to sit there and make special concentrations. I just do the job. It is a natural thing to me.'

In Monaco, that 'natural thing' enabled Michael to secure the first pole position of his career on a circuit which had been previously a private fiefdom of Ayrton Senna's (six wins in the previous seven years, an untouched record), and then go on to claim his fourth successive victory. As much as anything, it was not the performance of his car or even his by then acknowledged genius behind the wheel which was impressive: it was his head, his mental toughness, his maturity, his ability to handle all these pressures. At just 25, he was behaving with the sense and dignity that men twice his age were struggling to muster; and yet there was too an element of metronomic efficiency, a touch of ruthless ambition, which remained part of Michael as he grew up, so rapidly, in such a pressurized environment. No longer the boy-man, no longer possessing any hint of lost childhood, he had to be a leader even if he was a reluctant one. It was thrust upon him by virtue of being, as Martin Brundle put it, gifted with speed. But under the outer shell, the defensive skin of brisk good manners, lay the same Michael, a country boy from Kerpen, levelheaded and down-to-earth, struggling to reconcile all the conflicts.

At this time, Formula One was engulfed by fears and near-panic over safety standards. Press conferences; meetings in London, Paris and Monaco; inspection trips to circuits at Barcelona, Montreal, Magny-Cours and Silverstone; they all revolved together in a crazy whirl. Accusations flew in all directions. The rules were rewritten, revised and revised again. Millions wept at Ayrton Senna's funeral, which Michael, after due consideration, felt it was wisest not to attend. Testing continued. So, too, did the racing, but with a heavy heart, as the sport licked its wounds and repaired the massive damage inflicted. Michael's schedule following the Monaco Grand Prix reflects the time: on the Monday after his victory, he met Lauda, Berger and Fittipaldi to discuss safety matters; on Tuesday, he rested and went to his gym as usual; on Wednesday, he flew to Frankfurt for two days of promotional commitments with TAG Heuer, a demonstration of driving to some German jewellers at Hockenheim and a press conference to help build up the German Grand Prix; on Friday, he flew to Jerez, for testing until the following Tuesday; on Wednesday, he rested at home in Monte Carlo, and on Thursday morning he flew to Barcelona for the Spanish Grand Prix. In between, there were phone calls, long heart-searching discussions and ordinary everyday items of life to consider. Michael still had his sleepless nights and his worries, but he also learned to live again without carrying the guilt of that tragic Imola weekend with him. Willi Weber had broken the news of Ayrton's death to Michael and he knew how hurt he was. 'It hurt him so much,' he said. 'He cried like a little boy. He was very shocked – don't tell me this is a man without nerve or feelings.'

'I don't believe there is a single driver who has not had a lot of problems with what happened,' said Michael, who shed his tears alone, in private and away from the spotlight which was waiting for him. 'I believe in God, but I don't believe I have to go to church to prove that. If I have strong feelings for Ayrton, I can have them everywhere. I don't need to go to the funeral and show myself to be there. I had my own feelings about this. One reason why I didn't go was safety. The team told me not to go there. We have seen things happen in Germany and all over the world, where people have been attacked. I don't know how my situation would have been. Not just in Brazil, either, because even a German Ayrton Senna fan may have thought I was the cause of it. . . .'

Michael's comments, published originally in an interview with Mark Skewis for the British Grand Prix supplement of *Motoring News*, made back-page headlines in London's *Sun* newspaper on the eve of the British race in July. By then, the world had returned to something like normality. Michael reeled off victories in Canada and France, having finished second in the fifth race of the year at Barcelona, the Spanish Grand Prix, where he played a leading part in a threatened drivers' boycott of the race on safety grounds. The boycott did not take place because a temporary chicane was installed overnight and Michael, after taking pole position, finished the race second with only fifth gear working. It was a brilliant performance, as good as anything in his career, a drive stemming from his experience in sportscar racing as he was able to choose lines and manage his car in a way which defied belief. 'I don't know exactly what happened,' he said. 'I just know that it finally went into fifth gear and then everything stopped. I went in to the pits to ask the crew if they could fix it, but they couldn't do anything but change the tyres. I never imagined I would even be able to finish that race, so to be second was like a win. It was difficult in the beginning to take all the corners in fifth gear, but I managed to find a good line and keep up my lap times. In the pit-lane, it felt a bit like riding a horse!'

Michael shared his journey home to Monaco, from Barcelona, with Jochen Mass. According to Jochen, they talked of everything but motor racing, like two friends, the younger man sharing his thoughts with his former driving partner. Mass was impressed. 'I've given up thinking of ways I could improve him,' he said. 'He has gone too far. He is better by far than I ever was . . . so, why should I criticize him? Maybe I should tell him to wear a more modest watch, but why? There are some things in life you have to learn for yourself and he is only 25. You cannot be a 25-year-old 40-year-old you know. . . . He was innocent at Imola. No-one told him, he was misled. He has tried to work it all out for himself and he is getting there. We ask so much of him. Don't forget who he is. We see him in Monaco sometimes, for lunch, or to go out on the boat, and he is mentally strong, very articulate for his age, with a sweet girlfriend and a good family. You have to remember that too and give him proper consideration. He learns things his way.

We raced Le Mans in the night and I spoke to Michael and said, you guys are going too quick and he said, "No, I am not going too fast, I do it easy, there is no problem." The actual speed was not strange. It was that he got a bit upset, a bit temperamental and he said, "Nonsense, I'm not going too quick" and told me that if I could not go so fast that was my problem. That is what came through to me and I shut up; I laughed inside because I thought he would learn it all his way. And he did, because the car had a problem and he came back to me saying: "You were right, we were going too fast" and I liked that in him. He said he was sorry and he sounded a little arrogant too, but it was good. You need to be strong, to recognize your mistakes. But that is Michael. What you see is what you get. Straight and strong. Nice kid, amazing.'

By the time of Silverstone, he had won six of the opening seven races, including one, in France, that was the result of an exceptional slingshot start, a getaway which aroused later suspicions, and knew that another win – and with it a defeat for his most serious rival Damon Hill – might deliver a decisive psychological blow in the championship race. But it was not to happen that way. A strange and irksome mistake in passing Hill, who had pole position, on the warm-up lap, led to a stop-go penalty and, in turn (when it was ignored), a black flag. The repercussions were to rage for the next three months and cut a controversial hole through the third quarter of Michael's year, just as certainly as Imola had ended the first quarter with such devastating effect.

11 HOCKENHEIM

A Sad and Controversial Summer

> No. I saw a number five, but that was all, and I didn't know what it meant. I knew I had a five-second penalty, but I didn't know I had to come in.
>
> Michael Schumacher on whether he saw the black flag during the 1994 British Grand Prix.

To THE SOUTH FROM HEIDELBERG, surrounded by the forests of Baden-Wurttemburg which enclose the mist on cool damp mornings, lies one of Europe's fastest Formula One race circuits. It is a long stretch of asphalt, with straights, which test engine power and endurance, and chicanes, which test the brakes, connected by a series of slow corners through grandstands, which hold tens of thousands of people. This is the Hockenheimring. It is Germany's home Grand Prix track, 4.234 miles (6.815 kms) long, and one hot Sunday each July, when it hosts the premier race, it is packed with 150,000 noisy spectators. In the stadium section, the atmosphere can be intimidating, exciting or even frightening, depending on the state of your nerves, as fire crackers, flares or even rockets are released by the modern wave of motor racing fans in recognition of their hero, Michael Schumacher.

It was thus in 1992 and 1993. But in 1994 it was different. Michael, embroiled in disciplinary procedures after failing to respond to a black flag at Silverstone, was banned (the black flag being the most authoritative signal to a driver to come off the track and into the pits), but likely to race under appeal. His expected presence as the world championship leader, in a car with the potential to win, had guaranteed the organizers a sellout and he wanted to race. But before any final decision was taken, he had to be sure his decision to appeal was the right one for him and the team – instead of accepting the FIA's severe sanctions, announced in Paris on 26 July in the aftermath of the British Grand Prix at Silverstone. These all related to the same day, but amounted to a massive show of disciplinary strength by the ruling body in suspending Michael for two races, disqualifying him retro-spectively from the British race and fining the Benetton team $500,000 for 'failing on several occasions to obey the instructions of the officials at the 1994 British Grand Prix'. Michael, who had been summoned to Paris for the hearing, faced missing his home race at Hockenheim and the Hungarian Grand Prix in Budapest, if he did not appeal; but no decision came from the team or Michael until Thursday, 30 July, the eve of the German Grand Prix.

In Paris there had also been worse news for both Michael and Benetton in a further fine of $100,000 for failing, along with McLaren, to make their computer source codes available to the FIA after the tragic San Marino Grand Prix at Imola. It was in some respects a more salacious and damaging sanction than the others since it left open to speculation the possibility that Benetton, as the FIA put it, had a 'facility capable of breaching the regulations' contained in its system. In effect, it stimulated a welter of reports which, through innuendo or otherwise, suggested that Michael's runaway successes in the opening half of 1994 may have been due to help from the use of an illegal computerized driver aid, such as traction control. It was a black day indeed for Benetton and their top driver, a day which signalled the start of a long summer of discontent.

It had started with the formation lap at Silverstone when Michael passed Hill. This led to the stop-go penalty, the black flag, the ignorance of it and failure to obey it and, ultimately, an original fine for Michael of $250,000 for failing to stop and obey the flag. Clearly, given the announcements made in Paris, the FIA were anything but impressed by the actions of the British Grand Prix stewards as, in addition to multiplying the punishments heaped on Michael and his team, they also found Pierre

Aumonier had 'failed in his duties with regard to various points' as Silverstone's clerk to the course. Michael was unceremoniously stripped of his 33 point lead in the title race. It was trimmed to 27 and, with the prospect of a two-race ban to come, offered Hill a good chance to catch up and overhaul him.

After the race on 10 July, Michael had left Silverstone in a bitterly disappointed mood. As the parties and barbecues in the paddock swung into action, he had to swallow the realization that not only had he been given a stop-go penalty, he had also lost the race – and on the same day Germany was eliminated from the World Cup soccer finals in the United States. 'I felt sorry for the Silverstone crowd,' he said, 'because they were deprived, in the end, of the scrap they came to see. Once I was penalized, it was almost impossible for me to mount a realistic bid to beat Damon.'

He recognized what had happened and why, but found it difficult to accept. 'Sure, I did pass Damon on the formation lap and, yes, it is against the rules, but it was not the sort of thing that normally attracts so much trouble. I was completely unaware of the problems, in fact, and after the start I had a really good fight with Damon during the first part of the race. I was able to pick up time on the slower parts of the circuit, thanks to the handling of the B194, but on the straights he was just disappearing. Then, before my first pit stop, I was told about the five-second penalty. The way I understood it was that the time would be added on at the end of the race. I thought that was a bit strange. Then I was called in for the stop-go . . . I went in and, having been leading, found myself down in fourth place. To make matters worse, that was when gearbox problems began to develop . . . in the end I was happy to finish second.' In the end, too, Michael learned a harsh lesson in how important reliable and efficient team management was to his and Benetton's ambitions. The heated discussions during the race at Silverstone, the arguments with the officials and the ignorance of the black flag had hurt him more than anyone.

By the time of his Paris appearance, it had also become apparent to Michael that the introduction of stepped flat-bottom cars, as part of the rule changes which followed the Monaco

Grand Prix, were to reduce his advantage on the track. It seemed all sides were conspiring against him. During a 'new rules' test at the Paul Ricard circuit at Le Castellet in southern France, Michael was outpaced by Mika Hakkinen in a McLaren and also endured a nasty scare when he spun luridly in his admired canary-yellow Bugatti EB110 SS road car. He was, at the time, giving circuit rides to Ford engineers and, as he admitted, knew it had been a frightening moment. 'As I went into Signes, I braked, but there was nothing,' he was quoted as saying in a report in *Autosport*. 'I knew we would crash into the barrier if I did not slow down, so I put it into second gear. It was very close . . . I think I ought to have that car inspected very soon.'

To some neutral observers, it seemed that the championship was being restructured, during the midsummer series of rule changes and disciplinary actions, in order to even up Hill's chances. This was hinted at within the team during moments of particular pique, but no public statements were made. Benetton, at the time, was also heavily involved in final negotiations with Renault to secure a supply of their engines for 1995, something for which Michael had several times expressed his support after learning that even at his best he could not overhaul the power superiority of the Williams on certain circuits. Boosted by his championship dominance and his growing collection of expensive possessions and experiences – he had been thrilled to visit New York for the first time en route to Montreal where he reportedly arrived in cowboy boots and tassled jacket – Michael was finding himself increasingly pushed into a remote position. It was not one of his own making, but a natural consequence of the sequence of events which had been shaping the year; the explosions of July and August had hurt him far more deeply than he dared to show, but probably with beneficial long-term effects. However much the momentum of his success on the track added to his self-confidence as a driver, the events – right or wrong – off the circuit prevented him from growing too self-important.

Unimpressed, however, by the actions of the FIA in Paris, Michael decided to appeal and to race in Germany. The announcement came amid threats of blockades at Hockenheim, threats of trees being burned down and reports that other teams and drivers – Williams and Hill in particular – had been intimidated. After the race weekend was over, Hill admitted that he had been the subject of death threats. Michael, aware of all the chain reactions, made his decision to race based on the level of support for him and the event, and on his own feeling that he had been treated far too harshly by the authorities. 'I know some things have been done wrong and I know that in the Silverstone race I made some mistakes and I understand I have to be penalized for them, but still the penalty has been too hard,' he said.

The decision made, Michael found himself not only engulfed in racing once again, but also back at the centre of a new controversy as the FIA released another document which suggested, by innuendo, that the Benetton cars may have been running with an illegal 'launch control' system in their computer software at the time of the San Marino Grand Prix. The document, details of which were circulated throughout the press office, made it clear that nothing had been proved but did leave many questions unanswered. It was, plainly, another move in what was growing into a political and technical war between Michael's team and the ruling body. The popularly accepted theory was that, if the team had been found to have a form of traction control stored in their software, it might account for the excellence of some of Michael's starts, and his successes.

This 'war', it was widely believed, had started before the Spanish Grand Prix at Barcelona when Flavio Briatore wrote an open letter to the FIA president Max Mosley which severely criticized him and questioned his and the FIA's competence to run the sport in the wake of the terrible tragedies and the great debate over safety which had followed. Michael was, understandably, upset and angry as the new smears – issued in the form of a report by the FIA's Formula One technical delegate Charlie Whiting, which chronicled all the Benetton prevarications over supplying the key source codes to their computer systems – were timed to interrupt his and Benetton's preparations for his home race. Michael issued a prepared statement and later, confronted directly, said: 'I know we don't use any traction control. I know where these rumours are coming from and they had better watch themselves . . . I know that we don't have anything. We proved it to the FIA and there has been a statement from them that we don't have any traction control. What more can we do than proving, showing and being really willing to prove that we don't have anything? What more can we do? And still there are these rumours. The only thing I can think of is that they are jealous.'

Ross Brawn, the team's technical director, called a Saturday evening press conference and spoke convincingly and eloquently on Benetton's behalf. 'At no time have we tried to hide anything,' he said. 'The system they found was redundant, but we had to keep it in because of pressure of work. . . . There are a large number of deactivated devices within the software which we don't make the driver aware of, because they are irrelevant. I know Michael. He would not have used a system that was illegal with the consequences that would have brought. I am categoric on that point.' As for Michael's starts, these, he said, were down to research and practice during the winter, and perhaps a special clutch which could account for his performance in Spain. Briatore was also furious, his face as black as thunder. But he did not know that the most powerful storm of that weekend was to break during the race itself and continue for weeks to come.

Overpowered in qualifying, particularly by the Ferraris who took the front row for themselves, Michael's first race with the 'plank' – a 10mm strip of jabroc wood fitted under every car to create a 'stepped bottom' which reduced aerodynamic efficiency and in turn reduced downforce – resulted in his first retirement of the year with an engine failure after 19 laps, most of which he ran in second place behind eventual winner Gerhard Berger. By then, however, a worse disaster had affected Benetton: the sensational flash-fire which erupted when Jos Verstappen, his teammate, pulled into the pits for a refuelling stop after 15 laps. Barely two litres of fuel were spilt, but the immediate results were horrifying, with flames leaping 15 feet into the air. The pit crew were engulfed in them and it was to the team's great credit that no-one was seriously hurt and that the fire was extinguished in less than ten seconds. For Michael and Benetton, it was the worst possible end to a bad weekend of rumour, innuendo and politics. 'Nothing went right for us at Hockenheim, nothing at all,' he said. 'I was really upset about the fire, but thankful too that no-one was very badly hurt. Jos and five mechanics were taken to hospital, but only one guy was kept overnight. I hope we have none of these problems again. To me it was a personal insult to be accused of anything as I was. I believe we have proved we are beyond all reproach and I hope it is all at an end now, once and for all.'

But it was not. Not only did Michael still have to face his appeal in Paris on the black flag issue, but the team was told on Wednesday, 10 August that, after an investigation of the refuelling rig used on Verstappen's car at Hockenheim, it was believed they had deliberately removed a filter and, in the process, partly caused the terrifying fire which had engulfed their own driver. The charge came from the FIA which summoned the team to appear before another hearing, due on 19 October. Benetton responded to this by saying the filter was 'unnecessary and was removed with the full knowledge and permission of the FIA Formula One technical delegate'. A new furore broke, this time on the eve of the Hungarian Grand Prix at the Hungaroring near Budapest, a track to which Michael travelled with determination, but some concern. To help raise his morale, Michael's father Rolf and brother Ralf went with him to Budapest, and so too did one of Michael's oldest friends from Kerpen, Udo Irnich. Between them, and together with Corinna, they kept Michael's spirits up, enabled him to relax and to concentrate on his driving and to forget the escalating public controversies and the politics.

It proved to be a triumphant weekend, Michael taking pole position and winning the race to re-establish himself as the clear leader of the drivers' championship, but it was also something of a mirage, a brief respite from the whirlpool of problems in which he and Benetton were trapped. 'I feel my win in Hungary helped take away the pressure we all felt after Hockenheim, with so many claims being made about the refuelling fire. As soon as I sat in the car, I had a clear head, no problems at all. I just concentrated on the job and forgot about everything else. Before the weekend began, I thought I had probably experienced as much as anyone about politics and controversy in Formula One, but the things that happened in Hungary were something else.'

The background to the race had been all politics again as Benetton circulated an independent report, written by Peter Coombs, a director of Accident and Failure Technical Analysis Ltd, which supported Benetton's view that the removal of the fuel filter from the refulling rig did not cause the Hockenheim blaze and also questioned the integrity of the coupling systems supplied to the Formula One teams by the French company Intertechnique.

For Michael, however, there was only one course of action. He had to prepare for the next race, his favourite Belgian Grand Prix at Spa-Francorchamps, with single-minded determination, and also for the appeal hearing against his Silverstone punishments, which was due in Paris two days later. The Budapest triumph had left Michael 31 points clear of Hill with seven wins out of ten and fully justified the heavy testing programme that both he and Benetton had gone through with the new-rules car, complete with its skidblock 'plank'. These included a last-minute test at Silverstone, on the eve of opening practice, where a new three-dimensional rear wing was examined, a special creation for the high-downforce needs at the Hungaroring. Michael's performance in surviving the strident pressure in Hungary gained him new admirers and impressed some of the old. 'I like Damon and I respect what he has achieved in Formula One in a very short space of time,' said Martin Brundle. 'But I think Michael deserves to be world champion because he is so special. You would expect him to be phased by all the pressure he has been under, but he wasn't. He is just so strong in the head. Look at the lap he pulled out to get pole position on Saturday. The team didn't change a thing on his car, yet the guy goes out and gets an extra second from somewhere. That is bloody hard to do. It is a gift.'

For Spa-Francorchamps, Michael was positive and happy, but his enjoyment was an illusion. So too was his victory, a triumph that would have been the 10th of his career in his 50th race in Formula One. The circuit was filled with his supporters, and many too for teammate Verstappen who had finished third in Budapest. The rain on Saturday had given Rubens Barrichello in a Jordan-Hart the pole position, but Sunday belonged to Michael until he was retrospectively disqualified in another sensational episode, when his car was found to have an illegal amount of its skidblock 'plank' worn away. Understandably, Michael was baffled and upset. He felt he had won the race fair and square, but instead found that he was excluded from the result 48 hours before his appearance in Paris to appeal against his Silverstone misdemeanours. The news was stunning. Reporters from all over the world were left scrambling for information as it emerged at the race circuit five hours after the race had finished.

Michael had dominated the race, but spun across some kerbs on lap 19 when he was struggling with a handling problem with his car. The Benetton team said this was when the car's skidblock suffered the damage which meant it was undersized after the race, but this claim was not accepted by the FIA's delegate Charlie Whiting. He said the thinness of the skidblock was not attributable to the spin over the kerb 'because the accidental damage was clearly marked elsewhere'. The race stewards rejected Benetton's protests and concluded that 'not one of the defences offered was acceptable.' It was a devastating blow for Michael who was staying with friends when he heard the news, and it was compounded in Paris the following Tuesday when his appeal against the two-race suspension, imposed after the black flag episode at Silverstone, was rejected.

By then, Benetton's fuel filter appeal had been brought forward to 7 September, two days before the start of the Italian Grand Prix. That race at Monza and the Portuguese Grand Prix at Estoril were the two Michael was scheduled to miss through serving his ban. When the announcements were made, on a hot, late summer's afternoon in Paris, the pavement outside the Place de la Concorde was crowded and it was very clear that Michael was deeply upset at the outcome. On top of everything, with the loss of 16 points scored (at Silverstone and Spa-Francorchamps) and the potential of more at two further races, he knew that Hill and Williams had a perfect opportunity to cut a 21-point lead to just one if they could win at both Monza and Estoril. There were tears in his eyes as Michael grappled with the significance of these blows not only to his championship aspirations, but also to his reputation.

Flanked by his manager Willi Weber and by Tim Wright of the International Management Group (IMG), Michael struggled for words. 'I have to use this time to think about what to do,' he said. 'I am not going to make any decisions now, I need time to think about the future. I just don't know what I am going to do. I am shocked. I am disappointed and I am surprised. I really felt we had a good defence with good arguments.'

The severity of the punishments and the team's beseiged situation left Michael with much on his mind. His reputation and his future were at stake and he was under pressure to consider leaving Benetton, utilizing a clause in his contract to lever himself free. While he and his advisers pondered, with the German media unloading advice by the bucket, Benetton hired the celebrated British advocate, George Carman, to defend their interests in Paris at the hearing into the removal of the fuel filter. The team admitted they had removed the filter, but Carman produced a well-constructed explanation, also citing that another team, Larrousse, had allegedly been given permission to do so, in writing, by Intertechnique, that the removal was done without authority by a junior employee and that the team at no time attempted to disguise what they had done. The FIA decided to take no action and, at last, the regular trips to Paris for hearings were over. The team had also abandoned its plan to appeal against Michael's disqualification from the Belgian Grand Prix, an act which, given the vehemence with which they felt they should defend themselves, suggested an out-of-court agreement may have been reached on all matters.

Michael was therefore left to watch from the sidelines, actually as part of the RTL television team, as Hill sliced into his championship lead at Monza and Estoril with two successive victories. At the same time, he successfully disengaged himself from his three-year contract with Benetton and negotiated for a highly paid new contract which would end at the close of the 1995 season. Willi Weber was quoted in the popular German newspaper *Bild* as saying, on Michael's behalf, 'We told the Benetton team in writing that we will not continue driving under the current conditions.' The team answered by saying that 'Weber is not in a position to make such a claim,' and a protracted series of meetings began. Michael was not involved, choosing to miss testing and go away from the worry of Formula One to a health and fitness hotel in St Moritz to prepare for his return to action at the European Grand Prix at Jerez de la Frontera in Spain.

Dismayed at the possibility that the team may have acted in a way which infringed the regulations, without his knowledge, Michael was exercising his own right to control his future. In the end, Benetton had to concede to him and on 16 September they agreed to his demands. Michael was relieved it was over. 'We all make mistakes,' he said. 'But if one recognizes these mistakes, looks at them and learns from them, it is a good basis for the future. I will definitely drive for Benetton to the end of the current season and it is 99 per cent certain I will stay next year as well.' He confirmed too that it was 'decisive' for him that Benetton had not been shown to have cheated. In his mind, it was good enough. He could stay. Benetton had been given a lesson and, he hoped, they would learn it. Now, he could return, when allowed, to the business of the championship with a clear mind, focused on one thing: quickly adding to the single-point advantage he had remaining, with just three races to go.

12 ADELAIDE

THE END OF THE ROAD

What he did shows that Schumacher is a real driver, a racer. He did it just instinctively. He closed the door. It is the only thing he could do and he did it. It was an aggressive act of defensive driving.

> Alain Prost on the collision between Michael
> Schumacher and Damon Hill that handed
> the world championship to the German.

SUNSHINE AND FINE WINES, churches and pubs, restaurants and beaches make Adelaide, the main city of South Australia, a popular final destination on the Grand Prix calendar. The pubs seem to be on every corner, across every green park and down every road. They indicate that Adelaide is a homely city, but one which enjoys a drink and a party. And for that reason, it is a good place in which to conclude the Formula One world championship each year. No-one enjoys a celebration more than the Australians and they are fine organizers, enjoy good weather and love their sport. The 1994 Australian Grand Prix was the 10th staged in Adelaide and was a race with more significance than any other in the city since 1986. It was the final showdown between Michael Schumacher and Damon Hill, a down-to-the-wire confrontation to end one of the most tumultuous years on record.

After his two-race absence, Michael had returned to action in testing at Estoril immediately after the Portuguese Grand Prix. It was a vital test for him and the team as he had to prove he (and they) retained the zest and ability to become fully competitive again. Results at Monza and in Portugal had been disappointing and cynics were suggesting that all the early season success was due not just to Michael's driving ability, but also to his car. There were renewed hints at sinister aids within the technology. The Estoril test, with Paul Tracy, the Canadian IndyCar driver present, was important to dispel all the insinuations and Michael reacted in typical fashion by clocking fast times from the start, breaking off for a day of promotional work for Sanyo in Germany, and then flying back to top the times at the end of the week. His confidence restored, he had put the swagger back into the Benetton team as well.

Two weeks later, however, he was enticed, by the same weakness for extreme self-confidence, into an unnecessary and inaccurate series of critical comments about Hill, only 48 hours before arriving at the European Grand Prix. A group of British journalists, in Estoril to witness Nigel Mansell testing with Williams in advance of his much-vaunted return to Formula One, took the opportunity to sit down with Michael and discuss his prospects and his views on his rival. The answers were, in the parlance of Fleet Street's men, dynamite. The story was stored for use as a preview to the weekend's racing and then run in the London papers on Friday morning under headlines which suggested character assassination.

Michael claimed he no longer felt much respect for Hill, had been disillusioned by Hill's lack of sympathy and support for him during his long series of misfortunes and added, for good measure, that had Ayrton Senna still been alive, he would have run rings around the pair of them. Hill, in as dignified a manner as possible, brushed the comments aside, refused to be drawn in and said that if they were intended to destabilize him, then 'he [Schumacher] had better try a lot harder than that.' The story had been fanned into life in Germany as well in the weeks leading to the European race as the final three-race showdown was predictably being seen everywhere as a mini-championship season all on its own. It was even suggested in certain quarters in Germany that Michael was failing to co-operate with Damon on the return of the Spa-Francorchamps victor's trophy, but the truth was that it had been given to the Benetton team to hand on to Hill once he had been pronounced the rightful victor after the race.

'Now I know that when I get back to Jerez, it is going to be a real scrap,' Michael admitted after seeing Hill's victory in Estoril. 'Damon did a good job and drove very well . . . I think we will be fighting on level terms, but I think it is true too that Damon has not beaten me this season in any race without interference from outside.'

After his outburst in testing, Michael had to deliver on the track. And he did. He took pole position, he drove with speed and almost ruthless determination and he won the race by nearly 25 seconds, thanks to excellent strategy and pitwork. 'When Damon stopped, I was into the lead and I felt from then on that I could win,' said Michael afterwards, having admitted that he was struggling badly on his first set of tyres after Hill had made a flying start. 'Once I realized that his strategy was to do two stops to my three, it was even more clear for me. I knew I could push hard and pick up a lot of time. None of the back-markers caused me any trouble either and I was really able to enjoy my drive all the way to the chequered flag. For me, it was a very important win.' It was a devastating display of superiority and it put him five points ahead again in the championship with just two races remaining, the long-haul pair in Japan and Australia. Fit, concentrated, committed, Michael looked like a man in total control that weekend in Spain, even finding time not only to spend long hours working on improving his car and his lap times with his engineers, but also to support sponsors' promotional functions, including a public football match in the nearby Jerez stadium, and to take part in an orchestrated photo-call – requested by Bernie Ecclestone – with Hill to quell the escalating talk of a bitter rivalry between them. It was, however, at the track and in the hidden work areas of the motor home and the team's garage that Michael's best efforts were directed and appreciated. His ability to analyse his car and his performance put the team back on its feet.

'He's a complete professional,' said Ross Brawn, the technical director. 'During a Grand Prix weekend, he will think about nothing else but racing. He goes to bed at night thinking about his car and when he comes back in the morning he knows exactly what he wants to do. Nothing will divert him from that.' Corinna, in Jerez with Michael's dog, Jenny, understood this. So too, did his father and the rest of his family, who always left him enough space to work. As did the Benetton engineers and mechanics, who relished the valuable input from the man they had dubbed 'Brucie' because of his jutting, Bruce Forsyth-style chin. More than anything, Michael was liked and respected because he was successful and consistent. He rarely let them down.

'Most drivers perform well for 90 to 95 per cent of the time,' Brawn told Maurice Hamilton, in the *Observer*. 'But occasionally they have the odd day during testing where you wonder what's happening and you end up making no progress at all. Michael is amazing. You never question anything in terms of driver performance. If the car is going slower, it's because you've done something to make it slower and not because he is having a bad day.' To others, like engineer Frank Dernie who left Benetton for Ligier in 1994, Michael was 'a thinker' in a way that not many other drivers are. 'Or at least not to this extent. If you assume that they are all quick and have exceptional ability at the top level, then intelligent drivers, such as Prost and Piquet, are the ones who stand out. And Michael is certainly in the élite group.

'He adapts his style to try various things. You cannot pigeon-hole his style because I've seen him do them all. Look at the way he uses a throttle. There was a marked difference between Prost and Mansell in that Alain never jumped on the throttle like Nigel, but I've seen Schumacher do it both ways, depending on the circumstances. He will, if necessary, go back to his go-kart techniques. But he won't do so if he upsets the car too much.'

With a useful, but not comfortable lead in the championship to reassure him, Michael was in a good frame of mind for the final two races, until another unscheduled announcement, this time from his manager Willi Weber, caused further alarm for him and for Benetton. On this occasion, Weber told Adrian Warner of the Reuters news agency that the impending announcement of a new partnership between McLaren International and Mercedes-Benz would signal the creation of a 'dream team' which Schumacher would obviously regard as his number once choice for the 1996 season. 'He has never really broken off his contacts with Mercedes,' said Weber. 'Both sides have looked after the relationship. Both he and I have said this. There has always been a wish to work with Mercedes again.' Whether it was wise or not for Weber to say what he pleased on that day, 26 October, it was very apparent two days later, when Michael issued a statement of his own through the offices of Weber Management GmbH, that something had gone awry. In his own words, Michael wished 'to clarify recent rumours and speculations' and to 'confirm that I will be driving for Benetton for the 1995 season.'

On the same day, Mercedes' move to McLaren was confirmed in Stuttgart, and Benetton announced that Johnny Herbert was to succeed J. J. Lehto and Jos Verstappen as Michael's teammate for the final two races. Michael had raced with Herbert before, in his single excursion into Japanese Formula 3000, and knew he got on well with him. 'I have raced against him a lot so I know how talented he is – and I know about his sense of humour too!' said Michael.

Before Japan, Michael went to Singapore to acclimatize. It was vital for him. Knowing how much was riding on the race, how high the stakes were, he wanted to be as relaxed and focussed as possible. As a result, he arrived looking tanned and well, brisk and business-like, if a little stiff with tension. The frequent smiles, the firm handshakes and the polite manners remained, but there was a tangible urge to get on with the action and a reluctance to indulge in any small talk in the crowded, sloping and narrow paddock area between the garages and the temporary offices at the circuit. Hill, too, was tense. But with Mansell in increasingly influential form, he overcame his worst day, on Friday, to put together a genuinely memorable race performance in treacherous and wet conditions. This came, of course, after Michael had taken pole position, thanks to a wet Saturday, and after Jochen Mass, in Japan in his role as a television commentator for RTL, had jokingly hung up a 'no entry' sign to David Coulthard in Mansell's half of the Williams garage. The joke was related to rumours that Mansell had banned Coulthard and his manager Tim Wright of IMG from his area of the Williams pits because he wanted his mechanics' undivided attention. Since Wright was also associated with both Schumacher and Herbert, it all seemed a somewhat contrived way to unsettle Williams, if it was true. Predictably, Mansell and everyone at Williams denied it.

By race day, in the rain, the atmosphere was so tense on the grid it could almost be cut with a knife. Martin Brundle had been fastest in the morning warm-up, in the wet, in his McLaren-Peugeot, Mansell second, Hill fifth, Schumacher seventh; but not too much appeared to worry Michael or the Benetton camp. A ceremony in memory of Senna preceded the race which had attracted a crowd of 155,000 spectators, sitting bedraggled beneath their coloured plastic rainsheets.

At the start, with the championship there for the taking if Michael could win the race, the sky was heavy and when the lights flicked from red to green, he reacted by stamping hard, until he suffered too much wheelspin and, at the same time, swerved violently to the right. This was directly across Hill's line. On the television monitor screens, it looked a deliberate and dangerous move, but according to both drivers it was not so worrying. Hill resisted a challenge from Frentzen to hold on to second place through the opening three laps, until a downpour flooded the track and the safety car was sent out to lead the field at a unified pace. By then, several drivers, including Herbert, had lost their cars through aquaplaning on the straight.

Michael, his head heavy with concentration and his mind focussed by the belief that this was his race and his championship, led the field and, when the safety car peeled away after ten laps, he quickly opened up a clear lead. After 15 laps, however, the red flag was shown and the race was stopped as four more cars had slid off, including Brundle's McLaren which had collided with a track marshal, breaking his leg in the process. The stop only served to add to the tension as, on a wet track and with grey drizzle all around, the leading drivers decided that a rolling start from behind the pace car was to be the safest way to re-start the race.

Michael, his strategy of going for two pit-stops instead of one marginalized by the conditions and the reduction of the race distance to 50 laps, led again at the re-start, but almost immediately, he pitted and conceded the lead to Hill. With a clear track ahead instead of the plumes of spray thrown up by the Benetton, Hill was able to pull away while Michael, having rejoined the field, was seemingly held up by Mika Hakkinen in the second McLaren. The race was further confused by the stoppage as it now meant the on-track positions were different from the ones that counted, when the aggregate times were combined. Nonetheless, it was soon a clear fight between the two main protagonists once Hill had pitted. He led, but only on the circuit and not by enough to feel confident of winning when, quite unexpectedly, Schumacher made his second stop after 40 laps, leaving Hill with an overall lead of more than 14 seconds. There were ten laps to go in wet, but driveable conditions, and this meant that Michael had to reduce the gap by more than two seconds each lap to win.

On the track, Hill was more than half a lap ahead and it was only by means of radio and pit-board signals that the two drivers knew their respective positions and the gap as Michael cut it from 14 seconds down to 2.4 on the penultimate lap. Then, however, he ran into traffic, while Hill, on old tyres – one of which had been on for the full race distance – drove like a man inspired, to keep his car on the road and sufficiently far in front to win. In the end, he did so by 3.365 seconds, achieving exactly what was needed to take the championship all the way to Adelaide.

Michael's face, on the podium and in the post-race media conferences, told its own story. He was deeply disappointed, while Hill, understandably, was euphoric. Both men knew how high the stakes would be in Australia, what the risks were, how tired they felt and what further depths of commitment would be needed. The two drivers missed the Sunday night flights to Queensland and opted instead to travel the following day, Monday. Hill flew to Brisbane and was whisked off for a hectic 24 hours in the company of the former world motor-cycling champion Barry Sheene, while Michael, with Corinna, flew to Sydney. He spent Tuesday resting and out in a boat and on Wednesday enjoyed an outdoor lunch, during which he was slightly sunburned, before flying to Adelaide in the evening. By then, the crowds were gathering. The teams were fighting off the end-of-season fatigue which is normally banished by a week's break between the races and, as in Japan, there was a strong sense of tension and anxiety.

The Australian media were having a field day with comments from Hill about his contractual situation at Williams (he said he was unhappy and wanted a new one), and to begin with it seemed the greater pressure was on the Englishman. Hill, however, had the boost of a humorous Mansell in his team and the 41 year-old veteran was in a very good mood, displaying all the old enthusiasm which had helped him to win the 1992 title. Not only that, but with his vast experience, drawn from 184 Grands Prix, he had been there before and knew how to handle the pressure. Michael however, found that, unlike in Japan, he slept better and felt less nervous.

On Friday's opening day, Hill was quickest in the morning and Mansell in the afternoon when, with the pressure clearly telling on him, Michael spun heavily at turn four. He had been fastest on his first run and he badly wanted to regain pole from Mansell on his second. But the veteran Englishman, having thrown his car sideways to avoid a collision with Herbert's Benetton, showed all his experience and bravery by putting down a time that proved to be beyond Michael's reach. Michael had clocked 1:16.197, but Mansell did 1:16.179. It may have been a matter of only a few hundredths of a second, but it was a psychological blow in Williams' favour. Michael admitted that he was struggling with the handling of his car and did not like the height of the kerbs going into the chicane and that he had made a mistake – a mistake which cost him two wheels, the biggest crash of his season and pole position. 'I had a big fight with Mansell and I lost in the end. I don't know if I could have gone quicker . . . I like to think I could,' said Michael.

Saturday was wet. It meant the grid positions remained unchanged from Friday and that Mansell would start from pole position in front of the big crowd. Michael was second on the grid and Damon third. In the morning warm-up, Mansell was quickest, Michael third and Hill sixth, but no-one paid any attention. No-one knew the fuel loads and there was nothing of real significance to be learned. Overhead, the sky remained grey, the temperatures were cool and the paddock was alive with predictions and arguments. For several minutes before the start, Michael sat outside on a chest and concentrated quietly by himself. Here he was, on the other side of the world again, willing himself to fulfil those ambitions which had been nurtured in Korpen-Mannheim, on the kart track. On the grid, graffiti artists had scrawled 'rightful champion' on Michael's second spot and 'in memory of Ayrton' on Mansell's pole. Neither Hill nor Schumacher knew the tactics of the other and it was, with one point between them, as tight as it could possibly be for a showdown.

The race was a thriller which lasted for only 36 of the 81 laps. Mansell made a poor start, Michael flew by and Hill followed. The two contenders were nose-to-tail, even through a pit-stop which they took together after 18 laps. They were never more than two seconds apart and often less than half. They sliced through the traffic, weaved and raced, Hill's phenomenal speed and courage surprising even his own team. The rest of the field, as they had been throughout the year, were reduced to being bystanders until, on lap 36, it happened.

Michael, under pressure from Hill, colossal pressure, made a mistake. He ran wide on a kerb and hit a wall before returning to the track. He tried to hold on to his car and regain the racing line, but only succeeded in blocking Hill's approach to the next corner. The pair touched, Schumacher's car lifting off the ground and swerving away into a wall of tyres, while Hill, with his front end damaged, continued. He managed to reach the pits with a punctured left front tyre and damaged suspension before retiring. No-one, at first, could believe it, least of all Michael who only learned of the eventual outcome – that he was world champion by a single point – from a marshal and from shouts from the crowd as he walked back from the wreckage of his car at Stag corner, named after one of Adelaide's many pubs.

'I got caught out on a bump when the car stepped out and went sideways, but I caught it. Then I had to go on the white line and I had to use the run-off area,' said Michael. 'I went over the grass, touched the wall, but continued. Then I just wanted to turn into the corner and suddenly I saw Damon next to me and we just hit each other and I went up in the air. The steering was not right. I was a bit afraid because I thought I was going to roll over, but the car came back. This was the worst moment, being in a tyre wall and not being able to continue and yet seeing Damon driving on. They were the longest three laps of my life. I then heard on the loudspeakers that he had a problem, but I wasn't sure what kind of problem. But then, once I saw Mansell going by two or three times without Hill coming through, then I thought, that's it . . . !'

Michael was not certain he was the champion until he returned to the Benetton garage, with the help of a lift on a motor bike, where a celebration party had already started. 'It was a wild casino, so I knew what it meant. It was a great feeling,' he said, hugging Corinna, dancing with the mechanics and grinning from ear to ear.

The collision caused many observers to question if it had been a deliberate move by Michael, but Hill did not join the chorus and his dignity in defeat, at the end of such a tumultuous year, was an example. 'I didn't see him hit the wall,' he said. 'I saw him coming back across the grass and onto the track. I thought "Hello, you've slipped up there," but of course I thought his car was okay. But looking at the video just now it's clear his right rear suspension was damaged pretty badly and would have put him out of the race anyway. Of course, it's easy if you want to go back in time because I would have sat back and let him go, but. . . .'

There was no doubting what had happened or its significance. Michael had made a mistake but he had fought to defend himself, his position and his championship ambitions by instinctively closing the door, creating the impact which took both cars and both men out of the race. It barely mattered thereafter that Mansell went on to win and to secure the constructors' title for Williams who, like Michael, dedicated their honour to the memory of the man whose death had so dominated the year: Ayrton Senna. Michael, controlled and sober in his hour of triumph, was fully aware of how unsatisfactory it all looked and immediately after the race took the opportunity, as the newly-crowned champion, to apologize to Hill for the comments he had made during the test at Estoril. 'I said I didn't have much respect for him, then, but I was wrong. He has done a fantastic job in the last two races, a proper and a fantastic job. He has been a great rival.

'Winning this championship now feels like a dream. I don't know how to explain it. The emotions are in me, but I cannot really express them. . . . Early in the season, it had been clear to me that I was not going to win the championship, but that it was going to be Ayrton. But he hasn't been here for these last races and so I would like to take this championship and to give it to him. He is the driver who should have earned it. He had the best car and he was the best driver and those are my feelings about him. It was difficult at the time to show my feelings because I am not someone who likes to show his feelings on the outside, but I always thought about it. And now it is the right time to give something which I achieved, something which he should have achieved, and to give it to him. Thankyou.'

At the time of going to press, there was speculation that the FIA would strip Schumacher of his title on account of the incident in Adelaide. Most Formula One professionals however, including Frank Williams, expected the decision to stand. Even after his confirmation as World Champion, the controversy which had dogged Schumacher through the season refused to go away.

13

1995

IT TOOK TIME FOR the significance of being world champion to sink in. Adelaide was left behind; the wild revelry of the Benetton team, the controversies and the British media campaign, whipped up by the *Daily Mirror*, faded away. In their place came a calm feeling of achievement, an inner glow. For Michael Schumacher, it was a personal landmark. For Germany, it was a national one. And it brought with it a massive sense of celebration. The triumph made him a champion to a country that loves, lauds and heaps pressures upon its champions. Media event followed media event, television shows and interviews followed television appearances and photocalls in the build-up to the gala dinner, held at the Sporting Club in Monte Carlo, where he received his championship trophy, officially, from the President of the Federation Internationale de l'Automobile (FIA), Max Mosley. By then the temperature had dropped, both literally and metaphorically. The flash, snap, crackle of the media, the demands life of a Formula One world champion were put on one side and restful month of peace was allowed, except for the annual karting event at Bercy in Paris, which for kart-lover Michael was no more than a diversion from routine.

Typically, Michael used his brief period of quiet as an opportunity to train. He wanted to ensure his body was fine-tuned to perfection in readiness for his final season with Benetton, the team's first in partnership with Renault, the year in which he was to defend his title and establish himself among the ranks of double champions. During his enforced break through suspension in 1994, he had trained at altitude in Switzerland, where he learned several new techniques to add to his fitness regime. These new techniques were now put to serious use for the first time.

'My programme now is much more complex and I really feel better for it,' he said during a break in pre-season testing in Estoril. 'I do more exercise, but I do it differently and I get much better results from it. I don't want to tell you much more because a lot of the other drivers know that I train very hard and I need to keep it to myself . . .'

By early 1995, Benetton's factory workforce at Enstone were busy putting the finishing touches to the team's new car, the Renault-powered B195, which was launched amid much media attention at Treviso. Johnny Herbert was confirmed as Michael's team-mate and a lighter mood, influenced by his arrival and the start of a new season, began to prevail. Formula One was leaving behind its year of turmoil and tragedy and Michael, as world champion, was emerging as a thoughtful leader of a new generation of outstanding drivers.

From the same interview in Estoril, his comments on safety revealed a new sense of maturity. 'We used a lot of our experience last year in improving Formula One, but there are still a lot of other changes to complete. We talked about them over the winter and we shall just have to wait and see if they are achieved. But it is not only about the circuit. It is also about the cars. Both have to be improved and changed together in a sensible way. It is the only thing.'

Looking ahead, he admitted he was concerned by the prospect of travelling to Brazil for the first time since the death of Ayrton Senna. 'Going there without Ayrton is going to be very hard,' he said. 'Imola is not such a worry.' Asked about the pressures he felt, in defending the championship, he replied: 'I personally feel more relaxed because of this. I have won races. I have won the championship. I think there is more pressure to win on me, but at the moment I am still relaxed and I am looking forward to the first race. I had a relaxing winter and I coped with the pressure before that quite well. It does not upset me. I don't struggle with tension. Or with my work. I am not worried. We have a very good structure with the Benetton team and we do quality work. I know there is a lot of work to do with our new partnership with Renault and with the new car and I am ready for it.

'I am not fully satisfied. I still feel unsatisfied in many ways. I still expect a lot more and that is why I don't feel particularly fantastic about it. I am NOT over the moon or on top of the world! But that is normal for me. It has always been this way. When I won my first Grand Prix in Spa, it was a good feeling for me, but then I returned to normal very quickly afterwards. I don't have too many highs and lows, ups and downs. I am stable like that.'

Looking back on the championship, on the way it was won, left Michael frustrated. 'I have often thought about it,' he said. 'Quite a lot. I thought shit, there were so many opportunities for things to have gone wrong. I wouldn't have been the champion then. That worried me. But I am the champion and I feel quite satisfied now about the way it happened. There was a lot of heat in the situation at the time, but a lot of that has gone now. I have no problems about all those people who say I did it on purpose. They may now be asking why didn't he [Damon Hill] wait, try something later, or whatever. I am happy about all of this now.'

Even then, just a few weeks before the start of the new season, it was clear that there was no warmth in Michael's relationship with his chief rival. Both, in 1995, were to race with the same Renault V10 engines, on even terms, but as the opening race in Brazil loomed ever larger it seemed it was Hill's Williams which had all the extra power and speed. Benetton, predictably, had problems, most particularly with a hydraulic pump, but once this was resolved they quickly made up ground. In winter testing it was Williams who were most impressive, and they travelled to South America and the opening race at Interlagos filled with confidence. Their car was made-to-measure, they had done thousands of testing miles and each of their drivers was showing good form.

The only problem which seemed to be affecting Williams' confidence was the recurrent tonsillitis of David Coulthard, the young Scot who had been signed to partner Hill. Normally, Coulthard was a psychologically strong presence in the team, but his raw throat, hacking cough and fever had lowered his morale during a brief holiday at Angra dos Reis, up the coast from São Paulo towards Rio, before the race. Unfortunately, from Michael's point of view, the illness did nothing to dim his speed or that of his English team-mate. From the start, it was clear that 1995 had all the prospects of being as tough and competitive as 1994 for the chief protagonists for the title.

Hill had retained his dignity through the winter. He had won BBC Television's Sports Personality of the Year Award and made no complaints about the way 1994 had ended. He did not change his style as the new season approached. 'I've tried to forget what happened last year,' he said. 'It's irrelevant now. My only thoughts are on 1995, going to Brazil and opening a new chapter. But I certainly admit there may be an element of this race being treated as Adelaide Part Two . . . The interesting thing will be seeing how Michael copes if he is put under more pressure.' Hill denied suggestions in the media that he had breakfasted with Schumacher in Adelaide on the morning after their decisive collision. 'He was in the same building as me, having breakfast, and I just thought I'd better pop over and say hallo,' he admitted. 'I wanted to see what his face looked like when he saw me. I just said, "Well done – what does it feel like to be the world champion?" . . . I don't think he felt like a world champion by then, not at that point. I think it put him off his cereal . . .'

Within weeks, everyone was in Brazil. São Paulo was steaming, as ever, but the focus of attention was as much on the cemetery at Morumbi, where Senna lay buried, as on Interlagos. A strange atmosphere overshadowed the build-up to the opening race, a heaviness. The grief was past, but there were memorials, ceremonies, marks of respect for the late great champion. It affected everyone in different ways, but the Formula One paddock as a whole pulled together and went through it, for the most part without any further controversy, until the eve of the race itself. Then, unexpectedly, a new furore broke loose.

In a change to regulations, the Federation Internationale de l'Automobile (FIA) had introduced a different minimum weight calculation for the cars *and* their drivers. Instead of the car alone having to weigh 515 kilos, the car and its driver had to weigh a minimum of 595 kilos. This, in turn, made it less necessary for the drivers to be as light in weight as in the past. Indeed, it would be better for the teams if their drivers were heavier at the time of the pre-season weigh-in than later, when they were racing. The weight loss, it was felt, would be an advantage and was not likely to be detected because the FIA were in the habit, in the past, of weighing only the cars after a race and then adding to it the drivers' known weight (from the official weigh-in before the season or at the half-way mark).

As a result of all this, the pre-season weigh-in in Brazil was approached with more interest than usual. It produced some very interesting statistics, not least the revelation that Michael's weight was, unexpectedly, 77 kilos. The previous season he had scaled in at 69 kilos. Many eyebrows were raised in suspicion. Patrick Head, the technical director of the Williams team, suggested that such a differential, if translated into a weight-loss advantage to the Benetton team, could be worth 0.2 seconds per lap at Interlagos. In a race, that would be worth around 14 seconds and could help win a Grand Prix.

Michael denied all the allegations, particularly after he went on to finish first in the race and then found himself temporarily disqualified because of irregularities in his Elf fuel. It seemed the new season had started just as the 1994 season had ended: in controversy. When Michael was weighed again, contrary to convention, after the race, he was said to have lost slightly more than 5 kilos since being weighed on Thursday. There was nowhere to hide from the suspicious looks and pointing fingers as he retreated to the Brazilian resort of Bahia for a holiday during the ten-day break before the Argentine Grand Prix in Buenos Aires.

Michael, of course, was not the only driver to have gained a substantial amount of weight over the winter . . . so too had Gerhard Berger, Karl Wenglinger and Heinz-Harald Frentzen, but because of his status as champion and the controversies which had surrounded him and Benetton in 1994, the focus of all the unwanted attention was on him. He explained, later, that the weight increase was more marked than he had expected and resulted from various methods he had employed, like drinking several litres of water and eating heavily the night before, in order to give himself the best chance of being heavier. And, he added, he had trained much harder in the winter to put on more muscle, which weighs far more than fat . . .

In all sorts of ways, it was not a happy Brazilian Grand Prix for the man from Kerpen-Manheim, even though it did eventually produce his tenth Grand Prix win, albeit after an appeal in Paris against the disqualification. Coulthard, also, was disqualified for using irregular Elf fuel and later reinstated on appeal, although both his Williams team and Michael's Benetton team were deprived of their points scored for the constructors championship. Worse, however, in many ways for Michael and Benetton had been an incident at Interlagos on Friday when he had suffered a steering failure and crashed into a wall on the exit of the fast Ferrar Dura turn. For a brief time, it seemed that Benetton might withdraw their cars through fear of another similar and more serious accident (Michael had escaped unhurt), but they were able to solve the problem. 'It was a broken pin in the steering universal joint,' said Ross Brawn the following morning, after another of many long nights' work. 'It was a part we've used for three or four years and with which we had never previously had a problem. The car and the part were brand new, so we are strongly suspicious about a metallurgical fault. We've now got new parts on the car, to a slightly modified design, so we should be safe.'

In the end, Michael qualified second and Johnny Herbert fourth, a remarkable success in the circumstances. The race saw Hill retire, leaving Michael to win, but with the Elf controversy repeating the scenes of Spa-Francorchamps the previous year there was little for anyone to celebrate. It was confusion which won, with the result hanging in the balance until the appeals were finally heard. 'I think it was one of the hardest weekends I can remember for many years,' said Michael's race engineer Pat Symonds. 'I had about three hours' sleep over the whole period. A skid had come off Johnny's car on Saturday and it punched up into the moncoque, so we had to take the fuel cell out and repair it . . . and we'd done an all-nighter on Michael's car before that, so everyone was slow and tired. It just went on and on like that – everything that could happen seemed to.'

While Michael soaked up the sunshine in Bahia, the row over Elf's fuel escalated into a full-scale dispute with the FIA back in Europe. It was a good place for the world champion to be. He was out of the firing line, avoiding the media, but he could not avoid trouble of a different kind. This came when he went on a diving trip with his fitness expert Harry Hawelka, his hotel manager and a professional instructor. Manager Willy Weber and fiancée Corinna also went along, but stayed in the boat when the divers went underwater. When they resurfaced, the boat had gone – and Michael had to swim for more than an hour in the treacherous and tropical waters of the south Atlantic to find them. 'It was the worst hour of my life,' he said. 'I was really scared. When we came to the surface, there was no sign of our boat. We were a couple of miles off shore and I thought that the boat had put down an anchor. We could see it in the distance, but they could not see us – the waves were about two metres high and I was scared.' Michael's fitness served him well for, as his three companions tired and gave up the fight, he was able to go the full distance and organize their rescue. 'It was something that I never want to experience again,' he said.

The story made headlines in Europe on the eve of the Argentine race, where peace – political and metaphorical – was once again restored. Tanned and relaxed, Michael was in perfect condition for the first event in Buenos Aires for more than a decade. The sun shone and it was hot, but all the happiness seemed to be washed away with the heavy rains which began as soon as the cars were wheeled out of the garages for the first familiarization practice runs on Thursday. And it rained. Thick, heavy, wet downpours, slanting, grey and treacherous, turning the tight and tricky circuit into a sliding rink. Only Saturday morning produced a dry practice session, the rest were all wet. Michael spent the weekend searching in vain for balance and finally qualified third before then enduring a disappointing race, blighted by tyre problems which forced him to make three stops instead of the scheduled two. For consolation, he took third place and set fastest lap, but it was hardly satisfying stuff and the team admitted they were so overwhelmed by their workload with the new car and the work to be done with Renault that they had not prepared as well for the race as usual.

Back in Europe, meanwhile, the FIA appeal court met and overturned the Brazilian stewards' decision to disqualify Schumacher and Coulthard, prompting a verbal assault from

Ferrari in general and Gerhard Berger in particular. The Austrian had been severely critical of Schumacher and Elf after the Brazilian race, though he later established that some of the most ferocious comments attributed to him were not accurate or fair. A quarrel threatened to develop, but it petered out after a couple of weeks of banter in the German press. 'I can live with Schumacher being angry,' said Berger. 'If he wants a quarrel, he can have it . . .' It never became worse than that and by mid-season it was forgotten.

The sour taste remained in their mouths, however, until the San Marino Grand Prix at Imola, where more important memories filled the minds. The deaths of Roland Ratzenberger and Ayrton Senna had left deep scars and even the revisions to the circuit making it much safer than it had been, could not erase the spectre of the black May day there a year earlier. 'The circuit is not the same old-style Imola, but when I'm sitting here or I go outside, I know it is the same place as last year,' admitted Michael. 'However, to be honest, I'd have preferred it if we had gone somewhere else for this race.'

Five days' testing at Jerez in Spain had helped Schumacher and Benetton solve some of their reliability problems, and had also given them an opportunity to do some development of the B195 in advance of the Imola race. It seemed to pay off on Friday when Michael was fastest in opening qualifying, but his satisfaction was disturbed by a volley of criticism from Max Mosley, the FIA president, for the 'childish attitude' he had demonstrated by tampering with his weight for the pre-season weigh-in. Michael refused to be drawn into what promised to be an unpleasant revival of an old problem, but his weekend went downhill from then on. An accident on Saturday saw him lose a wheel at the Variante Alta and then, in the race, after leading from the start in the wet, he changed to slicks after nine laps and lost control on the crest of the hill before Piratella immediately afterwards. It was another heavy crash. There were no explanations, but both Michael's and the team's confidence was affected and it took a massive effort to repair that damage in the fortnight before the Spanish Grand Prix at Barcelona. The effort was made, however, and it worked.

By the time of his arrival at the Circuit de Catalunya, Michael had resolved that the Imola crash was 'my own stupid mistake'. He admitted it, but he added that he was not suffering from any undue pressure. It was suggested that he had been feeling the build-up of pressure in attempting to defend his hard-won title under duress, in a car that was difficult to handle and with speculation about his future dominating everything in the background. There was none of this about him, however, on Thursday afternoon when he sneaked into the Rothmans motor home for some of the delicious Austrian home-made biscuits which are the specialty of the house. The grin was as broad as ever and boyish happiness intact. The supposedly troubled Schumacher seemed to be carrying the world on his shoulders with *élan*.

It was something of a different story the following day. Much as expected, the two Ferraris were in dominant form and Alesi was delighting the crowd with his antics. Michael was four-tenths of a second off the pace, struggling for the right set-up and relishing nothing of his difficulties. His critics were rubbing their hands in preparation for a field day, but on Saturday they had to give up the idea. Having switched to experiment with Johnny Herbert's settings, Michael suddenly found his form, took pole comfortably and set up what proved to be a luxurious victory on Sunday afternoon. Using a two-stop strategy, he dominated from start to finish and was never in any danger, controlling the gap ahead of Hill's Williams much as he wished, pulling clear when he needed to, easing when he felt like it. It was a supreme return to form and Michael was as pleased to have Herbert joining him on the podium in second place as the British driver was himself after inheriting that position following the late retirement of Hill. It was certainly not all over, as some observers had suggested. Schumacher was back in the fight and with a vengeance.

His prospects were clearly brighter on the approach to the Monaco Grand Prix than they had been at any time since the start of the season. One of the main reasons was that the team were now confident they had overcome their most serious difficulties, in terms of reliability, with the car. Michael knew he had won in Monaco the previous year, too, and he was keen to repeat that feat, despite much media hype suggesting it would be Hill's turn to take the chequered flag on the circuit where his father was always treated and greeted like royalty. A shadow was thrown over the build-up to the race, however, when it was announced by McLaren and their veteran start Nigel Mansell that they were to part after an inauspicious union during the opening stages of the season. Mansell's departure was seen as tantamount to his retirement and, as such, it took some of the attention away from the build-up.

This did not bother Michael, however, and despite failing to take pole position he managed to win and deliver Renault's first victory on the streets of the Mediterranean principality in their history of Formula One competition. Alesi had dominated Thrusday's opening qualifying in his Ferrari, driving with great fervour and flair, but Hill took pole with an inspired effort on Saturday afternoon. Michael had good reason to rue his disappointment in qualifying: an accident in Saturday's free session, which resulted from him being touched by Heinz-Harald Frentzen's Sauber Ford, left him with damaged track rods and a bent rear wishbone. The damage was not fully discovered at first, but handling problems led Michael to diagnose serious repairs were required. As a result, considerable time was lost and this may have accounted for his inability to match Hill in final qualifying. It made no difference, however, to the outcome.

In the race, he made only one pit-stop and Hill made two. Once again, the story and the outcome were decided in the pit-lane where Benetton's superior strategy, allied to Schumacher's talented driving, did the trick. Afterwards, Michael suggested that he knew that Damon would be stopping twice, which was why he stuck with him through the opening laps even though he had a much larger and heavier fuel load. By the end, it was easy and he came home with a 35-second advantage and the championship firmly back in his sights.

For Hill, Monaco was a huge disappointment for which he heaped much blame on his team's absence of strategy for the occasion. After all that had been said earlier, it seemed the tables were turning, but Canada was to be another interesting test for both drivers. The beautiful city of Montreal was bathed in sunshine through most of the weekend, but for Sunday morning, when it rained enough to cause several upsets. Michael had claimed his third pole position in four races with some ease. He was quickest in both qualifying sessions and had few dramas on his way to finishing up three-tenths quicker than Damon Hill's Williams.

As if to prove how much more advanced they had become as the weeks went by, Benetton went to the trouble of flying in new front wings for both drivers on Saturday. Both drivers improved and it looked as if all was going to go to plan, with Michael leading by more than half a minute when mechanical problems intervened. The gearbox played up, the software went awry and it needed some fast work in the garage to reprogramme the car to ensure he finished the race in fifth place. It was scant reward for his superiority throughout the weekend. But there were some consolations – Hill, too, had wretched luck and was forced to retire with a failed hydraulics pump, a disappointment which left him demonstrating his displeasure with the Williams team in public before leaving the circuit.

As a result, Michael arrived in France for the resumption of the European summer season at Magny-Cours cushioned by a championship lead of seven points and knowing that Hill, not he, was under pressure. Both drivers had been at Silverstone in the days leading up to the race, preparing their cars for the British Grand Prix, but it was the Benetton boys who were happiest. They were introducing several new modifications to their machines for France, including a revised airbox, roll hoop and engine cover, and these changes, together with the revised front wing and a new engine from Renault, the RS7B, were expected to give them an excellent chance of victory. The expectations were correct.

Michael won again, this time after starting second on the grid alongside Hill, and opened up an 11-point lead as the team flew back to Britain in readiness for the British Grand Prix, where so many of the Benetton team's troubles had started in 1994.

In Magny-Cours, it was hot. Very hot. But the Benettons were in the pink and enjoying it. Michael improved his qualifying from Friday to Saturday and also continued to exude increasing amounts of the self-confidence that is synonymous with his mood in times of success. Although Hill dominated qualifying, he could not touch his rival in the race once he had, as usual, taken the lead during the first range of pit-stops. An early scuffle between them, when they almost touched on lap 13 as Hill led the way past a back-marker, had upset Michael. He suggested Damon had 'brake-tested' him deliberately, but such a notion was unnecessary in the aftermath of such a comprehensive win – again by more than half a second. Michael Schumacher was winning again with ease and his rivals' disarray was plain enough for all to see. The world drivers' champion was obviously not planning to relinquish his crown without a fight.

In Britain, it was an exceptional summer. At Silverstone, when the teams arrived in the week after the French race for final testing and preparation before the British Grand Prix, the sun shone with ferocious heat. There was a high blue sky, dazzling light and an air of almost Mediterranean aridity. The whole country was in shirt-sleeves and fears of a prolonged drought were worrying the farmers and market-gardeners. In the new paddock at the circuit, the heat merely added to the heavy atmosphere. The old grass paddock, once synonymous with the garden-party atmosphere of Silverstone, was gone. Instead, the drivers and their teams were cocooned inside high wire fencing that had been put up all around them at every other circuit in the world.

Like Damon Hill, Michael Schumacher went there to work. The heat was secondary to that objective. So, too, were the aesthetics of the paddock. Indeed, nothing other than lap times and a competitive performance really mattered to either of the two great rivals for the championship. Each knew this as well as the other, but a new tension had crept into their relationship in Magny-Cours and it was fostered by the media into a more aggressive and unpleasant war of words for the titillation of the public as the days till the British race began to diminish into single figures.

Michael had been harsh in his criticism of Damon after the race in France. He said the Englishman had been out of order. 'What

Damon did was not sporting and very dangerous,' said Michael. 'I was right behind him when he either lifted off slightly or even braked a little. I think he did it deliberately, and the next time he tries anything like that I will know what to do . . .' The threat was veiled, but it was sinister enough and it provided the media with exactly the feud they were looking for at the high-summer summit of the season, particularly as the British race at Silverstone was the subject of such intense speculation in print and already a 90,000 sellout.

Damon, not wishing to be dragged into a lengthy dispute, was careful not to provide further unnecessary words. Just as he had been entirely diplomatic about the incident in Adelaide which had ended the Australian Grand Prix the previous year and also ended his title hopes, he was to remain resolute in steering clear of further trouble this time. But the words he used to defend his own position were stronger than they had been in the past. 'Michael is a great driver,' he said. 'And he is more than capable of looking after himself on the circuit. I think he misjudged the manoeuver and gave himself a fright. If he wants to speak to me about it, I will be more than happy.'

Across the ashphalted new paddock, Michael was also busy talking. The 'brake-test' kept on returning to the conversations. 'Fortunately, I had quick reactions,' he said. 'I expected him to close me down on one side, which is allowed – I myself have done it in the past – but I wasn't expecting him to slow down. He lifted off, which in an F1 car is the same as going for the brakes on a road car – and you all know what happens when someone brakes suddenly in front of you on the road. I am not happy about it. It is not what you expect. You know there are a few tricks, but some of these should not be done in F1. I don't think he will do it again. I will make sure of that and so will the FIA. In the race, it made me more motivated. It made me furious.'

At the same time, during the same interviews at the Silverstone test, Michael sparked the next wave of words between them, at least in the media, when after being asked about his relationship with Damon he said: 'It is impossible for us to be friends. I find it difficult to understand him. Sometimes, I see him and he reacts normally and he says hallo. And the next time, he could be completely different. His mood is difficult to judge and it seems to change very often, while my mood stays more or less the same. I get on fine with David Coulthard, who always treats me the same, I never have a problem with him and we can have a laugh together . . .'

Michael's problems with Damon were no doubt exaggerated in the media, but the words he uttered were truly his. He made it clear that he could not envisage them developing a friendship and, as the Silverstone race loomed ever nearer, the tension between them that was apparent in the paddock grew greater. It was much worsened early in the week before the race when, in an interview with the British *Radio Times* magazine, Hill referred to Michael in disparaging terms, describing him as no more than a product of the Mercedes-Benz junior scheme and implying that he was merely a clone . . . The words went down like a lead balloon in Germany and earned the previously disciplined and sensible Hill few plaudits in the United Kingdom either. This, it seemed, was a deliberate and personal attack on his rival, but what seemed one thing on the surface was something else below. First, the interview was four months old and, second, the 'clone' comments were intended to compare a wide cross-section of modern drivers with the characters who had raced in the past. Sometimes, one and one do add up to three in print, a fact recognized by Hill, who apologized for the wrong impression created by his comments when he arrived at Silverstone on Thursday afternoon before the race.

By Sunday night, all thoughts of further apologies or any kind of reconciliation were gone, blown away by the furore which followed a stunning accident between the two protagonists for the championship during the race. The collision allowed Johnny Herbert to go on and claim the first victory of his career and ensure that the Mild Seven Benetton Renault team were top of the constructors' championship. Hill had dominated qualifying and started the race from pole position, thanks to his excellent Friday time (the Saturday session was effectively washed out by heavy rain). But, as so often before, his tactics were to be different from Schumacher's. In this case, two pit stops to one, a difference which ultimately led to their collision on lap 46 of the 61-lap race, with 15 remaining.

The key point in the race had been the pit-stops. Damon had made his second on lap 41, but when he exited the pit-lane it was to be on Michael's tail. With 20 laps remaining, Michael led but Damon had the fresher tyres and the question was: could he find a way past the world champion? The answer was inevitable, and said as much about the problems of overtaking in modern Formula One racing as about the drivers. The collision came at Priory on lap 46, when Michael took his usual wide line and Damon, from an unexpected position, lunged for the gap. As the cars met at the apex of the corner, the Williams hit the side of the Benetton, throwing both cars into the air. They came to a halt in the gravel trap.

'I think what Damon did was both stupid and unnecessary,' said Schumacher. 'There was no room for two cars there and it's not an overtaking place. If I hadn't been there, I think he'd have gone straight on into the gravel. He just came from nowhere. Even in front of your home crowd, I think you have to keep your temperament under control. It was more or less the same situation as at Adelaide last year, where he also tried to dive inside where there was no room . . .'

Hill was unrepentant. 'I thought I saw an opportunity that I could take advantage of,' he explained. 'But I'm afraid Michael is a harder man to pass than that. We had an accident which I would describe as a racing accident.'

The furore rumbled on and it was to much general astonishment that it was learned that each driver had been reprimanded severely by the stewards and cautioned that any 'future similar actions may result in severe penalties'. The blame was apportioned equally, much to Benetton's equal amazement, and their managing director, Flavio Briatore, made it clear he could hardly believe the decision. 'I'm sure I could have stayed ahead,' said Schumacher. 'He was on fresher tyres with the same fuel level, but towards the end the tyres would have levelled off and I would have pulled out a gap. I knew overtaking was very difficult and so I wasn't worried at all. I knew where I had to be quick – through Becketts and on all the long straights – and I was.'

To make matters worse in the aftermath of Silverstone, the

prospect of the next race at Hockenheim was something for Hill to approach with some trepidation. In 1994, there had been talk of intimidation and threats on him and the Williams team and it was likely to be worse this time, particularly after all the events in the British Grand Prix. This, after all, was the man who had accused Schumacher, Germany's hero, of being no more than a clone and who had then done the unthinkable by ramming him off the track as he led the race. Some of the comments from Briatore were hardly necessary either. Asked if he thought that the German fans would cause trouble at Hockenheim, as a result of the trouble at Silverstone, he replied: 'No, I don't. The German fans are more intelligent than Damon Hill.'

Schumacher, too, was concerned, and he made this clear not only well in advance of the German race – when, during testing at Silverstone, he had said that the last thing he wanted was any over-the-top 'support' from his fellow-countrymen – but also after the British race. It was a theme he repeated when he met the German media a week later in the build-up to the German Grand Prix. Talking at the Kerpen-Manheim kart-track, where he held his annual get-together, he said: 'I am pleading for fairness because anything else reflects badly on me. I cannot see that Hill wanted to take me off the road deliberately, although I cannot understand his manoeuvre and I am certainly puzzled as to why I was reprimanded.'

Interest in the so-called 'war of words' between the two drivers was at an all-time high and Michael appeared to have the strongest position, psychologically at least, particularly after it was revealed in the aftermath of Silverstone that Frank Williams had visited the Benetton garage to congratulate Johnny Herbert on his victory. It was alleged, also, that Williams had apologized for Hill's on-track behaviour, alluding to him as a 'prat' for the manner in which he had thrown the race away. Williams, however, was moved to issue a statement which said: 'Press reports alleging that I labelled Damon Hill "a prat" and apologized to the Benetton team after the incident are totally erroneous.'

The situation put Michael in a strong position, and he showed magnanimous concern for his rival's well-being at Hockenheim.

Referring to talk of death threats against Hill the previous year, he said: 'I still feel bad about that. We are doing a sport here. I have been fairly treated by the British fans wherever I have gone, so I expect the same from the Germans for Damon.' Hill himself had other concerns at this time. On the Wednesday after the British Grand Prix, his wife Georgie gave birth to their third child, a daughter named Tabitha. She had been expected on the day of the Silverstone race, but her late arrival gave her father plenty of diversions. The media were diverted, also, by the death of the greatest maestro of them all, Juan-Manuel Fangio, who died in Argentina less than 24 hours after the British Grand Prix.

Hill, as resolute after Silverstone as he had been diplomatic after Adelaide, agreed with a suggestion from Nigel Roebuck, in an interview for his Fifth Column in *Autosport*, that his reticence to speak out may not have been interpreted correctly. Indeed, it seemed that he had admitted his guilt in his part of the accident. Hill said: 'It probably didn't help that I tried not to inflame the situation by being diplomatic, in what I said, afterwards. That was then overtaken by comments Michael came out with. I think there's a feeling that I ruined a good race, and that may well be true, but you cannot judge unless you know something about it.

'In a race, you have very few chances to overtake and I took a chance on what I thought was a genuine opportunity. You have to bear in mind that at the time I was on fresh tyres, an advantage I wasn't going to have for long. He braked very early for Priory and he was well over to the right. When I came down the inside, I was relying on his recognizing that I was coming through and he, in my view, had a choice: he could move over, or he could stick to his line. That was my gamble, if you like, but I felt completely justified in doing what I did . . .

'I'm not known for being impetuous. In fact, I am usually accused of being too cautious. I took the view that there was only one approach to that race and that was to be aggressive and to take advantage of any opportunity I got. Michael was indicating to me, by the way he was driving, locking up into several of the corners, that he was rattled. It was important to try to get him, before he settled in with me behind him and also before my tyre advantage disappeared. I'm going to argue about the overtaking move: I just want people to understand that I will argue very strongly for what I did.'

The general reaction to Hill's explanation of the accident was a mixture of surprise and respect. Many paddock regulars felt he had been clearly in the wrong. Others were not sure. But the majority felt it was none of Schumacher's doing. Yet there was a grudging respect for the fact that Damon refused to change his view and would make no special, sympathetic attempt to modify the soured relationship between himself and Michael. At least, it was felt, he was being honest with himself and the public, though he modified his stance rather unexpectedly on the eve of the German Grand Prix when he suggested, in an interview with a German magazine, that it might be a good idea if he and Michael were to share one of the vintage cars used by the drivers in their parade lap before the German race on Sunday. Michael, testing in Jerez at the time, indicated that he would be agreeable to this. 'I generally thought it was a good idea,' he said. 'It would show the outside world that there is not the kind of war going on between us that some sections of the press are making out. Certainly, we are not friends and we don't have a relationship. There have been one or two occasions which I don't think have been very good, but that's always going to happen in motorsport. But there is certainly no war. It would have been a good sign to go together.'

Bernie Ecclestone, unfortunately, did not agree. Taking grasp of an opportunity which he perceived as ideal for him to lay down the law, he lambasted Hill for the proposal, vetoed the whole scheme, accused Damon of handling everything badly and warned him, too, that if he repeated such tomfoolery again he could face a serious ban and fine. If Hill had expected life to be strained and difficult in Germany, he did not expect his difficulties to include Ecclestone, the president of the Formula One Constructors' Association and vice-president (for commercial affairs) of FIA.

It was understood that Hill had telephoned Ecclestone after Silverstone to seek his advice. Ecclestone told him to telephone Schumacher and apologize, advice which Hill apparently chose not to take. Little wonder, then, that the Formula One ringmaster was unimpressed when a fresh idea for a rapprochement between the two championship protagonists was put forward. 'I think it's all a bit hypocritical,' said Ecclestone. 'It's a load of rubbish. Damon could easily have said last week, "Look, I made a mistake and I'm sorry it happened." If he says it wasn't his fault, but somebody else's, why does he want to sit in the car beside him? They nearly sat together in the gravel at Silverstone anyway. And, if they are in the same team next year, then they can sit side-by-side.'

His reference to 1996 was a sharp reminder that Michael and Damon were both involved deeply in discussions, with their own teams and others, about their future plans. Michael had been linked for months with a move to Ferrari, but had constantly denied it and been supported in his denials by Benetton. It was the same at Hockenheim, where he said: 'Last year, everybody thought that I was going to leave Benetton and go to McLaren Mercedes-Benz. A few days ago, everyone went with the idea that I was going to stay at Benetton. Now, they say that I'm going to Ferrari because some person has made some jokes and probably next week everyone will say I am going to Williams. It's like that in F1 . . . Usually, the silly season starts at Spa-Francorchamps, but this year, it has started a bit earlier. Many drivers' contracts run out this season and teams are without drivers for next year, so there's a harder approach to getting contracts done sooner.

'I want to leave my decision a bit later so that I can see which direction the teams I am looking at are going. The first priority for me has to be competitiveness because I'm sure other quick drivers are going to come into top teams and I don't want to be in a situation where I am struggling to win races . . .' Ironically, at about the same time, Ferrari's president, Luca di Montezemolo, made it more clear than ever before that Schumacher was close to being announced as Jean Alesi's replacement for 1996. In an interview published by the newspaper *La Stampa*, an organ owned by Fiat and regarded as the company's unofficial mouthpiece, he said: 'To win in Formula One, you need three things – a good organization, a great car and a great driver. In my role as president, I have a duty to bring home the best and Schumacher is undoubtedly the number one driver. I have a duty to think of him.'

The speculation and the hype helped to create a smokescreen, but it was soon blown away at Hockenheim by the sound and fury once the cars were on the track for Friday's opening practice session. A big crowd, of around 48,000, had assembled. The weather was warm, muggy and wet. There was tension in the air, even if not the acrimony reported by some British newspapers, which had suggested that Hill had been bundled into the boot of his car to travel in and out of the circuit for security reasons. The truth is that he was a passenger in a police car; a Mercedes-Benz at that.

Hill was not worried by events around him at all. Nor was Michael, around whom so much attention was focused; he should have been forgiven if he had become snappy. He was seeking victory to enlarge his lead in the championship and, though few others knew, he had other matters on his mind. No German had ever won a modern world championship Grand Prix on home soil before and much was expected of him, but it was not this which occupied his few moments away from the race – it was his forthcoming marriage to Corinna.

This was scheduled for the following week, but the business at hand occupied his thoughts most. Corinna was less conspicuous than usual, as both Michael's father and brother were with him at Hockenheim on Friday. No doubt, like many of the vast contingent of German supporters, they were hoping to see his Benetton B195 secure a strong provisional grip on pole position. However, after struggling to cope with the wrong gear ratios for the high-speed circuit, Michael finished up third-quickest behind the two Williams, and it seemed Benetton were in trouble this time. It was not easy all the way, however, for Damon. On a drying track on Friday morning, he had tried the circuit on slicks and instead ended up giving the public in the main part of the stadium section a perfect opportunity to goad him as he spun into a gravel trap.

The noise from the crowd was obvious and easy to understand. But Hill dispersed any bad feeling with his theatrical reaction – he waved with both arms, half bowed, and blew kisses to them. Then a couple of hours later he took overnight pole in 1:44.932, while Coulthard clocked clocked 1:45.306. Schumacher recorded

1:45.505. It was close. They knew it. The crowd knew it. The teams knew it. On Saturday morning, in hot sunshine, Michael was only sixth-fastest and it seemed Benetton were in trouble. But the team quickly got to work on damper adjustments and also managed to find a much better downforce-to-speed compromise which worked well in the final hour. It was a thrilling session of competitive motor racing which ended with Hill staying on pole, but Schumacher, pushing to the limit on every lap and sending up plumes of smoke each time he locked his left-front wheel as he came into the Sachs Curve, separating the two Williams. The trio were split by only 0.15 seconds. 'I didn't expect to run that close,' said Michael. 'This morning we struggled to make the car perform, and between the morning and the afternoon we improved much further than we expected. But the problem is typical of Hockenheim. You have to run low wing for top speed and still have some downforce in the stadium. Our car doesn't react too well with that kind of combination. At past races, we've always been down on speed to Williams. Our car doesn't have as much mechanical grip as theirs and it has been that way for the whole season. But the good thing with our car is that, if there is a problem, you can sort it out. The Williams looks quite good on the circuit and hopefully there is not much to come.'

Hill, under pressure for a good result after his disappointment at Silverstone, recognized that he had an opportunity to win, but predicted a close race. Ironically, in view of what was to follow, he added: 'We all have the same engine and therefore it is very difficult to make up any time except in the stadium. It's all down to how the car brakes. The stadium section has the only real corners and, with the car handling beautifully, I could take advantage there . . .'

Twenty-four hours later, he must have wished he had not tempted such providence. Starting from his third successive pole position, Damon made a perfect departure from the grid when the lights turned green, led the opening lap with confidence, and looked set to pull clear of the field when, on the first corner of the second lap, just as he came out of the stadium section, his race came to an end. 'It felt like the rear brakes came on a bit harder than before and it caught me out,' he said, after his Williams had stepped out of line, bumped across the run-off area and crashed heavily into the barriers. There had been 77,000 fans at the Hockenheimring on Saturday, but there were 128,000 on Sunday and it seemed each and every one of them was delighted. It was hot and the whole place seemed crazed by the sight of Michael's rival spinning out so early in what had been expected to become a difficult task for the home favourite. The fireworks, the crackers, the klaxons and the jeering were almost overwhelming as Hill trudged back towards the Williams garage.

Exactly how he felt then, nobody but Damon knew. He had lost the race and he had, it seemed, handed victory to Michael. The pair had shaken hands on the grid before the start, but had not travelled together on the parade lap. Indeed, Damon may have been glad, since the vintage vehicle which was used by the Benetton duo stopped and required a push. But now, here he was, finished. Race over. Michael, with a flexible two-stop strategy, was able to cruise to victory much as he would have wanted and later almost relished recounting his version of those opening laps. 'When I saw him go off, I couldn't believe it,' he said. 'I thought "great" – I thought about the first corner after the start. You know, everybody loses a lot of oil getting away from the grid and a whole pack of cars also stirs up dust. I knew the corner was going to be more slippery than normal and I braked early. Then, I saw Damon going sideways . . . Unfortunately, that was not the end of the story because I had another Williams driver pushing me very hard.'

Michael may not have intended it, but this was an exaggeration of Coulthard's part in the race. He drove sensibly and he finished second, but there was never any danger of him taking the lead and he eventually came home six seconds behind the Benetton which had slowed in the final lap before coming to a halt at the first corner after passing in celebration through the stadium. It seemed the victorious Schumacher had stopped to collect a flag, but sensibly bearing in mind that such habits had been banned, he rejected the entreaties of one fan on the circuit and, as he rejoiced in the car, unhappily stalled it. 'I wanted to stop for the flag,' he said. 'I was so emotional, but I remembered the rule and I accidentally stopped the car.' As a result, Michael was unable to propel himself through his victory lap and had instead to rely on the circuit truck to tow him. It was an irony, but one which gave him time to think, to consider his feelings and to contemplate how he might best describe them when he arrived in front of the media.

The Hockenheimring, predictably, was awash with celebrations. Rarely had the circuit seen so many flags, so many banners and so many sore heads at one time. The vast campsites joined as one in rising to greet their hero. The noise was almost deafening but 'Schumi' managed to retain his composure even though he found it difficult to find the words he needed. As ever, he was true to character: honest, simple, controlled and happy to win. The smile on his face on the podium as he celebrated with Coulthard and Berger told enough; Gerhard himself felt it and admitted it afterwards. The reception was quite extraordinary. This was a wild national party, something more than an ordinary victory for an ordinary racing driver.

'To be honest,' said Michael, eleven days later in Budapest, 'I've still not found the words to describe how it all felt. After I won this race, I struggled to find the words and even then, while I was there at Hockenheim, doing that victory lap, after the race, I tried to think about my feelings . . . but on the straight I just thought, "Why am I doing this?" because there was no way I could explain my feelings and, more than that, there was no reason for me, at that time, on the circuit, to think about it. I realized I should feel just happy and nothing else. There was no reason to explain it. Just enjoy it. Enjoy it. No words. I am not a man of words. I am not a journalist who has a vocabulary of words to explain things. My job is to be a racing driver. So, I did not even try. I forgot about the words and I just enjoyed that lap.

'It was so perfect, those few minutes, being towed by that truck, that I forgot everything although I was a little worried before that I may have broken some new rule and I might be disqualified again. I remember thinking, 'Oh, shit, what next!' and that is why I did not stop too long for the flag. Then I forgot it again and I just enjoyed sharing my happiness with the people all around the track. For me, that win meant as much as the world championship. Those spectators made it for me. It was like a dream, and afterwards, when I went back to Cologne and we went for dinner, it felt the same. We all enjoyed ourselves so much, myself and my friends, but we were quite tired and although we wanted to go out and have a couple of drinks, we really did not go for it. I think we stopped and went to bed by about twelve o'clock or one o'clock.'

Forty-eight hours later, of course, as only Michael knew, there was to be another special reason for his family to celebrate – his marriage to Corinna. Planned in secret, executed almost faultlessly, it eventually fell prey to the sort of media circus that both Michael and Corinna had hoped to avoid. As a result, it became the reason for a bizarre dodge-the-media series of events on Tuesday, 1 August, several disappointments eventually leading to a complete change of arrangements.

In the end, a civil marriage ceremony was performed in Michael's home town of Kerpen-Mannheim and a church wedding took place the following Saturday, 5 August, at a private chapel within the grounds at the Petersburg mansion, near Bonn, a place where the German government entertains foreign heads of state and where complete security could be assured.

'We planned to marry, as everyone does, in our own environment,' explained Michael. 'We wanted to be among our friends and our family. It was never intended to be a promotional thing in any way. It was a private decision, a private affair. I wanted to have it that way. Originally, we decided to do it in the Rathaus at Kerpen and everything was organized, but somehow (and I know how this happened) all our information was given away. It actually came from the church, so I was quite astonished at this. And they gave it away free! It meant there were so many media there . . . I just did not feel right, nor did Corinna. I was very upset. I could not enjoy it. I was not bothered about the people, the fans, but the media, the cameras, the way they go behind you and they hunt after you. It was something I was quite upset about.

'We still wanted to go ahead. But we wanted to do it at a place which was a bit more private. We nearly went and did it privately with some friends at their house, but the atmosphere was not right. In the end, I felt the right place to go was in the home town where I used to live, where I grew up, Kerpen-Mannheim. So we went there. Where all my friends are. Where we grew up. It was the press themselves that created all the confusion. If they had not made it so big, then I would have had no need to do anything, to change my plans. They just did not respect my views. So, it was up to them.

'As to the wedding party, we looked for somewhere which we knew would be very private for the whole weekend. I did not want any press at all. At the end of the day, they are only looking after someone's commercial interests. They publish things which are very interesting to sell, to give to spectators, for people to look at . . . But I did not see why they should make money out of me. I would have been upset to see many of these big companies making even more profit when there are so many people who need to be looked after and need help – and they get nothing. And so that is why I decided I wanted to make it private and why I wanted to control it myself. I wanted to know what was going on, which pictures were taken and where the money was going . . . I wanted it to go to charity – partly to UNICEF and partly to some other projects, some of which are completely private. But none of this money which was made from the fees charged to Bunte and RTL will go into my own pocket. None at all. I don't need the money. But I am able to control where the money goes so that the people who I feel need it the most will have it.

'Anyway, the atmosphere at the party after the wedding was just fantastic. The way we did it everyone had some fun. All the guests, all the people felt relaxed. We had 78 guests, I think. It was a great party. It went on until six o'clock in the morning and it was good. I am not a person who goes over the top, as you know, and so I did not that night. There was dancing and drinking and eating and . . . we also threw each other in the swimming-pool. Later on, of course, we all changed our clothes and carried on with the celebrations. It was perfect. Really nice. Both Corinna and I had wanted to marry in August and in Germany for the sakes of our friends and family. August is the month in Germany when sunshine is more or less guaranteed and that is why we married then and not at the end of the season. And I did not plan it any other way. We did not have a special holiday afterwards, but I did miss one test session. Just one – that is all. Then it was back to work in Budapest, of course.'

While Michael took the week off from Formula One, the Grand Prix business continued as usual. At Silverstone, Benetton were conspicuous by their absence as the Williams, McLaren, Ligier, Jordan, Tyrrell and Arrows teams began testing for the Hungarian Grand Prix. The most significant event at the British circuit was the début in a Formula One car of Canadian Jacques Villeneuve, who tested for Williams. His encouraging performance caught a great deal of attention and also led to him being signed by the team as Hill's team-mate for 1996. His test also gave Michael the ideal opportunity to complete his plans for the new season by indicating to Ferrari that he was set to accept their offer and, therefore, to leave Benetton at the end of the year. For Michael Schumacher, August 1995 was clearly a month of significant decisions and changes.

The Hungarian Grand Prix, at the Hungaroring, was to be one of the less memorable weekends. He went into the race with a 21-point advantage over Hill, but came out of it with that lead trimmed to 11. Damon won, Michael retired with a rare failure, a fuel-pump problem, and the title struggle was reopened with a vengeance. 'It is a very bumpy circuit and our car does not like these sort of bumpy tracks,' explained the defending champion. 'Williams did everything right. They had a good strategy, Damon drove well, nothing went wrong for them and they deserved to win.' It was generous and fair of Michael to laud the victor on this occasion, particularly as he had followed him through much of the race when they had to negotiate the notorious traffic. Third on the grid, Michael had followed the two Williams men into the first corner and from laps 13 to 74 before being forced to retire with faulty electronics. It was unwelcome but not a surprise, since refuelling had been a problem anyway at his first pit-stop, when Benetton had problems with their rig and could only load 18 litres. This caused a need for a second stop to top up the tank and, effectively, made it almost impossible for him to overhaul a flawless Hill.

The result swung the pressure back on to Michael – whose switch to Ferrari for 1996 was confirmed after the Hungarian race

– for the Belgian Grand Prix at Spa-Francorchamps, his favourite circuit. And, typically, he responded in brilliant fashion in arguably the greatest race of his career. Yes, he won and won well. But how he won! Problems in qualifying meant he lined up 16th on the grid, a novel experience he said he relished. 'It was a nice little surprise for me,' he said. 'I enjoyed being at the other end of the grid. It was quite funny in some respects because I could have a chat with [Roberto] Moreno and I felt very relaxed. I just thought "well, here you are, 16th, so just go for it." I was concerned at the gap in the championship, but I did not think worrying would do any good.

'I felt the championship would be very tough. I thought the Williams was better than our car and I could not see exactly what we could do, but I knew reliability and good strategy would help. I had had an accident in practice, but the team had my car ready by twenty past one. When it dried out and you could do times, I had a gearbox failure so it was, from my point of view, a bit of a mess.'

In the race, Michael demonstrated his magnificent talents for aggressive driving in the wet-dry conditions by carving through to challenge for the lead and then turning the race into a thrilling duel with Hill. In the changing conditions, it was almost unbelievable to see him defending his position as leader while racing on slicks in the wet, and there were plenty of incidents which caused the Englishman afterwards to lodge a complaint with the race stewards via his team. Hill's complaint was that Schumacher had weaved and banged wheels dangerously in defending his place as leader, but Schumacher saw it all quite differently. 'It was very satisfying to me,' he said. 'I was absolutely on the limit on the back straight and what I did I've seen many times before with Senna. He did it to me and he did it to Prost too. I thought it showed how special Senna was, so I learned from it and did the same things. I thought I was very fair, but the stewards did not. But the result of the race stood. I thought it was a great fight. He [Damon] was very upset, but I thought it was funny. To be honest, I laughed about it when he came to see me at the end of the race in a parc fermée and that probably aggravated him even more.'

After Belgium, it was clear that the momentum was once again with Schumacher and he carried it with him to Monza for the Italian Grand Prix, where another infamous collision between the two ended their parts in the race. Again, as at Silverstone, it seemed an impulsive Hill move was to blame, as he seemed to dive at a gap that did not exist on the approach to the chicane. Coulthard had led from the start, or more exactly the second start (as he had spun off on the original formation lap and then been reinstated after an accident of the grid), but he spun again at the second chicane, leaving Gerhard Berger leading in his Ferrari ahead of Schumacher and Hill. The Austrian was more than 2.8 seconds clear on lap 24 when the inevitable occurred – with Japan's Taki Inoue being blamed squarely for Hill for being in the wrong place at the wrong time and ruining his braking.

Michael was livid. His hopes of victory were ruined and he had to be restrained by a marshal after the accident when he motioned towards Hill. Together they travelled in a mini-bus back to the paddock, where Hill raged about Inoue's incompetence. He should not be out there,' he said. 'He had no idea of what he was doing.'

Michael said he was surprised to hear Damon's excuses. 'He tried to excuse himself for it by blaming someone else,' he said. 'I found this rather funny. I was not very happy. This time, I wanted him to say, "Sorry, I made a mistake" and then I would have had no problem with that because I don't think he did it on purpose. But I don't think it is right to make other people responsible.

'I know it is difficult with Inoue, as he moves around, but if you want to be a world champion then you have to handle that kind of situation in my view. I didn't know what was going on and I was very upset. It was the second time it had happened. I thought he was trying something silly again, like at Silverstone, so I told him what I thought.'

Psychologically, it was an important flashpoint in the season. Herbert won the race for Benetton, another inherited victory for a man losing his seat, but Damon was not to win another race until Adelaide. Schumacher was to go on and reel off a series of victories, after Coulthard won in Estoril two weeks later, and to take the title. 'I think I have more control in these kind of situations,' said Schumacher in Adelaide at the end of the year. 'When it is the other way around, he does it quite differently. It was clear, for example, that in Aida later in the season, he was not concentrating on the whole thing at the start, but only on me. But when I have fights with him, I concentrate maybe only 25 per cent on him and the rest of my mind is free to judge the situation.'

In Monza, protests were lodged. Tempers ran high. Words were inflamed. All of which led Benetton nowhere and left the sour relationship between Hill and Schumacher unchanged. Tensions remained high between them, but in Estoril, with Coulthard winning for the first time, it was to be Michael who gained by finishing second ahead of a disappointed Damon in third place. The Scot, recovering his best form, had emerged as a key new player in the championship run-in, and with the Williams team taking no action to force him to drive only in support of Hill, it was clear that Schumacher had an outstanding opportunity to virtually seal his second title at the next race, the European Grand Prix at the Nürburgring in Germany, close to Cologne, on 1 October. For Michael, who won, it was to be his finest hour, his greatest victory and his most famous flourish.

The old circuit at Nürburg had long been consigned to memory. The weather was damp, cloudy, cold and uninviting, and may of the paddock regulars had heavy colds. Two of them, Rubens Barrichello and Max Papis, took medicines which prompted allegations of drug abuse. It was a strange weekend, one surrounded by a frenzy of media hype in Germany. Yet, through it all, Schumacher marched on imperiously even though Coulthard secured pole position again and then led for the opening 12 laps. When he pitted for the first time, an inspired Jean Alesi took over in the Ferrari Schumacher would be driving in 1996. Alesi was inspired. He reeled off seven fastest laps in atrocious conditions and looked to be on course for the second win of his career, until Michael mounted the charge that was to make history. He had been second, comfortably, for most of the race, with Hill behind, and appeared to have no need to risk his six sensible points for the attraction of victory and 10. Indeed, with 10 laps remaining, he was nearly 14 seconds behind. Yet, he attacked. With 5 laps to go, he was three-tenths adrift and on Alesi's tail and on lap 65, of 67, he pounced, finding an impossible line and space at the Veedol Chicane, banging his wheels with the French-born Sicilian, forcing his way through. Schumacher won by 2.6 seconds and said it was the greatest win of his life, the day he clinched his second world title. Hill, who suffered and struggled, spun off and stood forlornly at the side of the track, one of his legs swelling with a hairline fracture of the fibula, to applaud him. It was the vanquished clapping the victor and they both knew it. 'In terms of fighting, of passing and of overtaking, that was the best win of my life,' said Schumacher.

After that, the rest was academic. Another supreme triumph of masterful tactics and composed racing in Aida brought victory in the Pacific Grand Prix to conclude the drivers' championship. It was the new order of things: Schumacher first, Coulthard second and Hill third. Flavio Briatore waved the German flag; Michael looked relieved and Damon sombre and stunned. 'It will sink in slowly, I suppose,' said Michael afterwards, before a wild party in the Aida hotel left him with a two-day hangover. 'But this victory and championship is as much due to the team and the crew as anyone. They have been unbelievable today – again. We are the only team that puts so much effort into our strategy and our pit-stops.'

Hill had attempted to fend Schumacher off in the first corner, but had succeeded only in allowing free passage to the Ferraris. Schumacher slipped back to fifth, but was up to fourth behind Coulthard, Alesi and Hill by lap 19 when the pit-stops began. Alesi, Hill and Schumacher went in together – and Schumacher came out first. Within a lap, he was up to second behind Coulthard, whose wrong switch of tactics from three stops to two gifted Michael the lead and the race. No wonder Benetton laughed all the way to the bar that night and again in Suzuka seven days later.

Michael, newly crowned as a double world champion, had recovered from his celebrations on a series of promotional appearances in Tokyo before returning south to dominate the Japanese Grand Prix. Pole position, victory and fastest lap followed in a performance that stamped him as the best and ensured that Benetton secured their first constructor's crown. To add to the team's pleasure, Johnny Herbert came home third and, despite knowing he was to be replaced in 1996 by Gerhard Berger, warmly congratulated the team on their success. The singing in the 'rog cabin' was memorable as the key men, the top drivers and their loyal followers caroused into the night. Williams, alas, ended with no finishers. Both drivers went off and the team faced a tough session with the media before returning to action in Adelaide at the final race.

Michael, as he said, had delivered his promises to the team: both titles and a glorious ending to the season. It set him up for a tilt at one more win, in Australia, to set a new record of 10 in an individual season. But, after a sunshine holiday with Corinna in Port Douglas, Queensland, he could not manage it. This time, a coming-together with Jean Alesi, when the Frenchman ran into him after 22 laps, ended the race for Schumacher. 'It was a stupid thing to happen,' he said. 'A silly move, but I could not have asked for a better season overall. It has been like a dream for me. And now I go to Ferrari, to face a new challenge, to try and revive the team and win again. I wish Benetton good luck for 1996 when, I hope, I will be looking out for their cars in my mirrors!'

MICHAEL SCHUMACHER FACT-FILE

KEY

DNS – Did not start
DQ – Disqualified
DNF – Did not finish (not classified)

1973 – 1987 KARTING

1984:	German Junior Champion
1985:	German Junior Champion
	Junior World Championship: Runner-Up
1986:	German Championship: 3rd
	European Championship: 3rd
1987:	German Champion
	European Champion

1988 – SINGLE SEATERS

1988:	Formula Konig German Champion
	German Formula Ford 1600 Championship: 6th
	European Formula Ford 1600 Championship: 2nd

1989 – GERMAN FORMULA THREE CHAMPIONSHIP WITH WTS

Date	Race	Car	Qual	Clas
April 16	HOCKENHEIM (D)	Reynard 893-Volkswagen	2	3
April 30	NURBURGRING (D)	Reynard 893-Volkswagen	5	3
May 28	AVUS (D)	Reynard 893-Volkswagen	5	3
June 11	BRNO (CZ)	Reynard 893-Volkswagen	8	5
June 18	ZELTWEG (A)	Reynard 893-Volkswagen	1	1
July 2	HOCKENHEIM (D)	Reynard 893-Volkswagen	2	3
July 9	WUNSTORF (D)	Reynard 893-Volkswagen	6	12
July 29	HOCKENHEIM (D)	Reynard 893-Volkswagen	4	19
August 6	DIEPHOLZ (D)	Reynard 893-Volkswagen	4	4
Sept 3	NURBURGRING (D)	Reynard 893-Volkswagen	6	5
Sept 24	NURBURGRING (D)	Reynard 893-Volkswagen	1	1
Sept 30	HOCKENHEIM (D)	Reynard 893-Volkswagen	2	3

OTHER FORMULA THREE RACES WITH WTS

NON-CHAMPIONSHIP GERMAN FORMULA THREE RACES

| March 18 | HOCKENHEIM (D) | Reynard 893-Volkswagen | 4 | 2 |
| April 1 | HOCKENHEIM (D) | Reynard 893-Volkswagen | 4 | 1 |

MACAU GRAND PRIX

| Nov 26 | MACAU (MK) | Reynard 893-Volkswagen | 6 | DNF* |

(*Won first heat but retired in second – therefore not classified in results)

Final Championship Positions

1	K WENDLINGER	164 points
2	H-H FRENTZEN	163 points
3	M SCHUMACHER	163 points

1990 – GERMAN FORMULA THREE CHAMPIONSHIP WITH WTS

Date	Race	Car	Qual	Clas
March 31	ZOLDER (BEL)	Reynard 903-Volkswagen	1	DNF
April 7	HOCKENHEIM (D)	Reynard 903-Volkswagen	1	19
April 21	NURBURGRING (D)	Reynard 903-Volkswagen	22	5
May 5	AVUS (D)	Reynard 903-Volkswagen	2	1
June 3	WUNSTORF (D)	Reynard 903-Volkswagen	1	1
June 30	NORISRING (D)	Reynard 903-Volkswagen	4	2
July 14	ZELTWEG (A)	Reynard 903-Volkswagen	1	1
August 4	DIEPHOLZ (D)	Reynard 903-Volkswagen	7	1
August 18	NURBURGRING (D)	Reynard 903-Volkswagen	1	1
Sept 1	NURBURGRING (D)	Reynard 903-Volkswagen	1	4
Oct 13	HOCKENHEIM (D)	Reynard 903-Volkswagen	2	2

Final Championship Positions

| 1 | M SCHUMACHER | 148 points |
| 2 | O RENSING | 117 points |

OTHER FORMULA THREE RESULTS WITH WTS

NON-CHAMPIONSHIP GERMAN FORMULA THREE RACE

| March 24 | HOCKENHEIM (D) | Reynard 903-Volkswagen | 2 | 1 |

EUROPEAN FORMULA THREE CUP

Sept 23	LE MANS (FRA)	Reynard 903-Speiss Opel	1	DQ**

(**Schumacher began original race in Reynard 903-Volkswagen, but after a first-lap crash he switched to his spare car powered by the Opel engine. He won the re-started race but was disqualified for switching engine types.)

FIA FORMULA THREE WORLD CUP

Nov 25	MACAU (MK)	Reynard 903-Volkswagen	2	1

EURO-MACAU-FUJI CHALLENGE CUP

Dec 2	FUJI (JAP)	Reynard 903-Volkswagen	2A	1

1990 – SPORTS-PROTOTYPE WORLD CHAMPIONSHIP WITH SAUBER MERCEDES

Date	Race	Car	Qual	Clas
April 8	SUZUKA (JAP)		DNS	DNS
April 29	MONZA (ITA)		DNS	DNS
May 20	SILVERSTONE (GB)	Mercedes-Benz C11	DQ	DQ
June 3	SPA (BEL)		DNS	DNS
July 22	DIJON (FRA)	Mercedes-Benz C11	3	2
August 19	NURBURGRING (D)	Mercedes-Benz C11	2	2
Sept 2	DONINGTON (GB)		DNS	DNS
Sept 23	MONTREAL (CAN)		DNS	DNS
Oct 7	MEXICO CITY (MEX)	Mercedes-Benz C11	2	1

(PARTNERED BY JOCHEN MASS THROUGHOUT)

Final Championship Positions

1 =	J SCHLESSER	49.5 points
	M BALDI	49.5 points
3	J MASS	48 points
4	A WALLACE	25 points
5 =	M SCHUMACHER	21 points
	K WENDLINGER	21 points
	J LAMMERS	21 points

1991 – SPORTSCAR WORLD CHAMPIONSHIP WITH MERCEDES

Date	Race	Car	Qual	Clas
April 14	SUZUKA (JAP)	Mercedes-Benz C291	3	DNF
May 5	MONZA (ITA)	Mercedes-Benz C291	6	DNF
May 19	SILVERSTONE (GB)	Mercedes-Benz C291	5	2
June 22/23	LE MANS (FRA)	Mercedes-Benz C11	4***	5
August 18	NURBURGRING (D)	Mercedes-Benz C291	5	DNF
Sept 15	MAGNY COURS (FRA)	Mercedes-Benz C291	3	DNF
Oct 6	MEXICO CITY (MEX)	Mercedes-Benz C291	2	DNF
Oct 27	AUTOPOLIS (JAP)	Mercedes-Benz C291	6	1

(***The top ten grid positions were reserved for normally-aspirated engines, so Michael's turbo-powered Mercedes actually started in 12th position)

(PARTNERED BY KARL WENDLINGER THROUGHOUT, EXCEPT LE MANS WHEN ALSO JOINED BY FRITZ KREUTZPOINTER)

Final Championship Positions

1	T FABI	86 points
2	D WARWICK	79 points
3=	P ALLIOT	69 points
	M BALDI	69 points
9=	M SCHUMACHER	43 points
	K WENDLINGER	43 points
	M REUTER	43 points

(Michael Schumacher also completed in the Norisring (June 30) and Diepholz (Aug 4) German Touring Car Championship Races in a Mercedes-Benz 190E)

JAPANESE FORMULA 3000 CHAMPIONSHIP WITH TEAM LE MANS

Date	Race	Car	Qual	Clas
July 28	SUGO (JAP)	Ralt-Mugen RT23	B2	2

1991 – FORMULA ONE WORLD CHAMPIONSHIP WITH TEAM 7-UP JORDAN AND CAMEL BENETTON FORD

Date	Race	Car	Qual	Clas
August 25	SPA (BEL)	Jordan Ford 191	7	DNF
Sept 8	MONZA (ITA)	Benetton Ford B191	7	5
Sept 22	ESTORIL (POR)	Benetton Ford B191	10	6
Sept 29	BARCELONA (ESP)	Benetton Ford B191	5	6
Oct 20	SUZUKA (JAP)	Benetton Ford B191	9	DNF
Nov 3	ADELAIDE (AUS)	Benetton Ford B191	6	DNF

Final World Championship Positions 1991

1	A SENNA	96 points
2	N MANSELL	72 points
3	R PATRESE	53 points
4	G BERGER	43 points
5	A PROST	34 points
12 =	M SCHUMACHER	4 points
	JJ LEHTO	4 points
	B GACHOT	4 points

1992 – FORMULA ONE WORLD CHAMPIONSHIP WITH CAMEL BENETTON FORD

Date	Race	Car	Qual	Clas
March 1	KYALAMI (SA)	Benetton Ford B191B	6	4
March 22	MEXICO CITY (MEX)	Benetton Ford B191B	3	3
April 5	INTERLAGOS (BRA)	Benetton Ford B191B	5	3
May 3	BARCELONA (ESP)	Benetton Ford B192	2	2
May 17	IMOLA (RSM)	Benetton Ford B192	5	DNF
May 31	MONTE CARLO (MON)	Benetton Ford B192	6	4
June 14	MONTREAL (CAN)	Benetton Ford B192	5	2
July 5	MAGNY-COURS (FRA)	Benetton Ford B192	5	DNF
July 12	SILVERSTONE (GB)	Benetton Ford B192	4	4
July 26	HOCKENHEIM (D)	Benetton Ford B192	6	3
August 16	HUNGARORING (HUN)	Benetton Ford B192	4	DNF
August 30	SPA (BEL)	Benetton Ford B192	3	1
Sept 13	MONZA (ITA)	Benetton Ford B192	6	3
Sept 27	ESTORIL (POR)	Benetton Ford B192	5	7
Oct 25	SUZUKA (JAP)	Benetton Ford B192	5	DNF
Nov 8	ADELAIDE (AUS)	Benetton Ford B192	5	2

Final World Championship Positions 1992

1	N MANSELL	108 points
2	R PATRESE	56 points
3	M SCHUMACHER	53 points
4	A SENNA	50 points
5	G BERGER	49 points

1993 – FORMULA ONE WORLD CHAMPIONSHIP WITH CAMEL BENETTON FORD

Date	Race	Car	Qual	Clas
March 14	KYALAMI (SA)	Benetton Ford B193A	3	DNF
March 28	INTERLAGOS (BRA)	Benetton Ford B193A	4	3
April 11	DONINGTON PK (EUR)	Benetton Ford B193B	3	DNF
April 25	IMOLA (RSM)	Benetton Ford B193B	3	2
May 9	BARCELONA (EP)	Benetton Ford B193B	4	3
May 23	MONTE CARLO (MON)	Benetton Ford B193B	2	DNF
June 13	MONTREAL (CAN)	Benetton Ford B193B	3	2
July 4	MAGNY-COURS (FRA)	Benetton Ford B193B	7	3
July 11	SILVERSTONE (GB)	Benetton Ford B193B	3	2
July 25	HOCKENHEIM (D)	Benetton Ford B193B	3	2
August 15	HUNGARORING (HUN)	Benetton Ford B193B	3	DNF
August 29	SPA (BEL)	Benetton Ford B193B	3	2
Sept 12	MONZA (ITA)	Benetton Ford B193B	5	DNF
Sept 26	ESTORIL (POR)	Benetton Ford B193B	6	1
Oct 24	SUZUKA (JAP)	Benetton Ford B193B	4	DNF
Nov 7	ADELAIDE (AUS)	Benetton Ford B193B	4	DNF

Final World Championship Positions 1993

1	A PROST	99 points
2	A SENNA	73 points
3	D HILL	69 points
4	M SCHUMACHER	52 points
5	R PATRESE	20 points

1994 – FORMULA ONE WORLD CHAMPIONSHIP WITH MILD SEVEN BENETTON FORD

Date	Race	Car	Qual	Clas
March 27	INTERLAGOS (BRA)	Benetton Ford B194	2	1
April 1	AIDA (PAC)	Benetton Ford B194	2	1
May 1	IMOLA (RSM)	Benetton Ford B194	2	1
May 15	MONTE CARLO (MON)	Benetton Ford B194	1	1
May 29	BARCELONA (ESP)	Benetton Ford B194	1	2
June 12	MONTREAL (CAN)	Benetton Ford B194	1	1
July 3	MAGNY-COURS (FRA)	Benetton Ford B194	3	1
July 10	SILVERSTONE (GB)	Benetton Ford B194	2	DQ
July 31	HOCKENHEIM (D)	Benetton Ford B194	4	DNF
August 14	HUNGARORING (HUN)	Benetton Ford B194	1	1
August 28	SPA (BEL)	Benetton Ford B194	2	DQ
Sept 11	MONZA (ITA)		DNS	DNS
Sept 25	ESTORIL (POR)		DNS	DNS
Oct 16	JEREZ (EUR)	Benetton Ford B194	1	1
Nov 6	SUZUKA (JAP)	Benetton Ford B194	1	2
Nov 13	ADELAIDE (AUS)	Benetton Ford B194	2	DNF

Final World Championship Positions 1994

1	M SCHUMACHER	92 points
2	D HILL	91 points
3	G BERGER	41 points
4	M HAKKINEN	26 points
5	J ALESI	24 points

1995 – FORMULA ONE WORLD CHAMPIONSHIP WITH MILD SEVEN BENETTON RENAULT

Date	Race	Car	Qual	Clas
March 26	INTERLAGOS (BRA)	Benetton Renault B195	2	1
April 9	BUENOS AIRES (ARG)	Benetton Renault B195	3	3
April 30	IMOLA (RSM)	Benetton Renault B195	1	DNF
May 14	BARCELONA (ESP)	Benetton Renault B195	1	1
May 28	MONTE CARLO (MON)	Benetton Renault B195	2	1
June 11	MONTREAL (CAN)	Benetton Renault B195	1	5
July 2	MAGNY-COURS (FRA)	Benetton Renault B195	2	1
July 16	SILVERSTONE (GB)	Benetton Renault B195	2	DNF
July 30	HOCKENHEIM (D)	Benetton Renault B195	2	1
August 13	HUNGARORING (HUN)	Benetton Renault B195	3	11
August 27	SPA (BEL)	Benetton Renault B195	16	1
September 10	MONZA (ITA)	Benetton Renault B195	2	DNF
September 24	ESTORIL (POR)	Benetton Renault B195	3	2
October 1	NURBURGRING (EUR)	Benetton Renault B195	3	1
October 22	AIDA (PAC)	Benetton Renault B195	3	1
October 29	SUZUKA (JAP)	Benetton Renault B195	1	1
November 12	ADELAIDE (AUS)	Benetton Renault B195	3	DNF

Final World Championship Positions 1995

1	M SCHUMACHER	102 points
2	D HILL	69 points
3	D COULTHARD	49 points
4	J HERBERT	45 points
5	J ALESI	42 points

INDEX

Aiello, Laurent 45, 47
Alboreto, Michele 30, 160
Alesi, Jean 119, 120, 122, 152, 161, 197, 198, 207, 217–219
Anderson, Gary 10, 83
Andretti, Michael 137
Aumonier, Pierre 168–9
Autosport 16, 37, 46, 170, 205
Auto Bild 50

Badoer, Luca 136
Baldi, Mauro 38–9, 40, 41, 108
Barnard, John 113
Barrichello, Rubens 8, 158, 159, 174
Bartelo, Michael 31–3
Bellof, Stefan 27, 121
Benetton, Luciano 112
Berger, Gerhard 68, 118, 123, 127, 160, 161, 172, 193, 196, 211, 216, 219
Bergmeister, Willy 223
Bernard, Eric 153
Betsch, Corinna 73–4, 115–16, 127, 132, 147–8, 161, 173, 181, 184, 187, 195, 208, 212, 213, 219
Bild 176
Blundell, Mark 144
Boutsen, Thierry 128
Brabham, David 110
Brawn, Ross 106, 112, 130, 140, 172, 180–1, 194
Briatore, Flavio 14, 89, 92, 98, 102, 112, 137, 145, 153, 161, 171–2, 203, 218
Brundle, Martin 12, 34, 39, 71, 113–14, 116, 118, 121, 122, 125, 128, 129, 153, 164, 174, 183
Bruynseraede, Roland 160
Buesing, Gustav 59, 63, 74
Byrne, Rory 98, 112, 146

Carman, Geroge 176
Cheever, Eddie 55, 121

Cheever, Ross 79
Coombs, Peter 174
Cooper, Adam 16, 37
Coulthard, David 182, 191, 194, 195, 202, 208, 210, 211, 216–218

Dalmas, Yannick 10
de Cesaris, Andrea 4, 5, 6, 9–12, 92
Dennis, Ron 137, 146, 148, 154
Dernie, Frank 181
Dilk, Guido 26–8
Dilk, Jurgen 6, 25–9
driver aids 118, 129, 143
Dungl, Willi 62, 70, 114, 116

Ecclestone, Bernie 180, 206, 207

Fabi, Teo 82, 107, 109, 110
Fangio, Juan-Manuel 123; 205
Ferte, Alain 39
Fijinaga, Yoshimi 51
FIA (Federation Internationale de Automobile) 65, 89, 154, 160, 161, 168, 170, 171–2, 173, 175–6, 192–196
Foster, Trevor 7, 10–12, 83, 96
Frentzen, Heinz-Harald 14, 44–6, 55, 60, 62–3, 64, 67, 68, 71–4, 193, 198

Gachot, Bertrand 2, 6, 15, 82
Gerd, Bodden 27
Giroix, Fabien 79
Grands Prix
    Argentinian 195
    Australian 130, 178, 185–8, 219
    Belgian 7, 26, 82, 86, 92, 127–8, 136, 174–5, 215
    Brazilian 111, 136, 190–193, 196
    British 76, 125, 136, 142, 143–4, 168–9, 200

Canadian 136, 142, 198
European 140, 142, 177, 179, 217
French 123–4, 136, 199
German 125, 126, 136, 168, 206
Hungarian 137–8, 144, 173, 214
Italian 76, 82, 90, 128, 175, 216
Japanese 104–5, 154, 182–4, 218
Macau 42–9
Monaco 32, 122–3, 138, 147, 197
Pacific 151, 153–6
Portuguese 128–9, 136, 145, 175, 178–9
San Marino 121, 136, 140–1, 156, 157, 168, 171, 196
South African 115, 137
Spanish 61, 120, 136, 141, 165, 171, 196
Grundy, Richard 43, 104–5, 139

Hakkinen, Mika 40, 44–9, 156, 170, 184
Hamilton, Maurice 181
Hawelka, Harry 105, 139, 140, 195
Head, Patrick 193
Herbert, Johnny 79, 182, 190, 194, 197, 202, 204, 216, 219
Hill, Damon 134, 136, 141, 144, 145, 149, 152, 153, 155, 166, 169, 171–2, 174, 175, 176, 178, 179–80, 183–4, 185–7, 191, 192, 194, 197–210, 214–218
Hill, Graham 149
Hunt, James 50

IMG (International Management Group) 77, 84, 86–8, 92, 99, 146, 175, 182
Independent on Sunday 149
Inoue, Taki 216
Irnich, Udo 24, 173
Irvine, Eddie 45, 153

Jakobi, Julian 88
Jardine, Tony 43
Johansson, Stefan 8, 85
Jones, Bruce 46
Jordan, Eddie 3, 6, 14–16, 66, 82–4, 85–9, 92–7, 100

Kaufmann, Wolfgang 34
Kramer, Gerd 15, 30

Lammers, Jan 39
Lamy, Pedro 160
Larrauri, Oscar 41
Lauda, Niki 22
Leberer, Josef 105
Lehto, J.J. 12, 148, 151, 159, 160, 182
Lohr, Ellen 34

McCormack, Mark 77
Mansell, Nigel 115, 118, 120, 123, 124, 127, 132, 179, 181, 182, 185, 186, 187, 198
Martini, Mauro 51
Mass, Jochen 33, 35, 37–40, 54, 60, 64–5, 68–70, 80–1, 127, 165–6, 182
Mirror 189
Modena, Stefano 121, 123
Montezemolo, Luca 207
Moreno, Roberto 77, 91–6, 103, 215
Mosley, Max 171, 189, 196
Motoring News 165
Muller, Jorg 38

Neerpasch, Jochen 6, 8, 14–15, 35, 54–60, 63, 66, 68, 77, 79, 83–8, 92–3, 97, 99–102, 114
Niedwitz, Klaus 74
Noack, Gerd 6, 22

Observer 181
Oliver, Jackie 17

Palmer, Kate 2
Papis, Max 217
Pareja, Jesus 109
Patrese, Riccardo 12, 118, 127, 132, 136, 137, 138, 142, 144, 146
Phillips, Ian 7, 8, 85–9, 94–5, 99
Piedade, Domingos 29–30
Piquet, Nelson 12, 90, 92–3, 104, 113, 116, 181
Price, Dave 14
Prost, Alain 4, 9, 47, 133, 134, 136, 141, 142, 145, 178, 181, 215

Racecourses
  Aida 151, 154–5, 218
  Autopolis 79, 81, 109
  Avus 34
  Brands Hatch 27
  Curcuit de Catalunya 197
  Diepholz 38
  Donington 136, 140
  Estoril 116, 136, 190, 216, 217
  Europa Motor Drom 19
  Fuji 42, 50–1, 53
  Hockenheim 15, 25, 30, 33, 40, 41, 44,
      62, 72, 125, 139, 144, 167, 170–3,
      174, 204, 207–209, 211
  Hungaroring 92, 126, 173, 214
  Imola 121, 157–60, 161, 166, 196, 197
  Interlagos 119, 151–2, 191–193
  Jerez 56–8, 60, 62, 68, 180
  Kyalami 117, 134
  Laval 45
  Le Castellet (Paul Ricard) 56, 62, 63,
      67, 72, 113, 170
  Le Mans 27, 40, 78, 82, 166
  Macau 40, 42–9, 53
  Magny-Cours 108–9, 124, 199, 200
  Mainz-Finthen 30
  Mexico City (Hermanos Rodriguez)
      40, 41, 68, 108, 117
  Monaco (Monte Carlo) 53, 142, 161
  Monza 89–90, 92–110, 144–5
  Norisring 37, 123
  Nurburgring 16, 30, 32–4, 38, 40, 41,
      62, 64, 65, 71, 82, 90, 108, 217
  Osterreichring 37
  Salzburgring 30
  Silverstone 3, 6, 7, 10, 16, 35, 36,
      64, 72, 76–89, 107–8, 124, 134,
      163, 166, 167, 168–9, 174, 200–
      203, 214
  Snetterton 79
  Spa-Francorchamps 1–17, 26, 77, 86,
      127, 138, 144, 174, 179, 215
  Sugo 79–80, 108
  Suzuka 105–7, 109, 154, 218
  Wunstorf 35, 37
  Zeltweg 31, 37, 72
  Zolder 33

Racing teams
  Arrows 214
  BMW 55
  Benetton 13, 14, 60, 77, 82, 87, 88–
      90, 99, 112–15, 121, 132, 133,
      136, 145–6, 148–9, 150–1, 168,
      170, 171–2, 173–7, 179, 187, 189,
      190, 193, 194, 196, 199, 208, 209,
      214
  Camel 68, 74, 104
  Camel Benetton Ford 7, 43, 133
  Ferrari 115, 196–198, 207, 214, 217
  Ikegami 51
  Jaguar 86
  Jordan 2, 13, 14, 16, 68, 74, 76, 82–3,
      89, 92–109, 214
  Larrousse 176
  McLaren 132, 134, 137, 142, 181–2,
      198, 214
  Mercedes (-Benz) 2–6, 15, 16, 32, 33,
      50, 51, 54–9, 60, 61–75, 82–3, 92,
      98–102, 110, 115, 158, 181–2
  Sauber 99, 101–2, 109, 115
  Sauber-Ford 198
  Sauber-Mercedes 35, 37–8, 56, 75, 82,
      115
  7-Up Jordan 2, 60
  Toleman 112
  Tyrell 214
  West Surrey Racing 40, 43
  Williams 132, 133, 135, 137, 149, 150,
      153–4, 158, 187, 191, 199, 204, 208,
      214, 219
  WTS 25, 31, 47, 150
  Yamaha 14, 98, 102
Radio Times 202
Ratzenberger, Roland 157, 159, 160,
      196
Reiss, Leo 67–8, 70
Rensing, Otto 34, 37, 40, 44, 78
Reuters 181
Robertson, Steve 50, 51
Rodgers, Fred 88–9, 94
Rosberg, Keke 8, 83, 106
Rosso, Victor 51
Runzheimer, Dr 140
Rydell, Rickard 51

Salo, Mika 29
Sauber, Pete 3, 15–16, 57–8, 66, 114–15
Schlesser, Jean-Louis 37–9, 41, 67, 78, 81, 109
Schmickler, Frank 31
Schulte, Christoph 31, 49, 50, 54, 57
Schumacher, Elisabeth 19, 21
Schumacher, Ralf 19, 173
Schumacher, Rolf 19, 21–2, 173
Senna, Ayrton 5, 15, 30, 47, 99, 102, 111, 118, 119, 123–5, 127, 128, 133, 134, 135, 136, 137–8, 141, 143, 144, 147, 149, 151–3, 154, 155, 157–65, 179, 187, 188, 190, 192, 196, 215
Sheene, Barry 184
Skewis, Mark 165
Stuck, Hans-Joachim 126
Sturm, Karin 64, 150
Sun 55
Surer, Marc 55
Symonds, Pat 98, 194

Tee, Steven 139
traction control 118–19, 135, 140, 141–2, 143, 154, 171
Tracy, Paul 179

Van Poele, Eric 4
Verstappen, Jos 148, 153, 172, 173, 174, 182

Villeneuve, Jacques 214
Villa d'Este 13, 94–5

Walkinshaw, Tom 65, 86, 89, 92, 96–7, 99–100, 106, 112, 151
Wallace, Andy 39
Warner, Adrian 181
Warwick, Derek 8, 16, 64–6, 82, 89, 108, 110
Warwick, Paul 65–6
Watkins, Professor 159
Weber, Willi 6, 8, 10, 14, 29–30, 41, 52, 55, 72, 77, 82, 85–6, 108, 117, 121, 144, 146, 150, 161, 164, 175, 176, 181–2, 195
Welti, Max 35–6
Wendlinger, Karl 14, 32–3, 55, 61, 67, 68–9, 78, 81, 87, 106–7, 108, 110, 114, 162–3, 193
Werner, Marco 37
Whiteways Technical Centre 113, 131
Whiting, Charlie 171, 175
Williams, Frank 153, 171, 175, 204
Williams, Richard 149
Winkelhock, Joachim 29, 32
Wright, Tim 175, 182

Zakowski, Peter 33
Zanardi, Alessandro 40, 94, 96–8, 141, 162